"*The Saints of Zion* is the go-to book for understanding the distinctive beliefs of the LDS Church. Drawing heavily from Mormon sources, Kerns compassionately, humbly, and carefully delineates where the Church has been and what she believes. Interested in Mormonism? You have come to the right place!"

—*J. D. Payne, associate professor of Christian ministry, Samford University*

"With a deep examination of LDS theology and history, *The Saints of Zion* makes abundantly clear that Mormonism is anything but historic Christianity. With this well-written, accessible work, Travis Kerns—a first-rate scholar on Mormonism—has done evangelicals a great service in making clear what the LDS church actually believes. If you want to know the truth about Mormons and Mormonism, *The Saints of Zion* is the place to start. I cannot commend the book or its author highly enough."

—*Jeff Robinson, senior editor, The Gospel Coalition*

THE
SAINTS
OF ZION

TRAVIS S. KERNS

THE
SAINTS
OF ZION

An Introduction to Mormon Theology

ACADEMIC

NASHVILLE, TENNESSEE

This work is dedicated to Staci, the love of my life and my true helpmeet from God. Without you, none of this would have been possible. I am thankful to the Lord every day for blessing me with you and am amazed at the depth of your love and support.

—◆—

The work is also dedicated to Shane and Dixie, without whose friendship life in Utah would be immeasurably more difficult. I am constantly astonished at your love for Christ and am eternally thankful he called you and your family from death to life.

—◆—

Similarly, this work would not have been possible without the friendship and teaching of Dr. Charlie Draper. Your end in this life came unexpectedly, but I know without a doubt you are worshipping at the feet of Jesus and glorying in him. Finally, this work is dedicated to Drs. Ted Cabal, Chad Brand, and James Chancellor. Without your constant support, encouragement, and teaching, especially while I was a graduate student and young professor at The Southern Baptist Theological Seminary, I would not be the man I am. Thank you for instilling in me the strong desire for scholarship, an insatiable appetite to understand another person's beliefs, and an unquenchable longing to see people in other faith traditions come to a saving knowledge of Christ.

—◆—

Maranatha, Lord Jesus.

Contents

Preface

I have been fascinated with the study of alternate faith traditions since I was a young man. Beginning in the 1980s, while in seventh grade, I found myself interested in what others believed and why they believed it. Although I grew up in Greenville, South Carolina, an area of the United States many would call the buckle of the Bible Belt, I still encountered people with non-Christian beliefs and discovered that I was very interested in their beliefs.

The study of the religions of the world and of minority religions in the United States took a serious, and academic, turn while I was a freshman at North Greenville University (then North Greenville College) in Tigerville, South Carolina. In 1996, with a course entitled "New Religious Movements and Minority Religions in America," Professor Chad Brand started me down a path of what would soon become a lifetime emphasis for ministry and scholarship. I was captivated by the belief systems of those in alternate faith traditions, especially the doctrines and history of the Church of Jesus Christ of Latter-day Saints. During my graduate studies at both the master's and doctoral levels, I focused as many papers, readings, and independent study courses on Mormonism, the religious tradition of the Church of Jesus Christ of Latter-day Saints, as possible. Academically, this course of study culminated in the writing of a PhD dissertation focused on Latter-day Saint philosophy, specifically, the notion of truth in epistemology.

As a professor at The Southern Baptist Theological Seminary in Louisville, Kentucky, I began taking students on short-term mission trips to Salt Lake City, Utah, in 2007. These trips deepened my interest in Mormonism and, more specifically, in Utah. This interest resulted in trips every summer to Utah, and in June 2012, my interest in Utah peaked and I felt more compelled than ever to move to Utah for full-time ministry. This was made real by a call from North American Mission Board president (and our former pastor) Kevin Ezell in the fall of 2012. My wife and I, along with our son, accepted the call to move to Utah early in 2013 and left Louisville in July 2013.

Utah has assuredly made my understanding of Mormonism more complete, as I am now immersed in Mormonism not only as a theological system but also as a cultural and sociological system. My unapologetic desire and calling in life is to see people come to a saving knowledge of the Jesus of the New Testament, and this includes members of the Church of Jesus Christ of Latter-day Saints, or, the LDS Church. My hope is that this work will move others to compassion and love for the people who make up the Church of Jesus Christ of Latter-day Saints, and, Lord willing, that it will also cause members of the LDS Church to rethink their beliefs and seek out the Jesus of the New Testament, free from Latter-day interpretations.

Acknowledgments

O ffering the proper acknowledgments at the outset of a book is, to say the least, difficult. I am reminded of an award show acceptance speech during which the winner thanks family, friends, and often "all the others I am forgetting." My wife, Staci, gave me constant encouragement, support, love, and time to research and write this work. Our son, Jeremiah, gave up his dad to countless hours of research. My parents, Bob and Donna Kerns, gave of their time, money, and energy to send me through years of academic training. My grandmothers, Bettie Albertson and Grace Elrod, showed me how to love Jesus without being ultimately concerned with just theology.

My first theology professor at North Greenville University (then College), Dr. Chad Brand, gave me a love for the Bible and theology. Similarly, Dr. Charles Draper gave me hours and hours of advice and training in all things Christianity. Likewise, Dr. Ted Cabal, my doctoral supervisor at The Southern Baptist Theological Seminary, instilled in me a love for apologetics, especially as an evangelistic tool and not as a way to win an argument. Dr. James Chancellor, a former professor at The Southern Baptist Theological Seminary, pushed me intellectually, forcing me to be able to defend my beliefs. He also ingrained in me a love for the sociology of religion, a topic I still find fascinating. Also, Southern Baptist Theological Seminary professors Jim Parker, Tim Beougher, Russell Fuller, and Rob Plummer helped me understand ministry, academics, and their proper role in life. To put it colloquially, three "brothers from another mother," Brian Payne, Barry Joslin, and Denny Burk, have been constant friends and have encouraged me throughout the years since we first were known as the "young guns" as new professors at Boyce College, the undergraduate school of The Southern Baptist Theological Seminary. Without their friendship, my life would be incomplete. I cannot thank God enough for putting these three brothers in my life. The publishing and editorial staff at B&H Academic deserve thanks for their patience and efforts. A special thanks goes to Chris Thompson and Jim Baird at B&H Academic for taking a chance on this work.

Finally, and probably most importantly, I want to thank the North American Mission Board (NAMB) of the Southern Baptist Convention for giving me grace and latitude to research and write this work. Steve Bass, Rick Curtis, and Kevin Ezell have been more than supervisors in my work for NAMB; they have been encouragers and supporters of my academic endeavors. Likewise, my NAMB Send City Missionary counterparts across the western United States have been particularly motivating and reassuring during my research and writing. Thanks be to God for his grace and mercy in putting all of these people in my life.

I would also like to acknowledge the work of Rulon T. Burton, specifically, his work *We Believe*. I am heavily indebted to his research and relied on his extensive bibliography.

Chapter 1

Introduction to Mormonism

T he Church of Jesus Christ of Latter-day Saints; Mormons; Latter-day Saints.[1] We encounter their missionaries riding bicycles through our neighborhoods. We see their commercials on television, promising happiness and a great family life. We work alongside them, live beside them, shop with them, but likely know relatively little about them. Our lack of knowledge about Latter-day Saint beliefs and practices is quickly shown in our usual questioning as to whether or not they still practice polygamy, a practice officially banned by the Salt Lake Church beginning in September 1890.

A lack of knowledge about Mormons, though, forces non-Mormons to ask deeper questions. Why does this lack of understanding exist? Should we do the hard work of trying to understand, as fully as possible, other faith communities around us? If we do the hard work, what is the ultimate purpose of the information we discover? How should we go about finding information? Should we seek to understand Mormonism in the first place? Or, more simply, why

---

[1] There are multiple groups of the Church of Jesus Christ of Latter-day Saints. The group being studied in this work is the largest of the Latter-day Saint groups and is headquartered in Salt Lake City, Utah. Other Latter-day Saint groups include the Community of Christ (known historically as the Reorganized Church of Jesus Christ of Latter-day Saints), headquartered in Independence, Missouri; the Church of Christ-Temple Lot, headquartered in Independence, Missouri; the Church of Jesus Christ of Latter-day Saints, Strangite, headquartered in Burlington, Wisconsin; the Restoration Church of Jesus Christ of Latter-day Saints, headquartered in Independence, Missouri; and the Church of Christ with Elijah Message, headquartered in Blue Springs, Missouri. For a short discussion of the various Latter-day Saint groups, see Frank S. Mead, Samuel S. Hill, and Craig D. Atwood, *Handbook of Denominations in the United States*, 12th ed. (Nashville: Abingdon, 2005), 346–53. For a more extended discussion, see Newell G. Bringhurst and John C. Hamer, eds., *Scattering of the Saints: Schism with Mormonism* (Independence, MO: John Whitmer, 2007).

should we focus a study on the Church of Jesus Christ of Latter-day Saints? Most fundamental, though, is the question, should we do the hard work of understanding?

The first issue we should address is the need for a better understanding of other faith communities around us. Hopefully, our attitude toward non-Christians is not one of apathy.[2] Unfortunately, as statistics for baptism rates among Protestants have dropped significantly over the past four to five decades, it seems that apathy is common among Christians.[3] Do we, as Christians, simply not care about the eternal fate of non-Christians? How might this apathy be remedied? Those who believe the Bible to be the Word of God, as we do, look to its pages for instruction and inspiration. It is to the Bible that we first turn, then, in order to right the drifting ship of our attitudes toward non-Christians.

There are a number of biblical examples of the proper attitude Christians should take toward non-Christians. Probably the greatest example of a Christian attitude toward non-Christians, especially in the context of evangelism, is found in the second half of Acts 17. After being run out of Berea by the Thessalonian Jews, the apostle Paul was sent by the believers to Athens. While waiting for Silas and Timothy to arrive, Paul was taken aback by the rampant idolatry found in the well-known, flourishing ancient city of Athens. So Paul found the local synagogue and proclaimed the message of Christ to the Jews in their place of worship. He also made his way to the local marketplace, a setting teeming with all types of people, but especially with non-Christians. There, Paul encountered a variety of beliefs. Being in such proximity to the Areopagus, Paul knew he would find any number of belief systems. J. R. McRay notes, "The western, Greek market lay due north of the Areopagus (Mars Hill) and contained the prominent temple of Hephaestus and the reconstructed Stoa (Colonnaded Porch) of Attalos, where poet and philosopher met to promenade

---

[2] It will be argued throughout this book that members of the Church of Jesus Christ of Latter-day Saints are not to be considered Christians in a soteriological sense due to the major theological differences with historic, orthodox Christianity. In other words, because of the significant differences between Mormon beliefs and historic, orthodox Christianity, any person holding to the theology of the LDS Church will not inherit the kingdom of heaven after death. This statement is not one of hatred or malice, but one of truth based in the Bible and of compassion.

[3] Most mainline Protestant denominations have been in decline for decades, the Southern Baptist Convention being one of the exceptions. However, for the majority of the twenty-first century, the Southern Baptist Convention has seen neither growth nor decline. See Peter Smith, "Southern Baptists Fret over Decline as Annual Meeting Begins," *USA Today*, June 10, 2008.

and talk."[4] Indeed, the belief systems in Athens were so varied, Luke tells us in Acts 17:16 that Paul's spirit was "deeply distressed." His provocation, the internal prompting of the Holy Spirit, led Paul to his unquenchable drive to share the message of Christ with all around him. Paul went further, though. He did not wait for the non-Christians to come to him; he went out in search of non-Christians in Athens. Remarkably, Paul's attitude toward the non-Christians was not one of anger or malice, as it had been toward Christians before his conversion (see Acts 7:54–8:3). Paul had been changed from the inside, a change wrought by the Holy Spirit, the same Spirit about whom Paul was now preaching. Paul was not engaged with non-Christians in order to win a debate or to score rhetorical points. He was interested in sharing the message of the risen Christ with those around him. His regular practice, upon entering a new town or city, was to find the local synagogue and share the gospel of Jesus Christ to those in the synagogue (see Acts 13:5, 14; 14:1; 17:1, 10, 17; 18:4, 19; 19:8). Paul's attitude was antithetical to apathy; he was eager to share. Paul went to the non-Christians; he did not expect them to come to him. Why? Because he was concerned for their souls.

Also central to this work is the question of why we should study the LDS Church in the first place. Is Mormonism really that important? Is it important enough to warrant the multiple books, articles, and so forth, devoted solely to studying Latter-day Saint beliefs? Put simply, *What's the big deal?*

Why Study the Church of Jesus Christ of Latter-day Saints?

Numerical Growth

The Church of Jesus Christ of Latter-day Saints is quickly becoming a player on the field of the world's major living religions.[5] Currently claiming more than 16 million members worldwide, including more than 100,000 missionaries, the LDS Church has experienced exponential growth since its humble beginnings in Palmyra, New York.[6] The LDS Church expanded from the north-

---

[4] J. R. McRay, "Athens," in *Dictionary of New Testament Background*, ed. Craig A. Evans and Stanley E. Porter (Downers Grove, IL: InterVarsity, 2000), 139.

[5] See note 1.

[6] In 1984, sociologist Rodney Stark wrote an article in which he argued that the LDS Church would "soon achieve a worldwide following comparable to that of Islam, Buddhism, Christianity, Hinduism, and the other dominant world faiths." See Rodney Stark, "The Rise of a New World Faith," *Review of Religious Research* 26 (1984): 18.

eastern United States to the western United States during the mid-1800s, but now the church has an international membership, with more members outside the United States than within. LDS scriptures promise that the newly formed Church would flourish; thus, the growth of the Church comes as no surprise to the LDS.[7]

Concerning the continuing growth of the LDS Church, sociologist Rodney Stark argued, "If, for example, we assume [Mormons] will grow by 30 percent per decade, then in 2080 there will be more than 60 million Mormons. But, since World War II, the Mormon growth rate has been far higher than 30 percent per decade. If we set the rate at 50 percent, then in 2080 there will be 265 million Mormons."[8] Numerous sociologists have analyzed Stark's projections, but Stark himself reassessed his projections in 1995 and concluded, "So far, so good."[9] More recently, in 2006, when asked about his projections, Stark said, "The [LDS] church liked the results and people who are against the [LDS] church are desperate to figure out why it won't happen. . . . Everyone takes the thing too seriously. I've tried to make clear all along that I was just trying to bring a little discipline to a lot of crazy conversations."[10]

What should be made of Stark's predictions and his own words from 1995 that his predictions are being met with higher-than-expected growth? After all, not everyone studying the LDS Church agrees with Stark's projections. At the 2002 meeting of the Association for the Sociology of Religion, Roger Loomis argued that "the growth rate of the [LDS Church] is decreasing and will probably continue to decrease in the future, with the total membership of the church never coming close to 280 million." Loomis explained further:

> [After 1989], the number of members and the number of missionaries had each increased by about 70%. To produce exponential growth, the number of converts would also need to increase by 70% over this time period to about 540,000 converts in the year 2001. Disappointingly, the number of converts in 2001 wasn't 70% higher than the 1989 level—it was 8% *lower*. In each of those 12 years, the church baptized

---

[7] See Doctrine and Covenants 1:23 and 6:6 on the website of the Church of Jesus Christ of Latter-day Saints, https://www.lds.org/scriptures/dc-testament/dc?lang=eng.
[8] Stark, "The Rise of a New World Faith," 23.
[9] Rodney Stark, "So Far, So Good: A Brief Assessment of Mormon Membership Projections," *Review of Religious Research* 38 (1996): 178.
[10] Cited in Peggy Fletcher Stack, "Keeping Members a Challenge for LDS Church," *Salt Lake Tribune*, June 22, 2006, http://www.sltrib.com/ci_2890645?IADID.

about 300,000 converts. This would indicate that the church is growing in a linear fashion, not an exponential one. In other words, the rate
of growth measured against the size of the Church is slowing down.[11]

Loomis concluded, "It's imaginable that the Mormon Church will grow at 50%
per decade for the next 78 years and will reach 280 million in 2080, but if it
were to then continue growing at that rate it would reach 16 billion in 2180 and
921 billion in 2280. At some point, circumstances *always* force exponential
growth to stop." He predicted that LDS growth would continue "linearly for
the next 15 or so years and then [begin] to slow down, eventually reaching a
maximum at 18.5 million members in 2031."[12]

Similar findings have been recounted. In a 2006 article in the *Salt Lake
Tribune*, Peggy Fletcher Stack reported that a 2001 survey conducted by the
Graduate Center of the City University of New York "discovered that about the
same number of people said they had joined the LDS Church as said they had
left it. The CUNY survey reported the church's net growth was zero percent."[13]
In another 2006 article in the *Salt Lake Tribune*, Matt Canham stated, "Statistics from other sources show the LDS growth worldwide has cooled. Official
church membership numbers in some key countries are much higher than the
LDS population identified by census counts."[14]

In a landmark study entitled *The Law of the Harvest: Practical Principles
of Effective Missionary Work*, David G. Stewart, a member of the LDS Church,
analyzed LDS growth rates and retention rates.[15] He wrote:

> LDS annual growth has declined from 5 percent in the late 1980s to
> less than 3 percent from 2000 to the present, even though the absolute
> number of missionaries has considerably increased over this period.
> The sharp decline in LDS growth rates occurred even at times with
> record numbers of missionaries serving. This declining growth comes
> in spite of unprecedented increase in opportunity.

[11] Roger Loomis, "Mormon Church Growth" (paper presented at the 2002 Association for the
Sociology of Religion, Chicago, IL), http://www.lds4u.com/growth2/Index.htm.
[12] Loomis.
[13] Stack, "Keeping Members a Challenge for LDS Church."
[14] Matt Canham, "Mormon Portion of Utah Population Steadily Shrinking," *Salt Lake Tribune*,
June 22, 2006, http://www.sltrib.com/ci_2886596.
[15] The remarks and statistics that follow are from David G. Stewart, *The Law of the Harvest:
Practical Principles of Effective Missionary Work,* accessed July 15, 2007, http://www.cumor-
ah.com/lawoftheharvest.pdf.

Stewart offered three reasons for the low rates of natural growth among the
LDS Church. First, he noted "a large majority of inactive members rear their
children outside of the Church. Second, many active international members
marry outside the Church, while many others remain unmarried. Finally,
birthrates have declined considerably among the core North American LDS
membership." This prompted Stewart to conclude, "The natural growth of
Latter-day Saints in the United States appears to be below the level required to
sustain a stable population."

Stewart also offered an analysis of organizational growth within the LDS
Church. He wrote, "Of all of the officially reported church growth statistics,
the number of stakes is the only indicator with any obligatory relationship to
actual member participation or activity, since stakes cannot be formed without a requisite number of active Melchizedek Priesthood holders."[16] Stewart
continued:

> The fact that stakes have been formed at a rate of less than one hundred
> every four years rather than one hundred or more each year demon-
> strates that only a fraction of converts become participating members.
> Respected LDS sociologist Dr. Armand Mauss observed: "The key
> to the church's future growth will be at least as much a function of
> retention as conversion. While our numbers continue to grow, the rate
> at which we are creating new stakes has noticeably slowed down. That
> is a clear indication of a retention problem."

He further discussed this problem with new convert retention in suggesting a
"worldwide LDS activity rate of 35 percent, or approximately 4 million individuals." Internationally, new convert retention is also a problem for the LDS
Church. Stewart noted, "Most international LDS members are not believing
semiactives who are simply undersocialized, but completely disassociated, inactive, or hostile individuals with no ongoing connection or commitment to the
Church." He added, "the areas with the most rapid numerical membership increase today, Latin America and the Philippines, are also areas with extremely
low convert retention."

Disagreement with Stark's projections reaches further than professionals
who study the LDS Church. Pleas for help with new convert retention from

[16] A ward is a local group of Latter-day Saints, usually numbering between 200 and 500. A
stake is a geographical grouping of wards (usually four to seven) into a larger ecclesiastical
unit.

LDS leaders also seem to mirror an unspoken disagreement with projections like those from Stark. During the April 1997 General Conference, then president Thomas S. Monson, first counselor in the First Presidency at that time, said, "Each new convert should be provided a calling in the Church. Such brings interest, stability, and growth."[17] At the same General Conference, former president Gordon B. Hinckley asserted, "A program for retaining and strengthening the convert will soon go out to all the Church. I plead with you, brethren; I ask of you, each of you, to become a part of this great effort. Every convert is precious. Every convert is a son or daughter of God. Every convert is a great and serious responsibility."[18] Similarly, in 1999, Hinckley exhorted Church members to make new converts a top priority. He wrote, "Having found and baptized a new convert, we have the challenge of fellowshipping him and strengthening his testimony of the truth of this work. We cannot have him walking in the front door and out the back."[19]

Not only do leaders within the LDS Church concern themselves with retention rates, they are also disquieted with the lack of growth of the Church through member-missionary work. In the past, member referrals of nonmembers were a significant piece of the work of LDS missionaries. However, referrals have dropped in recent times. While speaking to the Church membership, President Hinckley stated:

> The number of member referrals has declined in many areas because the matter does not receive attention. For instance, in the United States and Canada 42 percent of investigators came from member referrals in 1987. By 1997 that number had dropped to 20 percent. A similar decline is found across the world. Now brothers and sisters, this downward trend must be reversed. We need again to give this important matter its proper priority.[20]

Likewise, Elder M. Russell Ballard, a member of the Quorum of the Twelve Apostles, urges members to be participators in mission endeavors. He wrote,

---

[17] Thomas S. Monson, "They Will Come" (speech presented at the General Conference meeting of the Church of Jesus Christ of Latter-day Saints, Salt Lake City, UT, April 5, 1997), online at https://www.lds.org/general-conference/1997/04/they-will-come?lang=eng.
[18] Gordon B. Hinckley, "Converts and Young Men" (presented at the General Conference meeting of the Church of Jesus Christ of Latter-day Saints, Salt Lake City, UT, April 5, 1997), online at https://www.lds.org/general-conference/1997/04/converts-and-young-men?lang=eng.
[19] Gordon B. Hinckley, "Find the Lambs, Feed the Sheep," *Ensign,* May 1999, 107.
[20] Hinckley, 107.

"[O]ur current level of member-missionary work is inadequate. We can and must do better." He further added, "Member participation in missionary work has declined," and this decline "represents a decrease in the actual number of member referrals."[21]

Although Stark's projections have been questioned by sociologists, by others who study the LDS Church, and indirectly by statements from members of LDS leadership, still the LDS Church is a significant movement with more than 16 million members. Though the Church may not grow as quickly as some expect, the LDS Church still continues to grow and, therefore, deserves close study and examination, based, if for no other reason, on the number of adherents. Yet other reasons for studying the LDS Church exist.

Financial Affluence

Another reason to engage the LDS Church in the context of serious study is the financial affluence of the Church. Currently, the Church owns and operates a for-profit business holding company known as Deseret Management Corporation (hereinafter DMC). According to the DMC website, "DMC oversees the commercial companies affiliated with the Church, including Beneficial Financial Group, Bonneville International Corporation, Deseret Book Company, Deseret Morning News, Hawaii Reserves, Inc., Temple Square Hospitality Corporation, and Zions Securities Corporation."[22]

Of the seven companies managed by DMC, Beneficial Financial Group serves as the insurance corporation of the LDS Church. "Beneficial Financial Group was established in 1905. Although it began as a local company serving local needs, it has expanded to serve the entire western United States and parts of the Midwest and the East Coast. It is among the top 10 percent of American insurance companies."[23] Beneficial Financial Group's website explains further, "As of December 31, 2016, Beneficial's insurance in-force was $14.6 billion. Beneficial continues to maintain very high capital and surplus as a financial safety cushion to meet the company's future liability obligations. As of December 31, 2016, the company's capital and surplus was $177.4 million."[24]

[21] M. Russell Ballard, "Members Are the Key," *Ensign*, September 2000, 10.
[22] Deseret Management Corporation, "About DMC," accessed February 27, 2018, https://web.archive.org/web/20070928143117/http://www.deseretmanagement.com/?nid=9.
[23] Beneficial Financial Group, "Beneficial Financial Life Insurance," accessed January 24, 2018, https://www.insure.com/companies/beneficial-life-insurance.html.
[24] Beneficial Financial Group, "Financial Information," accessed February 28, 2018, http://www.beneficialfinancialgroup.com/about/financial_information.html.

A second company managed by DMC is Bonneville International Corporation, a media company, considered to be "a major national broadcasting group. The company owns and operates radio stations in Chicago; Washington D.C.; Seattle; Phoenix; St. Louis; Cincinnati; and Salt Lake City; plus KSL-TV in Salt Lake City, Bonneville Communications, Bonneville Satellite Company, and Bonneville Interactive Services."[25]

Third is Deseret Book Company, [26] an entity "committed to support the mission of The Church of Jesus Christ of Latter-day Saints by providing scriptures, books, music, and other quality products that strengthen individuals, families, and our society." Currently, Deseret Book Company owns Excel Entertainment (a music and media company), Shadow Mountain Press (book publishing), and "a full-service music and entertainment division [that] publishes some software, electronic products, and foreign translations of key titles." Similarly, "Deseret Book is both a publisher and retailer, and as such maintains a book club, retail stores, an online retail and informational Web site, and the Mormon Handicraft gift shops."[27]

Fourth, DMC manages Deseret News, a newspaper corporation that published its first newspaper on June 15, 1850. The *Deseret News* is described as "Utah's oldest continually published daily newspaper. Through its local and national print and digital products, the Deseret News offers news, analysis, and commentary on issues impacting families, including faith, education, media and culture, care for the poor, and financial responsibility."[28]

Fifth in DMC's corporate holding portfolio is Hawaii Reserves, Inc. This company "manages property affiliated with The Church of Jesus Christ of Latter-day Saints, located primarily in Laie, on the north shore of Oahu. This includes Laie Shopping Center as well as other commercial and residential

---

[25] Deseret Management Corporation, "Bonneville International Corporation," accessed February 27, 2018, https://web.archive.org/web/20070626085923/http://www.deseretmanagement.com/?nid=8&sid=471.

[26] The quotations in this paragraph are taken from Deseret Book, "About Deseret Book Company," accessed January 24, 2018, http://www.deseretbook.com/about.

[27] Deseret Book Company currently owns and operates 44 stores throughout the United States. By comparison, LifeWay Christian Resources of the Southern Baptist Convention currently owns and operates more than 170 LifeWay Christian Stores in the United States. Deseret Book Company, including its bookstores, is a for-profit business whereas LifeWay Christian Resources of the Southern Baptist Convention, including all LifeWay Christian Stores, is nonprofit.

[28] Deseret Management Corporation, "Deseret News," accessed January 24, 2018, http://deseretmanagement.com/our-companies/deseret-news/.

properties; Laie Cemetery and Hukilau Beach Park; subsidiaries Laie Water Company and Laie Treatment Works."[29]

Sixth is Temple Square Hospitality Corporation. According to their website:

Deseret Management Company corporation that provides hospitality services for all Temple Square guests. Its history traces back to the prestigious Hotel Utah, which was built in 1911. . . . In 1988, Temple Square Hospitality was organized to service the dining needs of those visiting Temple Square and Salt Lake City. Since then, it has grown into three catering facilities (including off-site catering), four restaurants, a bakery, and a full-service floral department. Known as the Hospitality Host at Temple Square, over 700,000 meals are served each year.[30]

The Lion House was constructed in 1856 under Brigham Young's leadership and serves as "a gathering place for receptions, group dinners, club meetings, and other events."[31] Constructed in 1911, the Joseph Smith Memorial Building served originally as a luxury hotel, but was renovated in the 1990s.

Finally, DMC manages Zions Securities Corporation, now known as Utah Property Management Associates (UPMA). Organized in 1922 as a small real estate management company, "the purpose of the company was to manage and operate several acquired properties. Since that time, UPMA has become a full-service real estate company and has been involved with many Church properties primarily in Utah and in several other states." The company is heavily invested in the development of downtown Salt Lake City and acts as "property managers for over 3 million sq. ft. of commercial buildings. UPMA accommodates some of the most prestigious tenants in the Salt Lake valley. Some of our well-known office buildings include Eagle Gate Plaza and Office Tower, Gateway Tower West, Social Hall Plaza, and Triad Center."[32] Similarly,

---

[29] Hawaii Reserves, Inc. Website, accessed January 24, 2018, http://www.hawaiireserves.com/index.htm.
[30] Temple Square Hospitality. Website, accessed February 23, 2018, http://www.templesquare.com/about-us.
[31] Deseret Management Corporation, "Temple Square Hospitality," accessed January 24, 2018, http://deseretmanagement.com/our-companies/temple-square-hospitality/.
[32] Utah Property Management Associates. Website, accessed February 23, 2018, https://utpma.com/about.

according to their website, UPMA manages 1,100 apartments in Salt Lake City and Ogden and 6,200 parking stall units in Salt Lake City.

A concise analysis of the business corporations of the LDS Church shows the financial wealth of the Church, but the contributions received from the tithes of individual Latter-day Saints, according to two scholars, contributes more to the coffers of the Church than do the businesses owned and operated by the Church.[33] Richard and Joan Ostling argued convincingly that the tithe income of the LDS Church provides the bulk of the Church's income. After interviewing LDS leaders, the Ostlings concluded:

> Though the church authorities steadfastly refused to provide aggregate numbers, certain things they said during the interviews turned out to be extremely useful. Most useful of all was [Presiding Bishop] Burton's remark that the tithe was "90 percent" of the church's income. Knowing the tithe, then, would indicate how much income the church makes from its other assets and also allow an estimate of the size of those earning assets.[34]

Due to the lack of official information offered by the Church, the Ostlings devised their own system by which the income generated by members' tithes may be estimated. They wrote, "So to find an estimate we looked for the closest comparable denomination of some size with a commitment to both open records and tithing, in order to examine contributions from both U.S. and (vastly different) international memberships. We settled on the Seventh-day Adventist Church, which emphasizes tithing and perpetuates a similarly disciplined, close-knit fellowship."[35] With respect to the Seventh-day Adventist Church, tithing records in 1995 indicated that the church received $989 per member in the United States and $77 per international member.[36] The Ostlings estimate, therefore, that since "the situations are roughly comparable, and while a straight correlation between the tithing of one church and the other is almost certainly inaccurate, we are convinced that the following projection errs on the

---

[33] The Ostlings made this conclusion after interviewing presiding bishop H. David Burton, who stated that "the tithe was '90 percent' of the church's income." Richard N. Ostling and Joan K. Ostling, *Mormon America: The Power and the Promise* (San Francisco: Harper, 1999), 396.

[34] Ostling and Ostling, 396.

[35] Ostling and Ostling, 396.

[36] Ostling and Ostling, 397.

conservative side."[37] When the membership numbers of the LDS Church are multiplied by the tithing averages based on the Seventh-day Adventist Church, the Ostlings conclude that the LDS Church received approximately $5.3 billion in 1995.[38]

Political Influence

Just as the Church is worthy of study due to its size and financial affluence, it is similarly worthy of study due to its political influence. One of the aspects of Joseph Smith's restoration of the supposed lost teachings of Christ was to restore the kingdom of God to earth, an inherently political entity. Klaus Hansen argued, "For faithful Latter-day Saints generally believed that, when Joseph Smith organized or rather restored the Church of Christ in 1830, he had also begun the establishment of the kingdom of God on earth, a kingdom that was to be identical with the church in the minds of most followers."[39] The Topical Guide to the standard works, a guide published by the LDS Church, includes forty-eight texts associated with the idea of the kingdom of God on earth.[40]

Indeed, the identification of the LDS Church with the political kingdom of God was not an idea foreign to Joseph Smith or the early leaders of the LDS Church. In 1842 Apostle John Taylor argued, "It has been the design of

---

[37] Ostling and Ostling, 397.

[38] Ostling and Ostling, 397. The tithing averages for members of the Seventh-day Adventist Church in 1995 was $989 per member in the United States and $77 per international member. Utilizing the same formula, and adjusting for inflation, the projection for LDS tithing income in 2016 should approach $8.3 billion. For inflation information, see Tim McMahon, "Historical Inflation Rate," Inflation.com, January 12, 2018, https://www.inflationdata.com/inflation/inflation_rate/historicalinflation.aspx.

However, to reassert one of the Ostlings' points, "A straight correlation between the tithing of one church and the other is almost certainly inaccurate." Thus, these types of projections should only be viewed as crude estimations and should in no way be understood to be absolutely precise or accurate.

For the purpose of comparison, the churches of the Southern Baptist Convention reported $11.5 billion in total receipts for 2015. However, the total income for the churches of the Southern Baptist Convention is not controlled centrally, as is the case with the LDS Church. For information concerning the 2006 Southern Baptist Convention total receipts, see http://www.bivocational.org/BIVO/Statistics/2006%20ACP/2006_SBC_ACP_Summary.htm (accessed January 24, 2018).

[39] Klaus J. Hansen, Quest for Empire: The Political Kingdom of God and the Council of Fifty in Mormon History (Lincoln: University of Nebraska Press, 1967), 4–5.

[40] Church of Jesus Christ of Latter-day Saints, "Topical Guide: Kingdom of God, on Earth," 2013 ed., LDS.org, accessed January 24, 2018, https://www.lds.org/scriptures/tg/kingdom-of-god-on-earth?lang=eng. See especially the following passages in the Doctrine and Covenants: 35:27; 38:9; 50:35; 65:2; 72:1; 76:107; 82:24; 90:3; 97:14; 105:32; and 138:44 (see note 7, above).

Jehovah . . . to . . . take the reigns of government into his own hand."[41] He also noted that God's taking of the "reigns of government" is "the only thing that can bring about the 'restoration of all things, spoken of by all the holy prophets since the world was—the dispensation of the fullness of times, when GOD shall gather together all things in one.'" Taylor concluded, "Other attempts to promote universal peace and happiness in the human family have proven abortive; every effort has failed; every plan and design has fallen to the ground; it needs the wisdom of God, the intelligence of God, and the power of God to accomplish this. The world has had a fair trial for six thousand years; the Lord will try the seventh thousand himself." Within the LDS worldview, the Lord trying "the seventh thousand himself" means the Latter-day Saints, and thereby the LDS Church, will gain control of the world's political systems.

Another early LDS leader who discussed the idea of the political kingdom of God was Apostle Parley Pratt. In November 1841 Pratt wrote a letter to Queen Victoria of England to inform her of a coming world revolution. Pratt noted:

Know assuredly that the world in which we live is on the eve of a *revolution*, more wonderful in its beginning—more rapid in its progress—more powerful in its operations—more extensive in its effects—more lasting in its influence—and more important in its consequences, than any which man has yet witnessed upon the earth . . . one [revolution] on which the fate of all nations is suspended, and upon which the future destiny of all the affairs of the earth is made to depend.[42]

The revolution to which Pratt was referring is nothing less than the complete and total destruction of all earthly kingdoms and the setting up of a new kingdom "under the immediate administration of the Messiah and his saints."[43]

Joseph Smith himself was concerned not only with the formation of the kingdom of God on earth, but also with the current political climate of his times. In the *Times and Seasons*, he sarcastically remarked:

---

[41] The quotations in this paragraph are from John Taylor, "The Government of God," *Times and Seasons*, July 15, 1842, 857.
[42] Parley Pratt, "A Letter to the Queen of England, Touching the Signs of the Times, and the Political Destiny of the World," *Times and Seasons*, November 15, 1841, 591.
[43] Pratt, 591.

O, Queen Victoria, and ye lords and commons of Great Britain, what think ye of a Republican Government? and how do you imagine your daughter will come out in her attempt at equal rights and reigning in righteousness? Pshaw! (will they answer.) your coffers are robbed with impunity; your citizens are mobbed, and driven like chaff from the threshing floor, and the government controlled by a set of money gambling, chicken hearted, public fed cowards, cannot redress you! . . . If there is any power in a Republican Government, in a real case of necessity, you have failed to find just men to exercise it.[44]

In the same editorial, Smith also offered his own personal view of God's coming government:

As the "world is governed too much" and as there is not a nation or dynasty, now occupying the earth, which acknowledges Almighty God as their law giver, and as "crowns won by blood, by blood must be maintained," I go emphatically, virtuously, and humanely, for a THE-ODEMOCRACY, where God and the people hold the power to conduct the affairs of men in righteousness.[45]

Smith not only believed God would usher in the kingdom of God on earth; he also believed God would use an earthly legislature to rule the earth. This so-called legislature was established in 1842 when Smith claimed to have received a revelation from God concerning the formation of such a body, known as the

---

[44] Joseph Smith Jr., "The Globe," *Times and Seasons*, April 15, 1844, 509. Concerning this letter to Queen Victoria, Klaus Hansen argued, "And yet the political implications of the kingdom of God Pratt and his fellow religionists hoped to establish were, potentially at least, a greater threat to Victoria's crown than all the turmoil stirred up by Chartists and anti-corn-law leagues which so annoyed and perplexed the Queen in the restless 1840's." See Hansen, *Quest for Empire*, 4.

[45] Smith, "The Globe," 510. Smith offered further consideration of the role of the United States government in his *General Smith's Views of the Powers and Policy of the Government of the United States*. Within this treatise he argued that Congress should be reduced to one-half its size, that state legislatures should pardon all inmates within the penitentiaries and that the penitentiaries should be "turned into seminaries," that Congress should pay all slave holders for their slaves in order to free the slaves, that military court-martial for desertion should be abolished, that a national bank should be formed, and, interestingly, that all lawyers should repent, "[obey] the ordinances of heaven, [and] preach the gospel to the destitute." Joseph Smith Jr., *General Smith's Views of the Powers and Policy of the Government of the United States* (Nauvoo, IL: John Taylor, 1844; Independence, MO: Community of Christ, 2003).

Council of Fifty.[46] LDS historian D. Michael Quinn argued that the "primary role of the Council of Fifty was to symbolize the otherworldly world order that would be established during the millennial reign of Christ on earth."[47] Similarly, Brigham Young University Religious Studies Center researcher Andrew F. Ehat argued that the Council of Fifty was Joseph Smith's "concrete description of the millennial government of God" or "the nucleus of a world government for the Millennium."[48] In practice, the Council of Fifty functioned mainly as "a working demonstration of the principles and pattern for a future kingdom of God on earth."[49] The Council of Fifty also functioned as the organizing body for Joseph Smith's presidential campaign when Smith declared his intention to run for the office of president of the United States in 1844. In the end, Kenneth Godfrey argued, "The Council of Fifty was viewed as the seed of a new political order that would rule, under Christ, following the prophesied cataclysmic events of the last days."[50] After the migrating Saints arrived in the Salt Lake valley, the Council functioned only sporadically and officially ceased to exist on May 14, 1945.[51]

---

[46] There is some disagreement as to the date of the formation of the Council of Fifty. Quinn noted that four different sources identify varying dates: April 7, 1842 (Council of Fifty minutes); March 10, 1844 (Wilford Woodruff and Franklin D. Richards); March 11, 1844 (William Clayton and Joseph Fielding Smith); and March 13, 1844 (Brigham Young). These four dates are all considered as viable "primarily because each source considered a different event as marking the Council's origin." It seems likely, however, that the Council, due to its own recorded minutes, understood its formation to be April 7, 1842; thus the 1842 date is utilized here. D. Michael Quinn, "The Council of Fifty and Its Members, 1844 to 1945," *BYU Studies* 20 (1980): 163–66.

The Council of Fifty was also known by other names. Quinn noted, "The official, revealed name of the Council of Fifty is 'The Kingdom of God and His Laws with the Keys and Power[s] [*sic*] thereof, and Judgment in the Hands of His Servants, Ahman Christ'"; however, the group came to be known simply as the Council of Fifty, based on the number of members. Other names by which this group was known include the Kingdom of God, the Kingdom, the K, Special Council, General Council, Council of the Kingdom, Grand Council, councils of the Gods, Council of 50—Kingdom, and Council of YTFIF. For a full accounting of the varying names of the Council of Fifty, see Quinn, 166–69.

[47] Quinn, 163.

[48] Andrew F. Ehat, "'It Seems Like Heaven Began on Earth': Joseph Smith and the Constitution of the Kingdom of God," *BYU Studies* 20 (1980): 253, 273.

[49] Kenneth W. Godfrey, "Council of Fifty," in *Encyclopedia of Mormonism*, ed. Daniel H. Ludlow (New York: Macmillan, 1992), in *GospeLink 2001* [CD-ROM] (Salt Lake City: Deseret, 2000).

[50] Godfrey.

[51] Quinn noted, "In theory, theology, and reality, the LDS Presidency and apostles always governed the Council of Fifty when it was functioning, and in the absence of the Council of Fifty, they continue as the apex of both Church and Kingdom on earth until the perfect world order

Though the Council of Fifty is no longer an officially functioning group, the LDS Church still has influence within the political world. Both United States senators and all members of the United States House of Representatives from the state of Utah are members of the Church. Along with the elected officials from Utah, former majority leader of the United States Senate Harry Reid (D-NV) is a member of the LDS Church, as is United States Senator Michael Crapo (R-ID). Also serving in the United States House of Representatives are Latter-day Saints from Alaska, Arizona, California, Idaho, New Mexico, and Oklahoma. Along with these national offices, two states have recently had Latter-day Saint governors: Massachusetts (Mitt Romney) and Utah (Michael Leavitt, Jon Huntsman Jr., and Gary Herbert).[52] Speaking about Governor Huntsman, one LDS scholar stated Huntsman is "indeed an active, practicing Latter-day Saint. His father, Jon Huntsman, Sr., is a general authority of the Church, a member of the Second Quorum of the Seventy."[53]

Of course, various religious groups, especially the Roman Catholic Church and varying Protestant denominations, can claim members of the United States Senate and House of Representatives as members of their respective groups; however, Latter-day Saint politicians have a connection to their faith unlike other religious politicians. The Latter-day Saint Temple Endowment ceremony includes the following passage:

> You and each of you covenant and promise before God, angels, and these witnesses at this altar, that you do accept the Law of Consecration as contained in the Doctrine and Covenants, in that you do consecrate yourselves, your time, talents, and everything with which the Lord has blessed you, or with which he may bless you, to the Church of Jesus Christ of Latter-day Saints, for the building up of the Kingdom of God on the earth and for the establishment of Zion.[54]

---

of the Millennium is established." Thus, eventually, the Council of Fifty came to be viewed as unnecessary. Quinn, "The Council of Fifty and Its Members, 1844–1945," 191.

[52] Collection: Inside Mormonism, "Mormon Politicians," Ranker, accessed January 24, 2018, https://www.ranker.com/list/mormon-politicians/famous-mormons.

[53] Robert L. Millet, e-mail message to author, March 20, 2007. Millet stated that most, if not all, of these politicians are active, practicing Latter-day Saints.

[54] Institute for Religious Research, "Mormon Temple Endowment Ceremony Text post-1990," http://www.irr.org/MIT/endowment.html; no longer accessible. After this text is read during the ceremony, all participants are instructed to bow their heads and answer yes. For an extended discussion of the LDS understanding of the kingdom of God and the establishment of Zion within the cultural and political context, see Robert L. Millet, "The Development of the Concept of Zion in Mormon Theology" (PhD diss., Florida State University, 1983), 134–81.

All resources and blessings, according to this passage from the Temple Endowment Ceremony, are to be used for the furtherance of the Church; political office is included in these resources and blessings.[55] Church members are also instructed to give their full allegiance to, and follow the instructions of, the president of the Church. Elder Dallin H. Oaks, then a member of the Quorum of Twelve Apostles, stated, "We are all subject to the authority of the called and sustained servants of the Lord. They and we are all governed by the direction of the Spirit of the Lord, and that Spirit only functions in an atmosphere of unity."[56] Similarly, Elder M. Russell Ballard of the Quorum of the Twelve Apostles stated, "If you will listen to the living prophet and the apostles and heed our counsel, you will not go astray." Ballard continued, "I caution you to not disregard the counsel of the President of the Church. . . . Study his words and strive to obey them. They are true and come from God."[57] Another LDS leader asked, "The prophet has my loyalty and he has my love, because how can I uphold the Lord unless I uphold him?"[58] The pledges to help build the Church and sustain the Prophet are paramount for the Latter-day Saint. Thus, the Latter-day Saint politician, specifically within the context of the United

---

[55] Robert Gottlieb and Peter Wiley argued, "Politics, beyond the making of money, is perhaps the Saints' most obsessive secular compulsion, and one that originated with the church itself." Church leaders have, in the past, attempted to influence congressional votes by contacting LDS politicians directly. Gottlieb and Wiley note a 1965 letter sent to all LDS politicians in Congress, asking them to vote in a specific way with regard to a pressing bill. Robert Gottlieb and Peter Wiley, *America's Saints: The Rise of Mormon Power* (New York: Harcourt Brace Jovanovich, 1986), 66, 81.

The bill in question was a repeal of section 14(b) of the Taft-Hartley Act, a bill that, if repealed, would allow states to enact right-to-work laws. The original Taft-Hartley Act was passed in 1947 and was the first time Congress had ever attempted to control labor unions and their formation. Basically, repealing the bill would allow labor unions, and, historically speaking, the Church had opposed labor unions up to that point. In 1965 the First Presidency sent a letter to both Utah senators, all Utah congressmen, and ten additional LDS congressmen from across the country, suggesting the congressmen and senators support the bill and oppose the repeal. One congressman, David King, after receiving the letter, publicly said he either needed to resign his seat or accept denying Church leadership because he fully supported the repeal. King voted for the repeal and was defeated during his next campaign. J. Kenneth Davies, "The Right-to-Work Movement," in *Utah History Encyclopedia*, accessed February 23, 2018, https://web.archive.org/web/20070811173059/http://www.media.utah.edu/UHE/r/RIGHTTOWORK.html.

In the end, the Eighty-Ninth United States Congress, the Congress with whom the repeal was filed, did not repeal section 14(b). Thus, the Congress acted on the repeal the way in which the Church had hoped. However, the actual influence of the letter sent by the First Presidency is unknown.

[56] Dallin H. Oaks, "Criticism," *Ensign*, February 1987, 70.

[57] M. Russell Ballard, "His Word Ye Shall Receive," *Ensign*, May 2001, 65.

[58] Loren C. Dunn, "Receiving a Prophet," *Ensign,* May 1983, 29.

States, is pressed to uphold the desires and needs of his or her constituents, the laws of the United States, the teachings of the Church, and the desires of the current president of the Church.[59]

As has been shown, the LDS Church is formidable as a religious, business, financial, and political force, thus making studies of the Church warranted and necessary. We must now turn to the question of the types of sources used to gather official doctrinal information of the LDS Church.

With reference to the faith community of the Latter-day Saints, though, is there a need for evangelicals to understand them better? As evangelicals, are we engaged or are we, as has been suggested, losing the battle? Carl Mosser and Paul Owen, in a 1998 article, fired a proverbial warning shot across the bow of evangelicalism and its relationship to the LDS Church and her scholars. Mosser and Owen noted, "In this battle the Mormons are fighting valiantly. And the evangelicals? It appears that we may be losing the battle and not knowing it."[60]

Readers may be aware of the vast number of books available detailing Latter-day Saint belief. Admittedly, there are a number of books, written by evangelicals, that seem to parallel the efforts of this work. Unfortunately, when LDS scholars and laity read the majority of these works purporting to explain the beliefs of the LDS Church, they do not recognize the beliefs as their own. Commenting on these types of explanatory works, Daniel Peterson, professor at Brigham Young University, wrote:

> Now, this leads to another rule. It seems to me that one of the rules of doing comparative religion stuff is that when you restate someone else's beliefs, that restatement ought to be recognizable to the person whose beliefs you are restating. You ought to be able to go to that person and say, "Now is this what you believe?" and the person would say, "Yes." The person might say, "That is not exactly how I would phrase it, but yeah, OK, given the change in language, that is what I believe." But if your intended target is always screaming, "But I don't

---

[59] This very idea has prompted one author to write, concerning former Massachusetts governor Mitt Romney's 2007 presidential campaign, "Romney should reassure us about his faith by unequivocally declaring that his primary loyalty is to the Constitution rather than to the LDS Church hierarchy." Laurie F. Maffly-Kipp, "A Mormon President?" *Christian Century*, August 21, 2007.

[60] Carl Mosser and Paul Owen, "Mormon Scholarship, Apologetics, and Evangelical Neglect: Losing the Battle and Not Knowing It?," *Trinity Journal* (1998): 179–205. Mosser and Owen are writing to evangelical scholars concerning evangelicals' lack of academic interaction with LDS scholars; however, the analogy holds true at the lay level as well.

believe that!" then the proper response is *not*, "Oh, yes you do!" This strikes me as a really, really illegitimate tool of comparative religion.[61]

Scholars outside the LDS Church draw the same conclusion that many works detailing Latter-day Saint beliefs are misleading. Three non-Mormon scholars, Francis Beckwith, Carl Mosser, and Paul Owen, concluded, "The traditional LDS theology described in many books on Mormonism is, on many points, increasingly unrepresentative of what Latter-day Saints actually believe."[62] A new approach is surely needed.

The Problem of Official Sources

The next question to which we must turn deals with the types of sources useful for the construction of Latter-day Saint doctrine. It should be obvious that the LDS Church demands further attention.[63] Unfortunately, most Christian works dealing with LDS doctrine are easily defeated by LDS scholars due to a significant lack of both original thought and primary, authoritative source material.

Within the realm of Latter-day Saint studies, however, there is a considerable problem when attempting to discern official Church doctrine and when trying to build LDS theology. For example, Robert Millet proclaimed, "One meets with great difficulty in categorizing or rubricizing Joseph Smith the Mormon Prophet, or for that matter Mormonism as a whole." He continued:

> It is not so easy to determine what is "traditional" or "orthodox" Mormonism. Orthodoxy has to do with a straight and proper walk, with appropriate beliefs and practices. In our case, it may or may not be a course charted by Joseph Smith or Brigham Young or some Church leader of the past. Some who claim to be orthodox on the basis of following the teachings of Brother Joseph—for example, members of polygamous cults—are not in harmony with the Church's constituted authorities and are therefore not orthodox. "When the Prophet Joseph

---

[61] Daniel C. Peterson, "Easier than Research, More Inflammatory than Truth," FairMormon, accessed October 7, 2004, http://www.fairlds.org/FAIR_Conferences/2000_Easier_than_Research_More_Inflammatory_than_Truth.html.

[62] Francis Beckwith, Carl Mosser, and Paul Owen, *The New Mormon Challenge* (Grand Rapids: Zondervan, 2002), 22.

[63] A recent work, *The New Mormon Challenge*, was the first serious, contemporary, major academic work by evangelical Christians investigating LDS doctrine. The work has caused many scholars to realize the need for more work in the area of LDS belief. See previous note.

Smith was martyred," President Harold B. Lee said in 1964, "there were
many saints who died spiritually with Joseph. So it was when Brigham
Young died; so it was when John Taylor died. We have some today willing to believe someone who is dead and gone and to accept his words
as having more authority than the words of a living authority today."[64]

Millet added further, "The Church is to be governed by current, daily revelation."[65] In attempting to determine how one might utilize the words of a past
leader, Millet commented, "To fix ourselves too tightly to the words of a past
prophet-leader—even Joseph Smith—is to approximate the mindset of certain
fundamentalist Protestant groups who reject modern divine communication in
the name of allegiance to the final, infallible, and complete word of God found
between the covers of the Bible."[66] Similarly, James Faulconer wrote, "The
church neither has an official theology nor encourages theological conjecture."
He continued:

> As individuals, we may find a theology helpful to our understanding,
> but no explanation or system of ideas will be sufficient to tell us what
> it means to be a Latter-day Saint. For a Latter-day Saint, a theology is
> always in danger of becoming meaningless because it can always be
> undone by new revelation.
>
> Except for scripture and what the prophet reveals, there is no au-
> thoritative *logos* [word] of the *theos* [God] for Latter-day Saints, and
> given that the prophet can and does continue to reveal things, there is
> no *logos* [word] of what he reveals except the record of those revela-
> tions. For LDS, the *logos* [word] is both in principle and in practice
> always changing, as reflected in the open canon of LDS scripture. In
> principle continuing revelation precludes an account of revelation as
> a whole. Thus, finally our only recourse is to the revelations of the
> prophet since, speaking for God, he can revoke any particular belief
> or practice at any moment, or he can institute a new one, and he can
> do those things with no concern for how to make his pronouncement
> rationally coherent with previous pronouncements or practices.[67]

[64] Robert L. Millet, "Joseph Smith and Modern Mormonism," *BYU Studies* 29 (1989): 65.
[65] Millet, 65.
[66] Millet, 65.
[67] James Faulconer, "Why a Mormon Won't Drink Coffee but Might Have a Coke: The Atheological Character of the Church of Jesus Christ of Latter-day Saints" (lecture, Brigham Young

As Millet and Faulconer have explained, determining a specific set of orthodox LDS beliefs is incredibly difficult. From which sources, then, can LDS beliefs be deduced?

In answering the question, "How do you decide what is your doctrine and what is not?" Robert Millet offered one formulation helpful to answer our original question concerning source authority. Millet wrote:

> In determining whether something is a part of the doctrine of the Church, we might ask: Is it found within the four standard works? Within official declarations or proclamations? Is it taught or discussed in general conference or other official gatherings by general Church leaders today? Is it found in the general handbooks or approved curriculum of the Church today? If it meets at least one of these criteria, we can feel secure and appropriate about teaching it.[68]

Gospel Principles, a work published by the Church, parallels Millet's assessment. In the chapter dealing with scripture, *Gospel Principles* states, "The Church of Jesus Christ of Latter-day Saints accepts four books as scripture: the Bible, the Book of Mormon, the Doctrine and Covenants, and the Pearl of Great Price. These books are called the standard works of the Church. The inspired words of our living prophets are also accepted as scripture."[69] Discussing living prophets further, *Gospel Principles* explains, "In addition to [the Bible, the Book of Mormon, the Doctrine and Covenants, and the Pearl of Great Price], the inspired words of our living prophets become scripture to us. Their words come to us through conferences, Church publications, and instructions to local priesthood leaders."[70] Similarly, Coke Newell wrote, "Revelations 'pertaining to the Kingdom of God' are recorded in the Scriptures—in the Bible, the Book of Mormon, *Doctrine and Covenants*, the *Pearl of Great Price*; in the General Conference talks given by general Authorities every six months; and in various other documents and official records of the church."[71]

University, Provo, UT, March 19, 2003).

[68] Robert L. Millet, *What Happened to the Cross? Distinctive LDS Teachings* (Salt Lake City: Deseret, 2007), 56. Millet also argued for the same sources of authority in another work, coauthored with Gerald R. McDermott. Robert L. Millet and Gerald R. McDermott, *Claiming Christ: A Mormon-Evangelical Debate* (Grand Rapids: Brazos, 2007), 31–32.

[69] Church of Jesus Christ of Latter-day Saints, *Gospel Principles* (Salt Lake City: Church of Jesus Christ of Latter-day Saints, 2009), 52.

[70] Church of Jesus Christ of Latter-day Saints, 55.

[71] Coke Newell, *Latter Days: An Insider's Guide to Mormonism, The Church of Jesus Christ of Latter-day Saints* (New York: St. Martin's, 2000), 259.

Therefore, in assessing official Church doctrine, the works attributed as officially binding and declarative, as the Church, its leaders, and scholars have defined them, will be used.[72] Also, when various LDS scholars or writers are surveyed, the opinions of those authors will be referenced as the *opinions* of those authors. For example, the works of LDS authors will not be referred to as, and should not be thought to be, official statements of LDS Church doctrine. This line of thinking is even shown in the front matter of many books published by LDS authors: "This work is not an official publication of The Church of Jesus Christ of Latter-day Saints. The views expressed herein are the responsibility of the author and do not necessarily represent the position of the Church."[73]

What's the Point?

As we have seen, the Church of Jesus Christ of Latter-day Saints is worthy of study. We have also seen a bold, biblical example of seeking out non-Christians and sharing the message of Christ with them. Likewise, we have explored the lack of understanding among non-Mormons concerning Mormon beliefs and practices. We know that Latter-day Saints deem many books about their doctrines to be false representations, and we understand which sources may be used to better understand Latter-day Saint beliefs. We must now ask a simple question: what's the point? Why go to all the trouble of researching, writing, editing, and reading a book about someone not like us? The answer to these questions is extremely simple, but not simplistic. It is our hope that the information presented will be used to understand Latter-day Saint doctrine more fully, which will then lead to furthering the work of sharing the gospel with members of the LDS Church.

---

[72] The use of Millet's system for the classification of material as authoritative does not lend authority to Millet. His system is being referenced due to his agreement with *Gospel Principles*, an official publication of the Church. In a private discussion with one current LDS mission president, two current LDS bishops, one current LDS stake president, and two former LDS stake presidents, all six men agreed that the explanation of *Gospel Principles* and Millet concerning LDS source authority was also their personal understanding of the sources from which official beliefs may be gleaned. The names and geographical locations of service of the six men will be kept private per their request.

Unless official church material is used for scriptural commentary, any commentaries referenced dealing with the four standard works should be understood to be the opinion of only the author(s) of the commentary and not official Church statements. Although they are not official statements of belief, they nonetheless represent a popular understanding of official beliefs.

[73] Millet, *What Happened to the Cross?*, iv.

It is not the contention of this work that Latter-day Saints be considered Christians in a soteriological sense; thus, the work of sharing the gospel with members of the LDS Church is necessary and urgent. This sharing of the message of Christ with members of the LDS Church should not, however, be done in a rude, contentious, or troublesome manner. First Peter 3:15–16 offers plain instruction here. When we present reasons for the hope of Christ found within us, we are to do so in a gentle, peaceable, and respectful way. Two people on different sides of an issue can, as the old saying goes, disagree without being disagreeable. Let us live in a 1 Peter 3 context, and let us continue our quest to understand Latter-day Saints in that same context.

Former LDS president Gordon B. Hinckley perhaps said it best when he wrote, "Ours ought to be a ceaseless quest for truth."[74] That ceaseless quest cannot end within the context of Latter-day Saint theology. The quest can only end when Latter-day Saints find the Christ of historic, orthodox Christianity. Evangelicals should daily pursue opportunities in which the historic, orthodox Christian faith can be presented to all non-Christians with the hope that God will change them from death to life.

---

[74] Gordon B. Hinckley, "The Continuing Pursuit of Truth," *Ensign*, April 1986, 2.

Chapter 2

Who, or What, Is God?

O ne of the most helpful innovations in philosophy is the movement toward thinking in worldviews. This ingenious philosophical process has
aided students and scholars alike in their understanding of all persons and their
beliefs. In his well-known work *The Universe Next Door*, Christian author
James W. Sire presents his appraisal of the major worldviews held by humanity. He writes:

> Formally stated, the purposes of this book are (1) to outline the ba-
> sic worldviews that underlie the way we in the Western world think
> about ourselves, other people, the natural world, and God or ultimate
> reality; (2) to trace historically how these worldviews have developed
> from a breakdown in the theistic worldview, moving in turn to deism,
> naturalism, nihilism, existentialism, Eastern mysticism and the new
> consciousness of the New Age; (3) to show how postmodernism puts
> a twist on these worldviews; and (4) to encourage us all to think in
> terms of worldviews, that is, with a consciousness of not only our own
> way of thought but also that of other people, so that we can first under-
> stand and then genuinely communicate with others in our pluralistic
> society.[1]

Thus, ultimately, Sire's catalog of neighboring universes deals exclusively
with worldviews and their consequences.

---

[1] James W. Sire, *The Universe Next Door*, 4th ed. (Downers Grove, IL: InterVarsity, 2004),
15–16.

Readers should immediately be asking one question, namely, about the definition of a worldview. Sire puts forth the following as his working definition of a worldview:

A worldview is a commitment, a fundamental orientation of the heart, that can be expressed as a story or in a set of propositions (assumptions which may be true, partially true or entirely false) which we hold (consciously or subconsciously, consistently or inconsistently) about the basic constitution of reality, and that provides the foundation on which we live and move and have our being.[2]

He moves further than this basic definition in order to help his readers understand meaning in the various phrases within. For example, he argues, "A worldview, therefore, is situated in the self—the central operating chamber of every human being. It is from this *heart* that all one's thoughts and actions proceed."[3] Similarly, he notes:

It is important to note that our own worldview may not be what we think it is. It is rather what we show it to be by our words and actions. Our worldview generally lies so deeply embedded in our subconscious that unless we have reflected long and hard, we are unaware of what it is. Even when we think we know what it is and lay it out clearly in neat propositions and clear stories, we may well be wrong. Our very actions may belie our self-understandings.[4]

Sire then moves to how one may determine one's own worldview, and, more importantly, the worldview of other people. He offers seven questions for making this determination: (1) What is prime reality—the really real? (2) What is the nature of external reality, that is, the world around us? (3) What is a human being? (4) What happens to a person at death? (5) Why is it possible to know anything at all? (6) How do we know what is right and wrong? (7) What is the meaning of human history?[5] A person's view of the world matters, and the filters through which individuals see the world are important to know. Put differently, worldviews are vital and provide the basis for our lives, both

---

[2] Sire, 17.
[3] Sire, 18.
[4] Sire, 19.
[5] Sire, 20. Though other sets of worldview questions have been advanced, it is Sire's framework through which the present study is grounded.

public and private. Our view of the world informs every question we have, every decision we make, and every action we take. In another work, considering the seven questions, Sire comments:

> When stated in such a sequence, these questions boggle the mind. Either the answers are obvious to us and we wonder why anyone would bother to ask such questions, or else we wonder how any of them can be answered with any certainty. If we feel the answers are too obvious to consider, then we have a worldview but have no idea that many others do not share it. We should realize that we live in a pluralistic world. What is obvious to us may be "a lie from hell" to our neighbor next door. If we do not recognize that, we are certainly naïve and provincial, and we have much to learn about living in today's world. Alternatively, if we feel that none of the questions can be answered without cheating or committing intellectual suicide, we have already adopted a sort of worldview—a form of skepticism that in its extreme form leads to nihilism.[6]

All of that to say, worldviews are important. Whether or not we take the time to think through our own worldview and the worldview of others, it is still true that every person operates within a worldview, whether knowingly or unknowingly. Taking the time to understand another person's worldview, especially another religious person's worldview, is vital to being an effective evangelist.

The purpose here is not to answer Sire's worldview questions in a systematic fashion from the perspective of the Church of Jesus Christ of Latter-day Saints, but to answer the first of Sire's questions and proceed from that answer. Indeed, Sire himself maintains that the first question, concerning prime reality, is the most important. In discussing how to answer the first question, he contends, "To this we might answer God, or the gods, or the material cosmos. *Our answer here is the most fundamental. It sets the boundaries for the answers that can consistently be given to the other six questions.*"[7] Indeed, the issue of deity is fundamental to any religious system, and that very much holds true for the Church of Jesus Christ of Latter-day Saints.

Though there is no official "systematic theology" for Latter-day Saints, they nonetheless have a short set of propositions put forward in the spring of

---

[6] James W. Sire, *Naming the Elephant* (Downers Grove, IL: InterVarsity, 2004), 21.
[7] Sire, *The Universe Next Door*, 20. Emphasis added.

1842 by Joseph Smith as core doctrines. That short set of propositions is called the Articles of Faith and may be found in any copy of the LDS standard works.[8] The first article reads, "We believe in God, the Eternal Father, and in His Son, Jesus Christ, and in the Holy Ghost."[9] In his monumental work on the Articles of Faith, LDS scholar James Talmage argued, "Since faith in God constitutes the foundation of religious belief and practice, and inasmuch as a knowledge of the attributes and character of Deity is essential to an intelligent exercise of faith in Him, this subject claims first place in our study of the doctrines of the Church."[10] Former LDS apostle Bruce R. McConkie wrote, "Man's purpose in life is to learn the nature and kind of being that God is, and then, by conformity to his laws and ordinances, to progress to that high state of exaltation wherein man becomes perfect as the Father is perfect."[11] Lowell L. Bennion, in his work *The Religion of the Latter-day Saints*, describes man's view of God as "significant" and "very important" to man's overall view of all things.[12] Indeed, one's view of deity is paramount and functions to set the boundary for the remainder of one's personally held convictions. As can be seen, not only from Sire's arguments but from LDS scholars as well, the doctrine of God is vital. Further, one could argue the LDS concept of God undergirds the entire LDS system of belief; thus, an examination of this doctrine is essential. We now turn our attention to the core belief and see how Latter-day Saints answer Sire's first question: What is prime reality—the really real?[13]

---

[8] Commenting on the Articles of Faith, LDS scholar B. H. Roberts wrote, "The combined directness, perspicuity, simplicity and comprehensiveness of this statement of the doctrine of the church is regarded as strong evidence of a divine inspiration operating upon the mind of Joseph Smith." B. H. Roberts, *A Comprehensive History of the Church of Jesus Christ of Latter-day Saints* (Provo, UT: Brigham Young University Press, 1965), 4:131. For an online version of the LDS Standard Works, see https://www.lds.org/topics/standard-works?lang=eng.

[9] Church of Jesus Christ of Latter-day Saints, "The Articles of Faith" (1842 Salt Lake City: Intellectual Reserve, 2013).

[10] James Talmage, *The Articles of Faith* (Salt Lake City: Signature Books, 2003), 27.

[11] Bruce R. McConkie, *Mormon Doctrine*, 2nd ed. (Salt Lake City: Deseret, 1979), 318.

[12] Lowell L. Bennion, *The Religion of the Latter-day Saints* (Salt Lake City: Church of Jesus Christ of Latter-day Saints, 1940), 26.

[13] This section is by no means meant to be a full-orbed systematic theology of the doctrine of God within Latter-day Saint thought. Space considerations simply do not allow for such a study. For more complete investigations of the Latter-day Saint doctrine of God, see Gordon Allred, comp., *God the Father* (Salt Lake City: Deseret, 1979); Talmage, *The Articles of Faith*, 27–54; Garland E. Tickemyer, "A Study of Some Representative Concepts of a Finite God in Contemporary American Philosophy with Application to the God Concepts of the Utah Mormons" (MA thesis, University of Southern California, 1954); James M. McLachlan and Loyd Ericson, eds., *Discourses in Mormon Theology* (Salt Lake City: Greg Kofford Books, 2007); A. C. Osborn, "The Mormon Doctrine of God and Heaven" (lecture, The Baptist

God the Father

"We believe in God, the Eternal Father." Thus begins the thirteen Articles of Faith, included within the LDS standard works. Originally published March 1, 1842, in a letter written by Joseph Smith, the Articles of Faith provide a standard creed for the LDS Church. The problem that arises immediately is the lack of clarity provided by the first part of the first of thirteen articles. Who, or what, exactly is this God? Doctrine and Covenants 130:22 offers a short answer to this question concerning God. The verse states, "The Father has a body of flesh and bones as tangible as man's." A more extended answer is found in Joseph Smith's King Follett discourse, a funeral message preached by Smith in 1844, two months before he was killed. In this message, Smith first articulated and nuanced his idea of God being an exalted man. Smith said:

> God himself was once as we are now, and is an exalted man, and sits enthroned in yonder heavens. If the veil were rent today, and the great God who holds this world its in [*sic*] orbit, and who upholds all worlds and all things by his power, was to make himself visible—I say, if you were to see him today you would see him like a man in form—like yourselves in all the person, image, and very form as a man; for Adam was created in the very fashion, image and likeness of God, and received instruction from, and walked, talked and conversed with him, as one man talks and communes with another.[14]

Orson Pratt, one of the early leaders of the LDS Church, agreed with Smith's understanding of deity. Pratt argued, "The true God exists both in time and space, and has as much relation to them as man or any other being. He has extension, and form, and dimensions, as well as man. He occupies space; has a body, parts, and passions; can go from place to place—can eat, drink, and talk,

---

Ministers' Conference of South Carolina, Darlington, SC, November 29,1898); Blake T. Ostler, *Exploring Mormon Thought: The Attributes of God* (Salt Lake City: Greg Kofford, 2001); Blake T. Ostler, *Exploring Mormon Thought: The Problems of Theism and the Love of God* (Salt Lake City: Greg Kofford, 2006); B. H. Roberts, *The Mormon Doctrine of Deity: The Roberts–Van Der Donckt Discussion* (Bountiful, UT: Horizon, 1903); Janice Allred, ed., *God the Mother* (Salt Lake City: Signature, 1997); Bruce E. Dana, *The Eternal Father and His Son* (Springville, UT: Cedar Fort, 2004); and Joseph W. Musser, ed., *Michael, Our Father and Our God* (Salt Lake City: Truth, 1945).

[14] Joseph Smith Jr., "How God Came to Be God," in *Joseph Smith: Selected Sermons and Writings*, ed. Robert L. Millet (New York: Paulist, 1989), 131–32.

as well as man."[15] Pratt, however, went further and added that God was once a man with a family. He explained, "Like man, he had a Father; and he was 'the express image of the person of the Father.'"[16]

Another early leader of the LDS Church who agreed with Joseph Smith was Brigham Young, the second president of the Church. In the context of a message delivered in the Tabernacle in Salt Lake City, Young declared, "Our God and Father in Heaven, is a being of tabernacle, or, in other words, he has a body, with parts the same as you and I have; and is capable of showing forth his works to organized beings, as for instance, in the world in which we live, it is the result of the knowledge and infinite wisdom that dwell in his organized body."[17] Similarly, Young also said, "We believe in one God, one Mediator and one Holy Ghost. We cannot believe for a moment that God is destitute of body, parts, passions, or attributes. Attributes can be made manifest only through an organized personage. All attributes are couched in and are the results of organized existence."[18]

Former LDS Church president Lorenzo Snow offered what has become an oft-quoted and likely one of the most recognized statements concerning the LDS understanding of the nature of God, a statement usually referred to as the Lorenzo Snow couplet. Recalling his patriarchal blessing given him by Joseph Smith Sr., Snow wrote:

> [Smith, Sr.] told me another thing that greatly surprised me. He said, "You will be great, and as great as you want to be, as great as God Himself, and you will not wish to be greater." I could not understand this, but years after in Nauvoo while talking upon a principle of the gospel, the Spirit of God rested powerfully upon me and showed me more clearly than I can now see your faces a certain principle and its glory, and it came to me summarized in this brief sentence: "As man is now, God once was; as God is now man may be." The Spirit of God was on me in a marvelous manner all that day, and I stored that great

---

[15] Orson Pratt, *The Essential Orson Pratt* (Salt Lake City: Signature, 1991), 52.

[16] Pratt, 52.

[17] Brigham Young, "Self Government—Mysteries—Recreation and Amusements, Not in Themselves Sinful—Tithing—Adam, Our Father and Our God," in *Journal of Discourses*, comp. G. D. Watt (London: Latter-day Saints' Book Depot, 1854), 1:4.

[18] Brigham Young, "Knowledge, Correctly Applied, the True Source of Wealth and Power—Unity of Jesus and His Father—Miracles—Slavery—True Charity, Etc.," in *Journal of Discourses*, comp. G. D. Watt and J. V. Long (London: Latter-day Saints' Book Depot, 1865), 10:192.

truth away in my mind. I felt that I had learnt something that I ought not to communicate to others.[19]

Of the couplet and the impact of this understanding of God on the life and ministry of Lorenzo Snow, his son wrote, "We cannot emphasize the fact too strongly that this revealed truth impressed Lorenzo Snow more than perhaps all else; it sank so deeply into his soul that it became the inspiration of his life and gave him his broad vision of his own great future and mighty mission and work of the Church."[20] Although Lorenzo Snow is given the primary credit for this couplet, Snow's son offers a more complete perspective. He wrote, "Let us understand clearly that while Lorenzo Snow, through a revelation from God, was the author of the above couplet expression, the Lord had revealed this great truth to [Joseph Smith] and to Father Smith, long before it was made known to Lorenzo Snow. In fact, it was the remarkable promise given to him in the Kirtland temple, in 1836, by the Patriarch, that first awakened the thought in his mind, and its expression in the frequently quoted couplet was not revealed to President Snow until the spring of 1840."[21]

Interestingly, President Snow, while visiting Brigham Young University, also offered insight into the deification of humans.[22] While touring Brigham Young University, Snow noticed children playing with clay, forming spheres out of the clay. Commenting to the president of Brigham Young University, President Snow said, "President Brimhall, these children are now at play, making mud worlds, the time will come when some of these boys, through their faithfulness to the gospel, will progress and develop in knowledge, intelligence, and power, in future eternities, until they shall be able to go out into space where there is unorganized matter and call together the necessary elements, and through their knowledge of and control over the laws and powers of nature, to organize matter into worlds on which their posterity may dwell, and over which they shall rule as gods."[23] Thus, Snow may be said to have believed

---

[19] Lorenzo Snow, *The Teachings of Lorenzo Snow*, ed. Clyde J. Williams (Salt Lake City: Bookcraft, 1984), 2. Though some contemporary LDS scholars argue the couplet is no longer valid, it has yet to be refuted by LDS leadership during a general conference.

[20] LeRoi C. Snow, "Devotion to a Divine Inspiration," in *God the Father*, comp. Gordon Allred, 185.

[21] LeRoi C. Snow, 185.

[22] Although the quote that follows does not deal directly with the LDS understanding of God, but with the LDS understanding of man, it is included here because the statement offers insight into Snow's understanding of God's nature before becoming God.

[23] LeRoi C. Snow, "Devotion to a Divine Inspiration," 188–89.

indirectly that God was once a human child, playing in a room with other children, in a sense, training to become the God he currently is.

In similar fashion, Lowell K. Bennion, former director of the Institute of Religion for the LDS Church, wrote:

> In the teachings of the gospel, God is not an absent ideal or idea; he is not law, force, matter, or nature; he is not simply the great Unknown. He is a *living God*, a conscious, sentient, intelligent being, a person with whom we associate the highest attributes of personality—intelligence, creativeness, goodness, and love—in their fullest development. All the prophets, in speaking of God, no matter what the occasion, make us feel that he is a real, objective personality in his own right, that he knows, loves, creates, and acts.[24]

So, like President Snow, Bennion understood God's very nature to be that of a glorified person.

This understanding of God's nature continues to be held in the present Church. LDS layman Bruce E. Dana wrote, "From all these inspired teachings, we are correctly taught that the Father's plan of salvation is an eternal plan; the same identical plan that allowed our Father to gain exaltation and become our Heavenly Father."[25] Dana continued:

> Thus, the divine patriarchal order of eternity, for those who become a God, is clearly set forth. We are most thankful that our Father, as a mortal man, proved faithful to the eternal plan of salvation that was operational by his Heavenly Father; the same identical plan used by all the Fathers before him. We are especially thankful that this eternal plan of salvation allows each of us the same opportunity, based on our faithfulness, to become like Heavenly Father![26]

The conclusion may be drawn, then, that the understanding of the Latter-day Saint God is simply that he was once a human being, a mortal, who lived on a planet like Earth.[27] The question then becomes, if God the

---

[24] Bennion, *The Religion of the Latter-day Saints*, 28.

[25] Dana, *The Eternal Father and His Son*, 22.

[26] Dana, 22.

[27] There is some speculation among scholars that mentions of Kolob in Abraham 3:1–16 in the Pearl of Great Price are discussions of the home planet of God the Father. Bruce McConkie, quoting from the book of Abraham explanation of Facsimile 2 in the Pearl of Great Price,

Father was once a man, does this impact his knowledge of things, specifically, his omniscience and foreknowledge? If God the Father was once a man and became God through a process of growth and learning, does God continue to grow and learn?

The Omniscience of God

Gospel Principles declares simply, "God is perfect. He is a God of righteousness, with attributes such as love, mercy, charity, truth, power, faith, knowledge, and judgment. He has all power. He knows all things. He is full of goodness."[28] James Talmage, a former member of the Quorum of Twelve Apostles, declared:

> God is omniscient. There is nothing in the physical or spiritual universe which He has not created; every property of matter He has ordained, every law He has framed. He possesses, therefore, a perfect knowledge of all His works. His power cannot be comprehended by man; God's wisdom is infinite. Being Himself eternal and perfect, His knowledge cannot be otherwise than infinite. To comprehend Himself, an infinite Being, He must possess an infinite mind.[29]

Marion G. Romney, former second counselor in the First Presidency, noted, "As a member of the Godhead, and being one with the Father and the Son, the Holy Ghost is, as are the Father and the Son, omniscient. He comprehends all truth having a knowledge of all things."[30] Bruce Dana concluded, "God has all knowledge, all wisdom, and all power. The Father and Son are truly omniscient Gods."[31] Seemingly, then, there is agreement among LDS scholarship and laity that God is omniscient. There is one historical example, however, showing a significant divergence over the omniscience of God. Specifically, this centers on the debates dealing with God's omniscience between Brigham Young and Orson Pratt.

The Young-Pratt debates. During the mid-1800s, Brigham Young sent LDS apostle Orson Pratt to Washington, D. C., to defend the Saints' belief in

---

argued Kolob is "nearest to the celestial, or the residence of God." See McConkie, *Mormon Doctrine*, 306.

[28] Church of Jesus Christ of Latter-day Saints, *Gospel Principles*, 6 (see chap. 1, n. 69).

[29] Talmage, *The Articles of Faith*, 43.

[30] Marion G. Romney, "The Holy Ghost," *Ensign,* May 1974, 90.

[31] Dana, *The Eternal Father and His Son*, 150.

plural marriage before the United States government. Pratt's mission was to publish a periodical, a newspaper in which he could defend Joseph Smith's teachings on plural marriage against the encroachment of the president and Congress of the United States. In his publication, *The Seer*, Orson Pratt offered his own opinions concerning the Latter-day Saint doctrines of plural marriage and the preexistence of man. Within his writings dealing with the preexistence of man, Pratt dealt briefly with the nature and attributes of God. One of the attributes with which Pratt dealt was God's knowledge. Pratt's motivation in working through the LDS doctrine of God was because "he saw his efforts as designed to reconcile teachings on the Godhead found in the Bible with those contained in the Mormon canon."[32] Bergera concluded, "Pratt's sympathies were clearly with those who questioned contradictions, as they saw them, in Mormon dogma. It was his desire that church teachings be amenable to human understanding and reasoning rather than a stumbling block."[33]

Orson Pratt clearly believed God to have all knowledge, past, present, and future. Indeed, for Pratt, God is truly omniscient in every sense of the word. When he dealt with the knowledge of God within the context of the preexistence of man, Pratt wrote:

> It has been most generally believed that the Saints will progress in knowledge to all eternity: but when they become one with the Father and Son, and receive a fulness [*sic*] of their glory, that will be the end of all progression in knowledge, because there will be nothing more to be learned. The Father and the Son do not progress in knowledge and wisdom, because they already know all things past, present, and to come. All that become like the Father and Son will know as much as they do, and consequently will learn no more. The Father and Son, and all who are like them and one with them, already know as much as any beings in existence know, or ever can know.[34]

Concerning the knowledge not only of God but also of the other gods in existence, Pratt contended:

---

[32] Gary James Bergera, "The Orson Pratt–Brigham Young Controversies: Conflict within the Quorums, 1853–1868," *Dialogue* 13 (Summer 1980): 11. For examples of LDS scriptures that teach that God is omniscient, see 1 Nephi 9:6; 2 Nephi 2:24; Mosiah 4:9; and Doctrine and Covenants 93:24.

[33] Bergera, 11.

[34] Orson Pratt, "The Pre-Existence of Man," *The Seer*, August 1853, 117.

Now we wish to be distinctly understood that each of these personal Gods has equal knowledge with all the rest; there are none among them that are in advance of the others in knowledge; though some may have been Gods as many millions of years as there are particles of dust in all the universe, yet there is not one truth that such are in possession of but what every other God knows. They are all equal in knowledge, and in wisdom, and in the possession of all truth. None of these Gods are progressing in knowledge: neither can they progress in the acquirement of any truth.[35]

In a lengthy, though intriguing and important, section regarding the argument that God will eternally progress in knowledge, Pratt offered a philosophical line of reasoning that God does not, and indeed cannot, progress in knowledge. Pratt argued:

Some have gone so far as to say that all the Gods were progressing in truth, and would continue to progress to all eternity, and that some were far in advance of others: but let us examine, for a moment, the absurdity of such a conjecture. If all the Gods will be eternally progressing, then it follows, that there must be a boundless infinity of knowledge that no God ever has attained to, or ever can attain to, throughout infinite ages to come. This boundless infinity of knowledge would be entirely out of the reach and control of all the Gods; therefore it would either not be governed at all, or else be governed by something that was infinitely Superior to all the Gods—a something that had all knowledge, and consequently that could acquire more. Have we any right to say that there is a boundless ocean of materials acting under such Superior laws that none of the Gods to all ages of eternity can be able to understand them? We should like to know what Law Giver gave such superior laws? If it be said that the laws were never given, but that the materials themselves eternally acted according to them, this would not in the least obviate the difficulty; for then there would be a boundless ocean of materials, possessing a knowledge of laws so infinitely superior to the knowledge of all the Gods, that none of them, by progressing for eternal ages, could ever reach it. This is the great absurdity resulting from the vague conjecture

---

[35] Pratt, 117–18.

that there will be an endless progression in knowledge among all the Gods. Such a conjecture is not only extremely absurd, but it is in direct opposition to what is revealed.[36]

Pratt concluded, "God and his Son, Jesus Christ, are in possession of all knowledge, and . . . there is no more truth for them to learn."[37] Similarly, he argued, "Therefore, the vague conjecture that God the Father can progress eternally in knowledge, is, as we have shown, not only absurd, but directly opposed to the revelations which He has given."[38]

Although Pratt envisioned a logical, reasoned doctrinal basis to the LDS faith, his philosophical nuances were not met with appreciation. In fact, Brigham Young, then president of the Church, viewed Pratt's thoughts as heretical. Commenting on the relationship between Young and Pratt, one author wrote, "Young, as president, feared the potential dangerous effects of Pratt's logic, while Pratt appreciated the value of a reasoned faith. The difference, one of emphasis, would become increasingly polarized."[39] When Pratt returned to Salt Lake City from Washington, D. C., he was met with concerns from Brigham Young. Bergera noted:

> Pratt returned to the Great Salt Lake Valley to deliver his homecoming report to Church leaders on 3 September 1854. Two weeks later to the day, Young privately reproached the Apostle during a prayer meeting of ranking general authorities. He warned Pratt that his interpretation of the omniscience of God "was a false doctrine & not true that there never will be a time to all Eternity when all the God[s] of Eternity will seace [*sic*] advancing in power knowledge experience & Glory for if this was the case Eternity would seace [*sic*] to be & the glory of God would come to an End but all of celestial beings will continue to advance in knowledge & power worlds without end."[40]

Then apostle Wilford Woodruff, present at the meetings between Young and Pratt, "recorded that the President 'told Brother Pratt to lay aside his Philosofical [*sic*] reasoning & get revelation from God to govern & Enlighten his

---

[36] Pratt, 118.
[37] Pratt, 118.
[38] Pratt, 119.
[39] Bergera, "The Orson Pratt–Brigham Young Controversies," 12.
[40] Bergera, 12–13.

mind more."[41] Two years after Pratt's return to Salt Lake City, on February 17, 1856, the Quorum of Twelve Apostles, engaged in a meeting, discussed the subject of the knowledge of God. Bergera commented:

> Young pointedly asked Pratt's opinion, of his belief that "intelligent beings would continue to learn to all Eternity." The outspoken Apostle, with customary frankness, responded that "he believed the Gods had a knowledge at the present time of ev'ry thing that ever did exist to the endless ages of all Eternity. He believed it as much as any truth that he had ever learned in or out of this Church." Young retorted that "he had never learned that principle in the Church for it was not taught in the Church for it was not true it was fals [*sic*] doctrine For the God[s] & all intelligent beings would never seace [*sic*] to learn except it was the Sons of Perdition they would continue to decrease until they became dissolved back into their native Element & lost their Identity."[42]

Similarly, Young stated, "When we use the term perfection, it applies to man in his present condition, as well as to heavenly beings. We are now, or may be, as perfect in our sphere as God and angels are in theirs, but the greatest intelligence in existence can continually ascent to greater heights of perfection."[43]

There was, then, in the early life of the LDS Church, a disagreement over the extent of the knowledge of God. Unfortunately for Young, however, his understanding of the knowledge of God did not take root within the doctrinal foundation of the Church. As quoted earlier, James Talmage believed God to be omniscient. Speaking of God the Father, Talmage wrote, "Being Himself eternal and perfect, His knowledge cannot be otherwise than infinite."[44] Likewise, Bruce McConkie noted simply, "God is *omniscient*."[45] Similarly, *Gospel Principles* declares, "God knows all things."[46] Robert Millet commented, "To say this another way, [Latter-day Saints] teach that God is all-powerful and all-knowing, but that he has not been so forever; there was once a time in an

---

[41] Bergera, 13.
[42] Bergera, 15.
[43] Brigham Young, *Discourses of Brigham Young*, comp. John A. Widtsoe (Salt Lake City: Deseret, 1954), 89.
[44] Talmage, *The Articles of Faith*, 43.
[45] McConkie, *Mormon Doctrine*, 545.
[46] Church of Jesus Christ of Latter-day Saints, *Gospel Principles*, 9.

eternity past when he lived on an earth like ours."[47] David Paulsen, professor of philosophy at Brigham Young University, noted:

> Latter-day Saints differ among themselves in their understanding of the nature of God's knowledge. Some have thought that God increases endlessly in knowledge as well as in glory and dominion. Others hold to the more traditional view that God's knowledge, including the foreknowledge of future free contingencies, is complete. Despite these differing views, there is accord on two fundamental issues: (1) God's foreknowledge does not causally determine human choices, and (2) this knowledge, like God's power, is maximally efficacious. No event occurs that he has not anticipated or has not taken into account in his planning.[48]

For Paulsen, and for many Latter-day Saints, a discussion of the omniscience of God cannot take place without mention of the freedom of the human will, an absolutely dominant belief within LDS theology. How, though, does the freedom of the will fit into the omniscience of God? Attention will now be turned to the question of the freedom of the will and how the LDS God may be fully omniscient without impacting the future decisions of his free creatures.

God's omniscience and human freedom. Human free agency and the foreknowledge of God have occupied places of prominence within LDS theological discussions since the founding of the Church. Yet the majority of scholars dealing with this issue have offered the same conclusion given by Maxwell: "Of course, when we mortals try to comprehend, rather than accept, foreordination, the result is one in which finite minds futilely try to comprehend omniscience. A full understanding is impossible; we simply have to trust what the Lord has told us."[49]

---

[47] Robert L. Millet, *The Mormon Faith* (Salt Lake City: Shadow Mountain, 1998), 29–30.
[48] David L. Paulsen, "Omnipotent God; Omnipresence of God; Omniscience of God," in *Encyclopedia of Mormonism* (New York: Macmillan, 1992), 3:1030.
    There is, within the issue of the omniscience of God, as Paulsen mentioned, an ongoing debate among scholars over whether or not God is omniscient. Some scholars, harking back to Joseph Smith for support, appeal to Smith's *The Lectures on Faith*, a series of talks given in Kirtland, Ohio, to Smith's "School of Prophets." However, as Kent Robson noted, "Any defense of the Omni-attributes based on *The Lectures on Faith* may thus rest on somewhat shaky ground." For an excellent discussion of this issue see Kent Robson, "Omnis on the Horizon," *Sunstone*, July–August 1983, 21–23.
[49] Neal A. Maxwell, "A More Determined Discipleship" (address delivered at Brigham Young University, October 10, 1978), *Ensign*, February 1979, 71.

Within Latter-day Saint scholarship, the issues of free agency and omniscience have been given serious consideration by writers such as B. H. Roberts, Sterling McMurrin, Blake Ostler, Neal Maxwell, and Kent Robson. B. H. Roberts, a member of the First Quorum of Seventy until his death, argued that God's omniscience does not include the future events of free creatures; God's omniscience covers only the past and present. Roberts wrote, "Not that God is Omniscient up to the point that further progress in knowledge is impossible to him; but that all knowledge that, all that exists, God knows. He is Universal Consciousness, and Mind—he is the All-knowing One, because he knows all that is known."[50] From Roberts, then, one may conclude that God's knowledge extends only to current events, not to future events.

Sterling McMurrin, a controversial Latter-day Saints philosopher who taught at the University of Utah, delved more into the God-and-time aspect of this debate. Through this investigation, McMurrin offered intriguing commentary that helps illuminate the questions raised here. First, McMurrin argued the LDS God is bound within space and time. He wrote, "Now Mormonism has always assumed the naïve concept of space and time as context for whatever is real. Accordingly, it denies eternity in the sense of timelessness, describing God as subject to both time and space." He noted further that, "God himself has the perspective of time, and whatever is in the world and whatever proceeds in the world is real for him genuinely and in its temporal process."[51] He went on to say:

> The doctrine of God's temporality is the most radical facet of Mormon finitism and certainly the most important, for by its very nature temporality involves process, as the concept of time can have meaning only as a measure or context for events. God is placed therefore not above or without, but within the ongoing processes of the universe. The ultimate immutability of reality is thereby denied, and world history, human history, human effort, human achievement, and human freedom take on a new meaning, for the future is real and unique, not merely from the perspective of men, but as well from the perspective of God.[52]

---

[50] B. H. Roberts, *Seventies Course in Theology* (Salt Lake City: Deseret News, 1911), 4:70.
[51] Sterling McMurrin, *The Theological Foundations of the Mormon Religion* (Salt Lake City: Signature, 2000), 39.
[52] McMurrin, 39.

Similarly, McMurrin wrote, "God is described in non-absolutistic terms as a being who is conditioned by and related to the world of which he is a part and which, because it is not ultimately his creation, is not absolutely under his dominion."[53] From McMurrin, then, one may conclude that God's knowledge is limited because of his temporality and his intimate connection to human events.

Blake Ostler, a lawyer in Salt Lake City, has authored two major works dealing with the LDS doctrine of God. In summarizing one of his chapters, Ostler declared, "A person cannot be significantly free if God exists and has infallible foreknowledge, and God cannot have foreknowledge if persons are genuinely free."[54] Ostler contended:

> Nevertheless, in this view God still has natural knowledge of all nec-essary truths and logical possibilities, middle knowledge of what free persons would *probably* do in the circumstances known to him and free knowledge of all things that God himself promises, plans or in-tends to bring about. Such knowledge includes knowledge of all things past, present, and future, known as they actually are at a given moment in time. God knows that what is past has occurred and has perfectly preserved the past in his infallible memory. God knows all things pres-ently occurring and that they are now actual. God also knows that all possible future events are potentially but not actually true. However, God does not know precisely which future choice of free agents will be actual, although he does have a complete knowledge of the proba-bility of such choices for any given individual.[55]

Therefore, according to Ostler, God does have foreknowledge of the choices of free human agents; however, that foreknowledge is of all possibilities and probabilities of future events, not the actual choices of free agents themselves.

Neal A. Maxwell, a former member of the Quorum of the Twelve Apos-tles, offered similar thinking. In an address at BYU, Maxwell stated, "Foreor-dination is like any other blessing—it is a conditional bestowal subject to our faithfulness. Prophecies foreshadow events without determining the outcome, because of a divine foreseeing of outcomes. So foreordination is a conditional

---

[53] McMurrin, 29.
[54] Ostler, *Exploring Mormon Thought: The Attributes of God*, 201.
[55] Ostler, 295–96.

bestowal of a role, a responsibility, or a blessing which, likewise, foresees but does not fix the outcome."[56]

Later in his address, he noted that "foreordination is clearly no excuse for fatalism, or arrogance, or the abuse of agency."[57] Likewise, Maxwell explained, "In ways which are not clear to us, [God] actually *sees*, rather than *foresees*, the future—because all things are, at once, present, before him!"[58]

Elsewhere, Maxwell noted that "God's omniscience is *not* solely a function of prolonged and discerning familiarity with us—but of the stunning reality that the past and present and future are part of an 'eternal now' with God!"[59] He also explained:

> Since . . . things are, for God, one "eternal now," it is to be remembered that for God to foresee is not to cause or even to desire a particular occurrence—but it is to take that occurrence into account beforehand, so that divine reckoning folds it into the unfolding purposes of God. . . .
>
> . . . Our agency is preserved . . . by the fact that as we approach a given moment we do not know what our response will be. Meanwhile, God has foreseen what we will do and has taken our decision into account. . . , so that His purposes are not frustrated. . . . The actual determinations, however, are made by *us* mortals using *our* agency as to this or that course of action.[60]

Maxwell concluded, "By foreseeing, God can plan and His purposes can be fulfilled, but He does this in a way that does not in the least compromise our individual free agency, any more than an able meteorologist causes the weather rather than forecasts it."[61] Thus, for Maxwell, God's omniscience is based on actually seeing what will happen in the future, seeing the future free decisions of humans. This seeing of the future does not cause, in any way, an event to be predetermined.[62]

---

[56] Maxwell, "A More Determined Discipleship," 71.

[57] Maxwell, 71.

[58] Maxwell, 72.

[59] Neal A. Maxwell, *All These Things Shall Give Thee Experience* (Salt Lake City: Deseret, 1979), 8.

[60] Maxwell, 12.

[61] Maxwell, 19.

[62] Maxwell's writing is replete with explanatory statements concerning the relationship between human free agency and God's knowledge. For example, Maxwell noted, "Ever to be emphasized, however, is the reality that God's 'seeing' is not the same thing as His 'causing' something to happen." Maxwell, 20.

Kent Robson, former professor of philosophy at Utah State University, contended that "God knows or does only those things which 'in any way are'—that is, only those things which can be known or done."[63] This understanding seems to limit God's omniscience. However, Robson commented, "We do not limit, in my opinion, the concept of omniscience or omnipotence in Mormon theology, or anywhere else, if we say that God cannot know or do what absolutely cannot be known or done."[64] Robson added:

> The issue is this: as Mormons we believe in freedom and free agency. In order for me to have freedom, I must have alternatives in my future that are *truly open* and not just *appear* to be open. Of course, I could think that I had alternatives when in fact God would know omni-temporally which alternative I would already select. But if it is the case that God knows that, then the future alternative choices I supposed to be open to me are not truly open. They are simply *apparent alternatives*. So, if God knows my every specific act, then I have no *real and meaningful* freedom.[65]

Robson has, as do all Latter-day Saints dealing with this issue, serious questions regarding God's full omniscience and man's freedom. In attempting to protect human freedom, he commented:

> In addition, given our free agency, it would be impossible for us ever to say, "We know that God expects us to be here on this day at this time doing what we are now doing, but we are going to reject this knowledge; we are going to attempt to foil God. We are going to rebel against what God knows as to what we will be doing here and now." For if God is totally omniscient, we must assert that he would know of our rebelliousness at this time and place. Of course, we could then say that if God knows of our rebelliousness, then we are not going to rebel; but then God would have known that also. In fact, it would be

He explained further that God's foreseeing the future is not an actual foreseeing, but more of a prediction based on God's knowledge of our premortal habits and personalities. Maxwell wrote, "Personality patterns, habits, strengths, and weaknesses observed by God over a long period in the premortal world would give God a perfect understanding of what we would do under a given set of circumstances." Maxwell, 20.

[63] Kent Robson, "Omnipotence, Omnipresence, and Omniscience," in *Line upon Line: Essays on Mormon Doctrine*, ed. Gary James Bergera (Salt Lake City: Signature, 1989), 68.

[64] Robson, 68

[65] Robson, 72.

impossible for God to be surprised, disappointed, thrilled, exhilarated, or overjoyed with what we do, because he would have known what every one of us would do in every specific action we ever undertake, now and in all of the future. Again, this argument is incompatible with free agency.[66]

Robson concluded, forthrightly, "If human freedom is compatible with God's omniscience—and there is no responsibility where there is no freedom—then we must choose which we consider to be more important: divine omniscience or human free agency and responsibility."[67] For Robson, the choice is clear: human free agency and responsibility are more important.[68]

From these Latter-day Saint scholars, then, the following conclusions concerning God's omniscience and human freedom may be drawn. First, human free agency is of paramount importance. Second, because human free agency is uplifted, God's full omniscience is necessarily modified. Third, since humans do indeed make free decisions, and since God's full omniscience of the exact events of the future is somewhat limited, God must make his plans based on what he predicts free human agents will decide in any given situation.

The question then becomes: if God must act in predictive ways, rather than in absolute ways, in writing his plans for the future, does this type of act affect his previous statements to humanity? Can God, in any real, substantive way, plan for the future? It does not seem so. Indeed, because the LDS God must be reactive when offering statements to humanity, the LDS doctrine of continuing revelation, something that will be discussed in a later chapter, is necessary based on the LDS doctrine of God.

God the Father: Conclusion

As stated at the beginning of this chapter, worldview thinking is critical. A person's worldview drives what he thinks, among other things, about himself, other people, his vocation, religion, family, marriage, politics, and morality. As Sire argued in *The Universe Next Door*, there is a small set of questions that one may use to determine his own worldview or the worldview of another person. The first question, "What is prime reality—the really real?" addresses the issue of God. And, as he argues, the answer to this question is the foundation

---

[66] Robson, 73.
[67] Robson, 73.
[68] Robson, 67.

to the answers for the other six worldview questions. When two people answer this first question similarly, they share a similar worldview foundation. When they answer differently, they share a different worldview foundation. However, it goes further than simply a worldview foundation. When two people answer the first question differently, they do not simply diverge on worldview foundations but on the entire worldview system itself. How, then, does this line of thinking affect our current discussion of the LDS understanding of God?

Based only on the understanding of God the Father, the LDS worldview is unique. The LDS God is believed, as many scholars quoted here have noted, to have been born and raised on a planet like Earth. The LDS God is believed to have progressed on that Earth-like planet to the point that, when he died in his physical existence, he gained an eternal glory that, according to Abraham 3 in the Pearl of Great Price, is, is near to, or is in some way related to a celestial body called Kolob. Now, reigning as God the Father, he rules over Earth as completely and totally free humans roam the planet. God the Father reacts to those humans as they learn and go about their lives and lives in his eternal existence as an exalted man with a physical body, parts, and passions, an existence any human male can achieve through being obedient to the commands of the teachings of Mormonism. This exalted man rules over Earth and all of its inhabitants alongside his celestial wife, and though not much is known about this Heavenly Mother, the couple is thought to be, at least in some ways, the First Family of the earth in the same way residents of the United States view the first family of our nation. Talmage summarizes the LDS view well: "I submit that to deny the materiality of God's person is to deny God; for a thing without parts has no whole, and an immaterial body cannot exist. The Church of Jesus Christ of Latter-day Saints proclaims against the incomprehensible God, devoid of 'body, parts, and passions,' as a thing impossible of existence."[69]

Jesus Christ the Son

When studying various religions around the world, Christians are always interested to hear what others think about the claims of Jesus. Jesus himself was interested in how humans answer this question when he asked the disciples, as recorded in Matt 16:13, "Who do people say that the Son of Man is?" Moreover, due to the exclusive nature of the teachings of Jesus and the focus of the entire Bible on Jesus, one's Christology is central. Passages such as Acts 4:12

[69] Talmage, *The Articles of Faith,* 48.

and John 14:6 make it abundantly clear that one's knowledge and acceptance of Jesus, as presented in the New Testament, are of utmost significance. Kevin Giles noted, "If we do not meet and know God in Christ, then we are without hope."[70] Gregg Allison wrote:

> The church has historically believed that "Jesus Christ was fully God and fully man in one person, and will be so forever." His deity is demonstrated by his own claims supported by his divine attributes and miraculous activities. His humanity is demonstrated by the virgin birth and his human attributes, activities, relationships, trials, and temptations. One peculiarity of his humanity was sinlessness, but this did not make him something other than human. Along with affirming the two natures of Jesus Christ, the church has also insisted that it was necessary for him to be fully God and fully man if he was to accomplish salvation for all of humanity.[71]

John Anthony McGuckin argued:

> The essence of the Good News that is the Christian gospel is that freedom brought to the world in the community of Christ, by the Lord's life-giving incarnation, ministry, death and resurrection, and the capacity this saving mystery (for it is a unified whole) confers on the redeemed for the true knowledge of God that illuminates, transfigures and vivifies the believer.[72]

Put simply, Christians show ultimate interest in a person's Christology because one's Christology has eternal implications.

Latter-day Saint Christology

We must first ask whether Latter-day Saints and traditional, orthodox Christians agree or disagree over Christological matters. Where, if any, is there agreement? Both sides agree that Jesus Christ was indeed a historical figure who lived 2,000 years ago. Both sides agree that Jesus Christ called apostles, performed miracles, and offered specific religious and moral teachings. Both

---

[70] Kevin Giles, *The Eternal Generation of the Son* (Downers Grove, IL: InterVarsity, 2012), 15.
[71] Gregg R. Allison, *Historical Theology: An Introduction to Christian Doctrine* (Grand Rapids: Zondervan, 2011), 365.
[72] John Anthony McGuckin, ed., *We Believe in One Lord Jesus Christ* (Downers Grove, IL: InterVarsity, 2009), xvii.

sides agree that Jesus Christ was tried by government officials, sentenced to death, actually died on a cross, and was literally raised from the dead on the third day. Both Latter-day Saints and traditional, orthodox Christians share significant agreement on the historical nature of Jesus Christ. Is there, then, disagreement? If disagreement is found, over what issue(s) does the disagreement center? The disagreement found between Latter-day Saints and traditional Christians does not primarily concern the historical person of Jesus. On the contrary, the disagreement primarily concerns the nature of Jesus.

Because the LDS Church is so often misunderstood and misrepresented and because Christology is so fundamental, the remainder of this section will focus on the Christology of the LDS Church as it is presented by LDS Church leaders, by LDS Church–approved curriculum, and by LDS scholars.[73]

Latter-day Saint Church Leaders on Christology. As noted earlier, a Latter-day Saint systematic theology is nowhere to be found. Indeed, the nature of the LDS faith decries such an attempt. However, numerous statements, proclamations, and talks have been given by LDS Church leaders since the LDS Church was founded in 1830, and a number of those statements, proclamations, and talks deal with the nature of Jesus Christ.

The first major statement by LDS Church leadership dealing with the nature of Jesus Christ was released on June 30, 1916, and is entitled "The Father and the Son: A Doctrinal Exposition by the First Presidency and the Quorum of the Twelve Apostles."[74] The editors of *Ensign* magazine noted some issues had erupted during the early twentieth century as to how Latter-day Saints should understand various scriptural passages in which God the Father and Christ the Son are discussed as one, and this confusion prompted LDS Church leadership to issue a statement. The editors wrote, "In the early 1900s, some discussion arose among Church members about the roles of God the Father and Jesus Christ. The First Presidency and Quorum of the Twelve Apostles issued the following in 1916 to clarify the meaning of certain scriptures where Jesus Christ, or Jehovah, is designated as the Father."[75] The statement lists four

---

[73] The standard works, in a direct fashion, are being purposefully left out of this section. Statements by LDS leaders, LDS Church publications, and LDS scholars are replete with references to the standard works; therefore, the standard works will be consulted indirectly rather than directly.

[74] This statement was originally printed in the *Improvement Era* newspaper in August 1916, but has been reprinted in a number of different publications. See Church of Jesus Christ of Latter-day Saints, "The Father and the Son," *Ensign,* April 2002, 13–18.

[75] Church of Jesus Christ of Latter-day Saints, "The Father and the Son," 13.

different meanings when the term *Father* is applied to God or to Jesus Christ: "Father as a literal parent," "Father as creator," "Jesus Christ the Father of those who abide in his gospel," and "Jesus Christ the Father by divine investiture of authority."[76] As a literal parent, the term *Father* is applied to God the Father in the sense that he "is the literal Parent of our Lord and Savior Jesus Christ and of the spirits of the human race."[77] As creator, the term *Father* is attributed to both God and Christ in varying ways. The leaders noted:

> God is not the Father of the earth as one of the worlds in space, nor of the heavenly bodies in whole or in part, not of the inanimate objects and the plants and the animals upon the earth, in the literal sense in which He is the Father of the spirits of mankind. Therefore, scriptures that refer to God in any way as the Father of the heavens and the earth are to be understood as signifying that God is the Maker, the Organizer, the Creator of the heavens and the earth.[78]

As creator, the term *Father* is attributed to Jesus in the sense that, in creation, "Jesus Christ, whom we also know as Jehovah, was the executive of the Father, Elohim, in the work of creation."[79] Further, the leaders asserted, "Jesus Christ, being the Creator, is consistently called the Father of heaven and earth in the sense explained above; and since His creations are of eternal quality He is very properly called the Eternal Father of heaven and earth."[80] The third use of the title "Father" is applied to Christ specifically with reference to salvation. The leaders wrote, "If it be proper to speak of those who accept and abide in the gospel as Christ's sons and daughters—and upon this matter the scriptures are explicit and cannot be gainsaid nor denied—it is consistently proper to speak of Jesus Christ as the Father of the righteous, they having become His children and He having been made their Father through the second birth—the baptismal regeneration."[81] The fourth way in which Christ is referred to as Father is by "divine investiture of authority." Here, the members of the First Presidency and Quorum of the Twelve Apostles noted:

---

[76] Church of Jesus Christ of Latter-day Saints, 14, 17.
[77] Church of Jesus Christ of Latter-day Saints, 14.
[78] Church of Jesus Christ of Latter-day Saints, 14.
[79] Church of Jesus Christ of Latter-day Saints, 14.
[80] Church of Jesus Christ of Latter-day Saints, 14.
[81] Church of Jesus Christ of Latter-day Saints, 17.

A fourth reason for applying the title "Father" to Jesus Christ is found in the fact that in all his dealings with the human family Jesus the Son has represented and yet represents Elohim His Father in power and authority. This is true of Christ in His preexistent, antemortal, or unembodied state, in the state which He was known as Jehovah; also during His embodiment in the flesh; and during His labors as a disembodied spirit in the realm of the dead; and since that period in His resurrected state.[82]

In an extremely telling concluding paragraph, the leaders wrote:

Jesus Christ is not the Father of the spirits who have taken or yet shall take bodies upon this earth, for He is one of them. He is The Son, as they are sons or daughters of Elohim. So far as the stages of eternal progression and attainment have been made known through divine revelation, we are to understand that only resurrected and glorified beings can become parents of spirit offspring. Only such exalted souls have reached maturity in the appointed course of eternal life; and the spirits born to them in the eternal worlds will pass in due sequence through the several stages or estates by which the glorified parents have attained exaltation.[83]

What can be gleaned concerning the nature of Christ from this early statement of LDS Church leadership? First, Christ cannot be determined to be a literal parent as the first of the four uses denotes. When Christ applies the title *Father* to himself, it must mean something different than that of a literal parent because only God (Elohim) carries that designation. Second, when Christ is referred to as Father in the context of creation, he is being referred to as the executive of the creation, having been given the power, by God, to perform the act of creating/organizing the world. Third, when "Father" is applied to Christ, it is sometimes applied in terms of his being the saving father of those who follow him. Fourth, and the most telling for the present study, is the investiture of the title "Father" to Jesus Christ. From this fourth way the term *Father* is used, one must conclude that these Latter-day Saint leaders believed Jesus to be a being who was not, in the beginning, equivalent with God the Father. This is plain in the concluding paragraph (quoted above) to the entire exposition. God

---

[82] Church of Jesus Christ of Latter-day Saints, 17.
[83] Church of Jesus Christ of Latter-day Saints, 18.

the Father is, in essence, greater than Jesus Christ because God has already undergone a resurrection and glorification, something Jesus had yet to undergo in his premortal existence.

The second major statement released by Latter-day Saint Church leadership came in the year 2000 and is entitled "The Living Christ: The Testimony of the Apostles."[84] Though shorter and much less nuanced than the 1916 statement, this proclamation has been distributed throughout the LDS Church and is cherished by its members. One of the first phrases in the statement is declarative of who Jesus Christ is and is most helpful to the present study. The proclamation states, "He was the Great Jehovah of the Old Testament, the Messiah of the New. Under the direction of His Father, He was the creator of the earth."[85] Though concise and seemingly straightforward, this sentence is telling, especially when combined with the teachings from the 1916 statement. When paired with the statement released nearly a century earlier, the 2000 proclamation declares Jesus and God the Father to be separate beings, united in purpose, but not in essence.

In summarizing LDS Church leader statements concerning the nature of Jesus Christ, a few comments may be made. First, these two statements make Jesus Christ and God the Father out to be two separate and distinct beings. Second, Jesus Christ and God the Father are not united in essence, but are united in purpose. Third, Jesus Christ is subservient to (and less than) God the Father, not in terms of traditional intra-Trinitarian subordination, but in terms of actual essence. Because God the Father has existed longer than Jesus Christ and because God the Father had undergone resurrection and exaltation when Jesus Christ was born, God the Father is a greater being than Jesus.

Latter-day Saint Church–Approved Curriculum on Christology. For the purpose of this section, the LDS Church–approved and printed curriculum *Gospel Principles* will be examined.[86] This manual is used for the purposes of adult Sunday school–type courses and is a standardized text throughout the entire LDS Church. *Gospel Principles* qualifies as an official statement of LDS Church doctrine because it is published by the LDS Church and is used in every local meeting house for teaching and instruction. It is not meant to be a

---

[84] See Church of Jesus Christ of Latter-day Saints, "The Living Christ: The Testimony of the Apostles," LDS.org, April 2000, https://www.lds.org/ensign/2000/04/the-living-christ-the-testimony-of-the-apostles-the-church-of-jesus-christ-of-Latter-day-saints?lang=eng.
[85] Church of Jesus Christ of Latter-day Saints, "The Living Christ."
[86] Church of Jesus Christ of Latter-day Saints, *Gospel Principles* (Salt Lake City: Church of Jesus Christ of Latter-day Saints, 2009).

statement of nuanced, systematic theology, but is meant to function as an adult Sunday school manual. Therefore, the statements found in *Gospel Principles* are purposefully succinct.

The discussion of Jesus Christ in *Gospel Principles* is set within the context of the premortal spirit world, a place Latter-day Saints believe all humans, including Jesus Christ, lived before being born on the earth.[87] Within this context, the manual reads, "When the plan for our salvation was presented to us in the premortal spirit world, we were so happy that we shouted for joy."[88] This plan of salvation, however, accounted for sin and the need for payment for that sin: "We needed a Savior to pay for our sins and teach us how to return to our Heavenly Father. Our Father said, 'Whom shall I send?' (Abraham 3:27). Jesus Christ, who was called Jehovah, said, 'Here am I, send me' (Abraham 3:27; see also Moses 4:1–4)."[89] After Jehovah proclaimed his willingness to be the Savior, Lucifer stepped forward and made the same proclamation. *Gospel Principles* declares, "Satan, who was called Lucifer, also came, saying, 'Behold, here am I, send me, I will be thy son, and I will redeem all mankind, that one soul shall not be lost, and surely I will do it; wherefore give me thine honor' (Moses 4:1)."[90] Continuing the storyline, the manual states, "After hearing both sons speak, Heavenly Father said, 'I will send the first' (Abraham 3:27). Jesus Christ was chosen and foreordained to be our Savior. . . . Heavenly Father chose Jesus Christ to be our Savior."[91] Similarly, a few chapters later, *Gospel Principles* devotes another section to its teaching on Jesus Christ. The manual notes, "Jesus is the only person on earth to be born of a mortal mother and an immortal Father."[92] Further, *Gospel Principles* teaches:

> [O]ur wise Heavenly Father prepared a wonderful, merciful plan to save us from physical and spiritual death. He planned for a Savior to come to earth to ransom (redeem) us from our sins and from death. Because of our sins and the weakness of our mortal bodies, we could not ransom ourselves (see Alma 34:10–12). The one who would be our Savior would need to be sinless and to have power over death. There are several reasons why Jesus Christ was the only person who could

---

[87] Church of Jesus Christ of Latter-day Saints, *Gospel Principles*, 9–12.
[88] Church of Jesus Christ of Latter-day Saints, 13.
[89] Church of Jesus Christ of Latter-day Saints, 13.
[90] Church of Jesus Christ of Latter-day Saints, 13.
[91] Church of Jesus Christ of Latter-day Saints, 15.
[92] Church of Jesus Christ of Latter-day Saints, 53.

be our Savior. One reason is that Heavenly Father chose Him to be the Savior. He was the Only Begotten Son of God and thus had power over death. . . . Jesus also qualified to be our Savior because He is the only person who has ever lived on the earth who did not sin. This made Him a worthy sacrifice to pay for the sins of others.[93]

From *Gospel Principles*, then, a limited (but important) set of beliefs may be drawn concerning Jesus. First, there was a time in history when Jehovah was not the Messiah. Or, said slightly differently, there was a time in history when Jehovah was not the Christ. Second, there was a time in history when Jehovah and Lucifer competed for the title "Messiah." Latter-day Saints may argue that Lucifer would have never been chosen to be Messiah, so the competition was not completely open; however, the fact remains: Jehovah and Lucifer both made requests of God the Father to be the Messiah. Third, God chose Jehovah to be the Messiah at a specific point in the past because Jehovah agreed to complete the plan for salvation according to God's determined means. Thus, Jehovah is not the Savior by essence or being but by God's choosing and, to use a phrase from the 1916 LDS Church leadership statement, by divine investiture.

Latter-day Saint Scholars on Christology. The number of Latter-day Saint scholars has increased exponentially over the recent past, with the vast majority of contemporary professors and scholars receiving degrees from well-known and well-respected major universities. Nonmembers studying the LDS Church can be overwhelmed by the sheer amount of writing being produced by LDS scholars. Thus, choosing which scholars to survey can be difficult. However, two scholars stand out in Latter-day Saint life as both well-known and well respected: James E. Talmage and Robert L. Millet. Talmage served as a member of the Quorum of the Twelve Apostles from 1911 until his death in 1933 and is best known in Latter-day Saint circles for his works *Jesus the Christ* and *The Articles of Faith*. Robert Millet was a professor at Brigham Young University and served as Abraham Smoot University Professor and also previously served as dean of the School of Religious Education and as Richard L. Evans Chair of Religious Understanding. Millet has written more than fifty books and hundreds of articles. Most Latter-day Saints know of his work and

---

[93] Church of Jesus Christ of Latter-day Saints, 59–61. Another manual used by Latter-day Saints, though in their homes instead of the local meeting house, is entitled *Gospel Fundamentals*. This manual contains the same teachings as *Gospel Principles*. See Church of Jesus Christ of Latter-day Saints, *Gospel Fundamentals* (Salt Lake City: Church of Jesus Christ of Latter-day Saints, 2002), 5–20.

likely have at least one of his works in their personal libraries. Millet's influence on contemporary Latter-day Saints cannot be overstated.

James E. Talmage. In the introduction to his work *Jesus the Christ*, Talmage wrote, "Instead of beginning our study with the earthly birth of the Holy Babe of Bethlehem, we shall consider the part taken by the Firstborn Son of God in the primeval councils of heaven, at the time when He was chosen and ordained to be the Savior of the unborn race of mortals, the Redeemer of a world then in its formative stages of development."[94] This reinforces the ideas presented earlier, namely, that Latter-day Saints believe there was a time in the past when he was named the Christ. Concerning the entire event, Talmage argued:

> Satan's plan of compulsion, whereby all would be safely conducted through the career of mortality, bereft of freedom to act and agency to choose, so circumscribed that they would be compelled to do right— that one soul would not be lost—was rejected; and the humble offer of Jesus the Firstborn—to assume mortality and live among men as their Exemplar and Teacher, observing the sanctity of man's agency but teaching men to use aright that divine heritage—was accepted. The decision brought war, which resulted in the vanquishment of Satan and his angels, who were cast out and deprived of the boundless privileges incident to the mortal or second estate. In that august council of the angels and the Gods, the Being who later was born in flesh as Mary's Son, Jesus, took prominent part, and there was He ordained of the Father to be the Savior of mankind.[95]

Here, then, Talmage defines for readers his understanding that, at one point in the past, Jesus was not the Messiah and then at some later point, Jesus was made the Messiah. The natural question here surrounds the Latter-day Saint use of the word *eternal* to describe Jesus as the Christ. Plainly, according to Latter-day Saint thought, Jesus has not always been the Christ; therefore, how can he be described as eternal? Talmage answered, "As to time, the term being used in the sense of all duration past, this is our earliest record of the Firstborn among the sons of God; to us who read, it makes the beginning."[96] Similarly, in an interesting comment concerning John 1, Talmage argued:

---

[94] James Talmage, *Jesus the Christ* (Salt Lake City: Deseret, 1990), 3.
[95] Talmage, 8.
[96] Talmage, 8.

The passage is simple, precise and unambiguous. We may reasonably give to the phrase "In the beginning" the same meaning as attaches thereto in the first line of Genesis; and such signification must indicate a time antecedent to the earliest stages of human existence upon the earth. That the Word is Jesus Christ, who was with the Father in that beginning and who was Himself invested with the powers and rank of Godship, and that he came into the world and dwelt among men, are definitely affirmed.[97]

Thus, it may be concluded that Talmage believed Jesus to be a being who existed "in the beginning with the Father," but understood in such a way that Jesus existed "at the beginning of the plans for the earth with the Father." Similarly, like the previously examined proclamations and *Gospel Principles*, Talmage is in agreement that at some point in the past, Jehovah was not the Messiah but then was made the Messiah because he showed a willingness to follow God the Father's plan.

Robert L. Millet. As stated above, Robert Millet has exerted a tremendous influence on contemporary Latter-day Saint thought through his writings and through his teaching career at Brigham Young University. His writings are well researched, nuanced, and theological. Much of his writing focuses on explaining Latter-day Saint thought to both members and nonmembers. Of greatest interest to this section is his work on the doctrine of the Trinity.

In an article entitled "God and Man," Millet noted, "[Latter-day Saints] believe the doctrine of the Trinity represents a superimposition of Hellenistic philosophy on the Bible and that the simplest and closest reading of the four Gospels sets forth a Godhead of three distinct beings and three Gods—not three coequal persons in one substance or essence."[98] He added, "If the Nicene theologians meant to convey that the Father and Son are possessed of the 'same substance' or 'same essence' in the sense that they are both possessed of divinity, of an equal divinity, of a divine nature, then Latter-day Saints would agree. Jesus Christ is the Son of God. Jesus Christ is God the Son. He was fully human and fully divine."[99] Similarly, he wrote:

---

[97] Talmage, 9.
[98] Robert L. Millet, "God and Man," in *No Weapon Shall Prosper*, ed. Robert L. Millet (Salt Lake City: Deseret, 2011), 352.
[99] Millet, 353.

[Latter-day Saints] believe the Father, Son, and Holy Spirit are one in that they constitute one Godhead. We believe they are one in that they possess all of the attributes of godliness in perfection. We believe they are one in the sense that theirs is a covenantal relationship, a relationship established before the world was. Joseph Smith explained that this "everlasting covenant was made between three personages before the organization of the earth, and relates to their dispensation of things to men on the earth; these personages . . . are called God the first, the Creator; God the second, the Redeemer; and God the third, the witness or Testator." Finally, they are one in the scriptural sense that the love and unity among the three distinct personages is of such a magnitude that they are occasionally referred to simply as "God."[100]

He concluded, in agreement with James Talmage:

The one-ness of the Godhead, to which the scriptures so abundantly testify, implies no mystical union of substance, nor any unnatural and therefore impossible blending of personality. Father, Son, and Holy Ghost are as distinct in their persons and individualities as are any three personages in mortality. Yet their unity of purpose and operation is such as to make their edicts one, and their will the will of God.[101]

A question naturally arises here: is this covenant between the three persons an everlasting, or eternal, covenant? In another work, Millet responded to such questions. He wrote, "My colleague Stephen Robinson has pointed out further that 'in both Hebrew and Greek the words for "eternity" denote neither an endless linear time nor a state outside of time, but rather "an age," an "epoch," a "long time," "world," or some other such term—even a "lifetime," or "a generation"—always a measurable *period* of time rather than *endless* time or timelessness.'"[102]

In summarizing Millet's view, a few points may be made. First, Latter-day Saints do not believe in the traditional Christian doctrine of the Trinity. Second, Latter-day Saints believe the three members of the Godhead to be united in various ways, but not in terms of union of being. Third, Latter-day Saints believe the three members of the Godhead are united through a covenant relationship,

---

[100] Millet, 354–55.
[101] Millet, 356.
[102] Robert L. Millet, *Getting at the Truth* (Salt Lake City: Deseret, 2004), 102.

making them long-lasting promise keepers with each other. Fourth, Latter-day Saints believe the Godhead to be eternally covenanted together, but not outside of time. The three members of the Godhead, and their relationship with each other, exist within time, and the length of their relationship could, if such an instrument existed, be measured.

Jesus Christ: Conclusion

To say that Latter-day Saint Christology is complex would be an understatement. Latter-day Saints and traditional Christians can agree on the actual existence of a historical figure named Jesus of Nazareth and that this historical person lived, breathed, traveled, taught, was crucified, and was raised to life after death. About these issues there is no question. However, when it comes to the actual nature of Jesus Christ, there is significant disagreement. Traditional Christianity understands Jesus Christ to be eternally one with the Father and the Spirit, both in purpose and in being. Latter-day Saints understand that oneness to be in purpose only. Traditional Christians believe Jesus to have always been Jesus the Christ, the second member of the Trinity, in a timeless sense. Latter-day Saints believe Jesus was at one point in time not Jesus the Christ, the Messiah. Likewise, Latter-day Saints believe Jesus was, at one point in the past, adopted as the Messiah. Traditional Christians believe Jesus to be the second person of the triune God, a relationship characterized by more than mere covenant between the three persons. Latter-day Saints believe Jesus to be a member of the Godhead, a relationship, started at a point in the past, by covenant.

Thus, though there are points of agreement, there are significant points of disagreement. We disagree over the interpretation of scriptural passages, we disagree over what the early Christians believed, and we disagree over theological points. Of those disagreements, however, the disagreement over the nature of the central figure of the Christian faith is the most significant. Both Latter-day Saints and traditional Christians claim to follow Jesus. Both claim Jesus as their own. One has "Jesus Christ" in its church title. The other calls itself "the Christian church." But in the end, who is this Jesus? One's answer to this question has eternal ramifications. Jesus is the second person of an ontologically united Trinity. Jesus is fully human and fully divine. Jesus is the Lion and the Lamb, the Alpha and the Omega. Jesus is, as Peter answered, the Messiah, the Son of the living God (Matt 16:16).

The Holy Spirit

Commonly referred to as the Holy Ghost by Latter-day Saints, this third member of the Godhead is an immaterial spirit that testifies of the existence of God the Father and Jesus Christ the Son. Doctrine and Covenants 130:22–23 reads, "The Father has a body of flesh and bones as tangible as man's; the Son also; but the Holy Ghost has not a body of flesh and bones, but is a personage of Spirit. Were it not so, the Holy Ghost could not dwell in us. A man may receive the Holy Ghost, and it may descend upon him and not tarry with him."

As we explore the doctrine of the Holy Ghost, it is most helpful to think through this in a structural pattern, dealing with specific attributes of this third member of the Godhead.

The Holy Ghost Is a Spirit

As noted above, Latter-day Saints believe the Holy Ghost to be a personage of spirit. First Nephi 11:11 reads, "And I said unto him: To know the interpretation thereof—for I spake unto him as a man speaketh; for I beheld that he was in the form of a man; yet nevertheless, I knew that it was the Spirit of the Lord; and he spake unto me as a man speaketh with another." Again, Doctrine and Covenants 130:22–23 reads, "The Father has a body of flesh and bones as tangible as man's; the Son also; but the Holy Ghost has not a body of flesh and bones, but is a personage of Spirit. Were it not so, the Holy Ghost could not dwell in us. A man may receive the Holy Ghost, and it may descend upon him and not tarry with him." Bruce McConkie, commenting on these verses, wrote:

> The *Holy Ghost* is the third member of the Godhead. He is a Personage of Spirit, a Spirit Person, a Spirit Man, a Spirit Entity. He can be in only one place at one time, and he does not and cannot transform himself into any other form or image than that of the Man whom he is, though his power and influence can be manifest at one and the same time through all immensity. He is the Comforter, Testator, Revelator, Sanctifier, Holy Spirit, Holy Spirit of Promise, Spirit of Truth, Spirit of the Lord, and Messenger of the Father and the Son, and his companionship is the greatest gift that mortal man can enjoy. His mission is to perform all of the functions appertaining to the various name-titles which he bears. Because he is a Spirit Personage, he has power—according to the eternal laws ordained by the Father—to perform essential and unique functions for men. In this dispensation, at least,

nothing has been revealed as to his origin or destiny; expressions on these matters are both speculative and fruitless.[103]

Similarly, McConkie wrote, "We learn these truths relative to the Gods we worship: 1. They are three in number, three separate persons: the first is the Father, the second, the Son; and the third, the Holy Ghost. They are three individuals who meet together, counsel in concert, and as occasion requires, travel separately through all immensity. They are three holy men, two having bodies of flesh and bones, the third being a personage of spirit."[104] Like McConkie, James Talmage explained, "The Holy Ghost, called also Spirit, and Spirit of the Lord, Spirit of God, Comforter, and Spirit of Truth, is not tabernacle in a body of flesh and bones, but is a personage of spirit; yet we know that the Spirit has manifested Himself in the form of a man."[105] Likewise, Talmage wrote, "That the Spirit of the Lord is capable of manifesting Himself in the form and figure of man, is indicated by the wonderful interview between the Spirit and Nephi, in which He revealed Himself to the prophet, questioned him concerning his desires and belief, instructed him in the things of God, speaking face to face with the man."[106] During the April 1916 Annual General Conference in Salt Lake City, Elder Chares W. Penrose, a member of the Quorum of the Twelve Apostles, said concerning the Holy Ghost, "The Holy Ghost as a 'personage of spirit,' whom Jesus Christ said he would send from the Father, and who would not come unless Jesus went away (John 16:7) was not and is not a 'being of tabernacle,' but, without a body of flesh and bones, he represents both the Father and the Son and is one of the Godhead."[107] During the April 1921 Annual General Conference, Elder Penrose spoke again concerning the Holy Ghost. He stated:

The Holy Ghost is a personage of spirit, as Jesus was when he was Jehovah. . . . [Jehovah] was a personage of spirit, and he came here to the earth that he might be exactly like his brethren and like his Father, and have a body made of the lower elements of the universe. . . .

[103] McConkie, *Mormon Doctrine*, 359.
[104] Church of Jesus Christ of Latter-day Saints, *Teachings of the Latter-day Prophets* (Salt Lake City: Church of Jesus Christ of Latter-day Saints, 1986), 228–29.
[105] Talmage, *Articles of Faith*, 41.
[106] Talmage, 165.
[107] Church of Jesus Christ of Latter-day Saints, *Conference Report* (Salt Lake City: Church of Jesus Christ of Latter-day Saints, 1916), 22.

But about the Holy Ghost, what about that? Why, he is a personage of spirit, an individual, a being, and he bears witness of the Father and of the Son and makes them plain to man. He is called by the Savior, the "Comforter."[108]

Before becoming president of the Church, Joseph Fielding Smith, then a member of the Quorum of the Twelve Apostles, wrote:

The Holy Ghost is the third member of the Godhead. He is a Spirit, in the form of a man. The Holy Ghost is a personage of Spirit, and has a spirit body only. His mission is to bear witness of the Father and the Son and of all truth. As a spirit personage the Holy Ghost has size and dimensions. He does not fill the immensity of space, and cannot be everywhere present in person at the same time. He is also called the Holy Spirit, the Spirit of God, the Spirit of the Lord, the Spirit of Truth, and the Comforter.[109]

Thus, from these various texts and LDS leaders, we can conclude Latter-day Saints believe the Holy Ghost to be a spirit being who can, when need arises, take on the form of a man. We can also conclude, as did McConkie, that there is no information given in Latter-day scriptures or from Latter-day prophets concerning the origin of the Holy Ghost.

The Holy Ghost and Power for Speech

We now turn to the various responsibilities of the Holy Ghost, and the first we will examine is the giving of power for speech. Several texts from the Book of Mormon, Doctrine and Covenants, and the Pearl of Great Price are helpful here. First Nephi 10:17 reads:

And it came to pass after I, Nephi, having heard all the words of my father, concerning the things which he saw in a vision, and also the things which he spake by the power of the Holy Ghost, which power he received by faith on the Son of God—and the Son of God was the Messiah who should come—I, Nephi, was desirous also that I might see, and hear, and know of these things, by the power of the Holy

---

[108] Church of Jesus Christ of Latter-day Saints, *Conference Report* (Salt Lake City: Church of Jesus Christ of Latter-day Saints, 1921), 12–13.
[109] Church of Jesus Christ of Latter-day Saints, *Doctrines of the Gospel Student Manual* (Salt Lake City: Church of Jesus Christ of Latter-day Saints, 1986), 11.

Ghost, which is the gift of God unto all those who diligently seek him, as well in time of old as in the time that he should manifest himself unto the children of men.

Likewise, 2 Nephi 33:1 reads, "And now I, Nephi, cannot write all the things which were taught among my people; neither am I mighty in writing, like unto speaking; for when a man speaketh by the power of the Holy Ghost the power of the Holy Ghost carrieth it unto the hearts of the children of men." Similarly, Doctrine and Covenants 50:21–22 reads, "Therefore, why is it that ye cannot understand and know, that he that receiveth the word by the Spirit of truth receiveth it as it is preached by the Spirit of truth? Wherefore, he that preacheth and he that receiveth, understand one another, and both are edified and rejoice together." Finally, Moses 5:58 reads, "And thus the Gospel began to be preached, from the beginning, being declared by holy angels sent forth from the presence of God, and by his own voice, and by the gift of the Holy Ghost."

Like the above quoted texts, LDS leaders have discussed their understanding of the Holy Ghost and his power over speech. Elder J. Reuben Clark, a member of the Quorum of the Twelve Apostles, said, "How shall we know when the things they have spoken were said as they were 'moved upon by the Holy Ghost'? I have given some thought to the question, and the answer thereto so far as I can determine, is: We can tell when the speakers are 'moved upon by the Holy Ghost' only when we, ourselves, are 'moved upon by the Holy Ghost.' In a way, this completely shifts the responsibility from them to us to determine when they so speak."[110] Similarly, President Brigham Young taught, "The preacher needs the power of the Holy Ghost to deal out to each heart a word in due season, and the hearers need the Holy Ghost to bring forth the fruits of the preached word of God to his glory."[111]

Thus, from the scriptural texts and the LDS leaders, we can say Latter-day Saints believe the following to be true: First, the Holy Ghost is involved in giving power to offer heavenly information. Second, the Holy Ghost is empowered to provide listeners with the ability to determine whether information being presented is authoritative or not. And, third, the Holy Ghost is involved in giving the listener the ability to understand, completely, the message being

---

[110] Church of Jesus Christ of Latter-day Saints, *Doctrine and Covenants Student Manual* (Salt Lake City: Church of Jesus Christ of Latter-day Saints, 1981), 144.
[111] John A Widtsoe, comp., *Discourses of Brigham Young* (Salt Lake City: Deseret Book, 1941), 333.

sent out. Indeed, for the Latter-day Saint, the Holy Ghost is an active presence in speech.

The Holy Ghost and Knowledge

Not only is the Holy Ghost involved in speech; he is also involved in the giving of knowledge. Again, surveying various LDS scriptural texts and general authorities will be helpful. First Nephi 10:19 reads, "For he that diligently seeketh shall find; and the mysteries of God shall be unfolded unto them, by the power of the Holy Ghost, as well in these times as in times of old, and as well in times of old as in times to come; wherefore, the course of the Lord is one eternal round." Likewise, 2 Nephi 26:13 states, "And that he manifesteth himself unto all those who believe in him, by the power of the Holy Ghost; yea, unto every nation, kindred, tongue, and people, working mighty miracles, signs, and wonders, among the children of men according to their faith." Probably the most-used verses from the Book of Mormon, especially by Latter-day Saint missionaries, and therefore probably the most oft-heard verses from the Book of Mormon are Moroni 10:4–5. They read, "And when ye shall receive these things, I would exhort you that ye would ask God, the Eternal Father, in the name of Christ, if these things are not true; and if ye shall ask with a sincere heart, with real intent, having faith in Christ, he will manifest the truth of it unto you, by the power of the Holy Ghost. And by the power of the Holy Ghost ye may know the truth of all things."

Latter-day Saint general authorities have added to this discussion as well. At the 1967 Semi-Annual General Conference in Salt Lake City, Elder Marion G. Romney argued:

> One who receives the witness of the Holy Ghost has a sure knowledge that God lives; that he is our Father in heaven; that Jesus Christ is our Elder Brother in the spirit and the Only Begotten Son of the father in the flesh, our Savior and Redeemer. Such a one knows that the universal order in the heavens above, in the earth beneath, and in the waters under the earth, all give evidence that God lives; he knows that the testimonies of the prophets concerning the Father, Son, and Holy Ghost are accurate and true. Secure in this knowledge, his life has purpose.

The gospel of Jesus Christ becomes for him what Paul said it is, "The power of God unto salvation."[112]

Similarly, albeit years earlier, Elder James Talmage wrote:

> The Office of the Holy Ghost in his ministrations among men is de-scribed in scripture. He is a teacher sent from the Father; and unto those who are entitled to His tuition He will reveal all things necessary for the soul's advancement. Through the influences of the Holy Spirit the powers of the human mind may be quickened and increased, so that things past may be brought to remembrance. He will serve as a guide in things divine unto all who will obey Him, enlightening ev-ery man, in the measure of his humility and obedience; unfolding the mysteries of God, as the knowledge thus revealed may effect greater spiritual growth; conveying knowledge from God to man; sanctifying those who have been cleansed through obedience to the requirements of the Gospel; manifesting all things; and bearing witness unto men concerning the existence and infallibility of the Father and the Son. And not alone does the Holy Ghost bring to mind the past, and ex-plain the things of the present, but His power is manifested likewise in prophecy concerning the future. . . . The power of the Holy Ghost then, is the spirit of prophecy and revelation; His office is that of en-lightenment of the mind, quickening of the intellect, and sanctification of the soul.[113]

President Brigham Young added, "Our faith is concentrated in the Son of God, and through him in the Father; and the Holy Ghost is their minister to bring truths to our remembrance, to reveal new truths to us, and teach, guide, and direct the course of every mind, until we become perfected and prepared to go home, where we can see and converse with our Father in Heaven."[114] Finally, Elder Bruce McConkie declared:

> True it is that honest truth seekers come to know of the truth and di-vinity of the Lord's work by the power of the Holy Ghost: they receive a flash of revelation telling them that Jesus is the Lord, that Joseph

[112] Church of Jesus Christ of Latter-day Saints, *Conference Report* (Salt Lake City: Church of Jesus Christ of Latter-day Saints, 1967), 137.

[113] Talmage, *The Articles of Faith*, 167–68.

[114] Widtsoe, *Discourses of Brigham Young* (1941), 26.

Smith is his prophet, that the Book of Mormon is the mind and will and voice of the Lord, that the Church of Jesus Christ of Latter-day Saints is the only true and living church upon the whole earth. They gain a testimony before baptism. But it is only after they pledge their all in the cause of Christ that they receive the gift of the Holy Ghost, which is the heavenly endowment of which Jesus spoke. Then they receive a fulfillment of the promise: "by the power of the Holy Ghost ye may know the truth of all things." (Moroni 10:4–5) Then they will receive the "spirit of revelation," and the Lord tells them in their heart and in their mind whatsoever he will. (D&C 8:1–3)[115]

Therefore, from these Latter-day texts and leaders, we can understand Latter-day Saints to believe the following as it relates to the Holy Ghost and knowledge: First, the Holy Ghost manifests the truthfulness of Christ to those who believe. Second, the Holy Ghost will reveal the truthfulness of Mormonism to those who ask for that revelation. Third, the Holy Ghost is given the responsibility to give those with LDS testimonies surety of faith.

The Holy Ghost as Comforter and Companion

Third, the Holy Ghost functions as a constant source of comfort and companionship for the Latter-day Saint. Doctrine and Covenants 35:19 reads, "Wherefore, watch over him that his faith fail not, and it shall be given by the Comforter, the Holy Ghost, that knoweth all things." Similarly, Doctrine and Covenants 121:46 reads, "The Holy Ghost shall be thy constant companion, and thy scepter of righteousness and truth; and thy dominion shall be an everlasting dominion, and without compulsory means it shall flow unto thee forever and ever."

An early Latter-day Saint member of the Quorum of the Twelve Apostles, Parley P. Pratt, made similar notes concerning the Holy Ghost and companionship. He wrote:

The gift of the Holy Ghost quickens all the intellectual faculties, increases, enlarges, expands, and purifies all the natural passions and affections, and adapts them, by the gift of wisdom, to their lawful use. It inspires, develops, cultivates, and matures all the fine-toned sympathies, joys, tastes, kindred feelings, and affections of our nature. It

---

[115] Church of Jesus Christ of Latter-day Saints, *Doctrines of the Gospel Student Manual*, 45.

inspires virtue, kindness, goodness, tenderness, gentleness, and charity. Such is the gift of the Holy Ghost, and such are its operations when
received through the lawful channel—the divine, eternal priesthood.[116]

In similar fashion, Elder John A. Widtsoe noted:

> The gift of the Holy Ghost confers upon a person the right to receive,
> as he may desire and need, the presence, light and intelligence of the
> Holy Ghost. It gives, as it were, an official claim upon the mighty
> assistance and comforting assurance of the Holy Ghost. When the ser-
> vants of the Lord display a spiritual power beyond the command of
> man; when the grief-laden heart beats with joy; when failure is con-
> verted into victory, it is by the visitation of the Holy Ghost. It is the
> Spirit of God under the direction of the Holy Ghost that quickeneth all
> things. Latter-day Saints have received, under the hands of those di-
> vinely empowered, this inexpressibly glorious "gift," which will lead
> them if they are fitted, into the companionship of the Holy Ghost, and
> win for them intelligence and power to win joy in life and exaltation
> in the world to come. Those who have been so blessed have not always
> understood the greatness of that which has been given them, or have
> not earnestly sought its help. So powerful a gift, with such boundless
> promise, justifies every attempt to cleanse body and soul. Certain it
> is, that only with the aid of the Holy Ghost shall we be able to rise to
> the heights of salvation of which we dream and for which we pray.[117]

From these texts and general authorities, then, we can gather that Latter-day
Saints believe the following as true concerning the Holy Ghost and companionship: First, the Holy Ghost is a comforter and will be with believers during
good times and bad. Second, the Holy Ghost is a companion and will, similarly, be with believers during good times and bad. Third, the companionship of
the Holy Ghost gives the Latter-day Saint the ability to grow in his or her faith
and humanity in real, tangible ways.

---

[116] Church of Jesus Christ of Latter-day Saints, 45.
[117] Church of Jesus Christ of Latter-day Saints, *Teachings of the Latter-day Prophets*, 276–77.

The Holy Ghost and Scriptural Revelation

Next, we turn our attention to the role of the Holy Ghost in the giving of scriptural revelation.[118] Doctrine and Covenants 68:1–4 states:

> My servant, Orson Hyde, was called by his ordination to proclaim the everlasting gospel, by the Spirit of the living God, from people to people, and from land to land, in the congregations of the wicked, in their synagogues, reasoning with and expounding all scriptures unto them. And, behold, and lo, this is an ensample unto all those who were ordained unto this priesthood, whose mission is appointed unto them to go forth—and this is the ensample unto them, that they shall speak as they are moved upon by the Holy Ghost. And whatsoever they shall speak when moved upon by the Holy Ghost shall be scripture, shall be the will of the Lord, shall be the mind of the Lord, shall be the word of the Lord, shall be the voice of the Lord, and the power of God unto salvation.

Elder Bruce McConkie weighed in on this issue as well. He wrote:

> Prophetic utterances, both oral and written, are scripture. "To some it is given by the Holy Ghost to know that Jesus Christ is the Son of God, and that he was crucified for the sins of the world." (D&C 46:13) Testimonies borne by such persons, when moved upon by the Spirit, are scripture. In fact, all the elders of the Church, by virtue of their ordination, are called "to proclaim the everlasting gospel, by the Spirit of the living God," with this promise: "Whatsoever they shall speak when moved upon by the Holy Ghost shall be scripture, shall be the will of the Lord, shall be the mind of the Lord, shall be the word of the Lord, shall be the voice of the Lord, and the power of God unto salvation." (D&C 68:1, 4) And as it is with elders on earth, so it is with their fellow servants beyond the veil. The words of the angels of God in heaven are scripture, for, "Angels speak by the power of the Holy Ghost; wherefore, they speak the words of Christ." (2 Nephi 32:3) Such scripture as is canonized—meaning, at the present moment, the Bible, the Book of Mormon, the Doctrine and Covenants, and the

---

[118] Because an entire chapter of this work is devoted to scripture, this section will be necessarily concise.

Pearl of Great Price—comes from prophets who held positions of leadership and trust in the Lord's earthly kingdom. It is binding upon the Church and the world and is the standard by which all men shall be judged when they shall stand before the pleasing bar of the great Jehovah to receive according to their works.[119]

We can therefore conclude that Latter-day Saints believe the Holy Ghost has an integral part in the issuing of revelation from heaven. Indeed, as Doctrine and Covenants puts it, when speakers are moved upon by the Holy Ghost, they can and do speak scripture. And as McConkie wrote, all ordained elders of the LDS Church have the ability to speak scripture while performing their duty to proclaim the message of the LDS Church to the world.

The Holy Ghost as Revealer of Heavenly Father and Jesus Christ

Finally, we turn to the role of the Holy Ghost as revealer of Heavenly Father and Jesus Christ. Based on the sheer number of Latter-day Saint scriptural references and the words of LDS leaders, this is the most important role of the Holy Ghost. First Nephi 12:18 states, "And the large and spacious building, which thy father saw, is vain imaginations and the pride of the children of men. And a great and a terrible gulf divideth them; yea, even the word of the justice of the Eternal God, and the Messiah who is the Lamb of God, of whom the Holy Ghost beareth record, from the beginning of the world until this time, and from this time henceforth and forever." Second Nephi 31:18 reads, "And then are ye in this strait and narrow path which leads to eternal life; yea, ye have entered in by the gate; ye have done according to the commandments of the Father and the Son; and ye have received the Holy Ghost, which witnesses of the Father and the Son, unto the fulfilling of the promise which he hath made, that if ye entered in by the way ye should receive." Similarly, 3 Nephi 15:23 states, "And they understood me not that I said they shall hear my voice; and they understood me not that the Gentiles should not at any time hear my voice—that I should not manifest myself unto them save it were by the Holy Ghost." Also in the Book of Mormon is another helpful text, Moroni 8:9: "And after this manner did the Holy Ghost manifest the word of God unto me; wherefore, my beloved son, I know that it is solemn mockery before God, that ye should baptize little children." Doctrine and Covenants 1:39 teaches, "For behold, and lo, the

---

[119] Church of Jesus Christ of Latter-day Saints, *Teachings of the Living Prophets* (Salt Lake City: Church of Jesus Christ of Latter-day Saints, 2010), 86.

Lord is God, and the Spirit beareth record, and the record is true, and the truth abideth forever. Amen." From the Doctrine and Covenants 20:26–27, we learn:

> Not only those who believed after he came in the meridian of time, in the flesh, but all those from the beginning, even as many as were before he came, who believed in the words of the holy prophets, who spake as they were inspired by the gift of the Holy Ghost, who truly testified of him in all things, should have eternal life, as well as those who should come after, who should believe in the gifts and callings of God by the Holy Ghost, which beareth record of the Father and of the Son.

Likewise, Doctrine and Covenants 42:17 reads, "For, behold, the Comforter knoweth all things, and beareth record of the Father and of the Son." Finally, from the Pearl of Great Price, Moses 1:24, we find, "And it came to pass that when Satan had departed from the presence of Moses, that Moses lifted up his eyes unto heaven, being filled with the Holy Ghost, which beareth record of the Father and the Son."

In similar fashion, Latter-day Saint leaders have added their voice to the discussion concerning the Holy Ghost as revealer of Heavenly Father and Jesus Christ. Elder Joseph Fielding Smith, before becoming president of the Church, said, "The Holy Ghost is the third member of the Godhead. He is a Spirit, in the form of a man. The Holy Ghost is a personage of Spirit, and has a spirit body only. His mission is to bear witness of the Father and the Son and of all truth."[120] Smith also declared:

> We know what has been revealed and that the Holy Ghost, sometimes spoken of as the Holy Spirit, and Comforter, is the third member of the Godhead, and that he, being in perfect harmony with the Father and the Son, reveals to man by the spirit of revelation and prophecy the truths of the gospel of Jesus Christ. Our great duty is so to live that we may be led constantly in light and truth by this Comforter so that we may not be deceived by the many false spirits that are in the world.[121]

Similarly, Elder George F. Richards, during the Semi-annual General Conference in October 1931, said, "This is the office of the Holy Ghost, who

---

[120] Church of Jesus Christ of Latter-day Saints, *Doctrines of the Gospel Student Manual*, 11.
[121] Church of Jesus Christ of Latter-day Saints, *Teachings of the Living Prophets*, 271.

is a personage of spirit, one of the trinity of the Godhead. It is his mission and office to bear witness of the Father and of the Son and of the truth of all things."[122] Finally, Joseph Smith, in his well-known *Lectures on Faith*, argued, "Though our first parents were driven out of the garden of Eden, and were even separated from the presence of God by a vail [*sic*], they still retained a knowledge of his existence, and that sufficiently to move them to call upon him. And further, that no sooner was the plan of redemption revealed to man, and he began to call upon God, than the Holy Spirit was given, bearing record of the Father and Son."[123]

Therefore, from the surveyed Latter-day scriptures and leaders, we can surmise the following to be the case for Latter-day Saints with respect to the Holy Ghost's role: the Holy Ghost's main role is indeed to reveal Heavenly Father and Jesus Christ to those who are earnestly seeking for them.

The Relationship of the Godhead

Having surveyed the Latter-day Saint understanding of Heavenly Father, Jesus Christ the Son, and the Holy Ghost, the natural question now becomes how these three beings relate together to form what Latter-day Saints call the God-head. Article of Faith 1 states simply, "We believe in God, the Eternal Father, and in His Son, Jesus Christ, and in the Holy Ghost." Historically, orthodox Christians argue for the Trinity, but Latter-day Saints adamantly refuse to ac-cept this doctrine. How, then, do Latter-day Saints understand the relationship between Heavenly Father, Jesus Christ, and the Holy Ghost?

Again, a short survey of Latter-day scriptures will be helpful, along with a survey of LDS leaders. Second Nephi 31:21 reads, "And now, behold, my beloved brethren, this is the way; and there is none other way nor name given under heaven whereby man can be saved in the kingdom of God. And now, behold, this is the doctrine of Christ, and the only and true doctrine of the Father, and of the Son, and of the Holy Ghost, which is one God, without end. Amen." Likewise, Mosiah 15:4 states, "And they are one God, yea, the very Eternal Father of heaven and of earth." Ether 12:41 notes, "And now, I would commend you to seek this Jesus of whom the prophets and apostles have writ-ten, that the grace of God the Father, and also the Lord Jesus Christ, and the

---

[122] Church of Jesus Christ of Latter-day Saints, *Conference Report* (Salt Lake City: Church of Jesus Christ of Latter-day Saints, 1931), 101.
[123] Joseph Smith, *Lectures on Faith* (Salt Lake City: Deseret Book, 1985), 2:24–25.

Holy Ghost, which beareth record of them, may be and abide in you forever. Amen." Finally, Doctrine and Covenants 20:26–28 reads, "Not only those who believed after he came in the meridian of time, in the flesh, but all those from the beginning, even as many as were before he came, who believed in the words of the holy prophets, who spake as they were inspired by the gift of the Holy Ghost, who truly testified of him in all things, should have eternal life, as well as those who should come after, who should believe in the gifts and callings of God by the Holy Ghost, which beareth record of the Father and of the Son; which Father, Son, and Holy Ghost are one God, infinite and eternal, without end. Amen."

Former Latter-day Saint president Joseph F. Smith stated, "We believe in the Godhead, comprising the three individual personages, Father, Son, and Holy Ghost."[124] Similarly, Elder Joseph Fielding Smith, before becoming president of the Church, noted, "This reference [Doctrine & Covenants 20:27–29], then, to the three as one God, must be interpreted to mean that they constitute one Godhead or Supreme Council, composed of three separate Personages, the Father, the Son, and the Holy Ghost."[125] Continuing in the same line of thought, Smith argued:

I make bold to say that there is not within the lids of the Bible one single passage which can properly be construed to uphold the popular but erroneous doctrine that the Father and the Son and the Holy Ghost are in substance one, a spirit, or essence, and without body or parts or passions, incomprehensible and invisible. To the contrary, I maintain that throughout the scriptures there is ample evidence in numerous passages, teaching that the Eternal Father and his Son Jesus Christ and the Holy Ghost are separate entities, perfectly distinct and in person independent from each other. This is the doctrine clearly stated by our Savior. It is their epistles to the ancient saints. Any doctrine to the contrary contradicts what is plainly written and is a misinterpretation of these teachings.[126]

Similarly, Elder Bruce McConkie explained:

---

[124] Church of Jesus Christ of Latter-day Saints, *Conference Report* (Salt Lake City: Church of Jesus Christ of Latter-day Saints, 1907), app. 4.
[125] Church of Jesus Christ of Latter-day Saints, *Melchizedek Priesthood Personal Study Guide* (Salt Lake City: Church of Jesus Christ of Latter-day Saints, 1972), 10.
[126] Church of Jesus Christ of Latter-day Saints, *Teachings of the Latter-day Prophets*, 228.

We learn these truths relative to the Gods we worship: 1. They are three in number, three separate persons: the first is the Father, the second, the Son; and the third, the Holy Ghost. They are three individuals who meet together, counsel in concert, and as occasion requires travel separately through all immensity. They are three holy men, two having bodies of flesh and bones, the third being a personage of spirit. 2. They are one and dwell in each other, meaning: They have the same mind one with another; they think the same thoughts, speak the same words, and perform the same acts—so much so that any thought, word, or act of one is the thought of the other. 3. They possess the same character, enjoy the same perfections, and manifest the same attributes, each one possessing all of these in their eternal and godly fulness. 4. Their unity in all things, their perfect oneness in mind, power, and perfections, marks the course and charts the way for faithful mortals, whose chief goal in life is to unite together and become one with them, thereby gaining eternal life for themselves. 5. Our Lord is the manifestation of the Father, meaning: God is in Christ revealing himself to men so that those who believe in the Son believe also in the Father, and into such the Father gives the Holy Ghost, and they being thus purified in Christ are fit to dwell with him and his Father forever.[127]

Finally, Elder Orson Pratt argued, "The Godhead may be further illustrated by a council, consisting of three men—all possessing equal wisdom, knowledge, and truth—together with equal qualifications in every other respect. Each person would be a separate distinct person or substance from the other two, and yet the three would form but one council."[128]

In summary, then, we can deduce that Latter-day Saints believe the following concerning the relationship among the Godhead: First, there is no such doctrine in Mormonism as the historic, orthodox doctrine of the Trinity. Second, there is in Mormonism a belief that the members of the Godhead function together, within a relationship, to carry out various plans on the earth. Third, the members of the Godhead function together in a council, and when one member of that council reveals information, he does so on behalf of the entire council. Fourth, each member of the Godhead possesses equal knowledge and attributes. Fifth, the council of the Godhead makes the plans and charts the

---

[127] Church of Jesus Christ of Latter-day Saints, 228–29.
[128] Church of Jesus Christ of Latter-day Saints, 229.

path for humanity. Finally, sixth, the members of the Godhead are fully separate and distinct from each other, three separate beings who counsel together
for the decisions that shape the course of humankind.

Conclusion

Having surveyed the Latter-day Saint doctrines of God the Father, Jesus Christ
the Son, the Holy Ghost, and the relationship between the three, a few conclusions may be drawn. First, the Latter-day Saint understanding of the doctrine
of God is dramatically different from that of historic, orthodox Christianity.
Keeping James Sire's worldview questions in mind, Latter-day Saints would,
by definition, have to answer the first question differently than historic, orthodox Christians. This entails, simply, that the Latter-day Saint deity is different
from the historic, orthodox Christian deity, meaning the two worldviews are
different. Second, the Latter-day Saint understanding of God is drawn, not
from the pages of the Bible, but mainly from the pages of Latter-day scripture,
revelation, and the inspired interpretation of that revelation by LDS leaders.
When passages from the Bible are discussed or referenced, those passages are
interpreted in light of Latter-day scripture and the interpretation of Latter-day
Saint leaders. Third, maybe the most dreadful conclusion that might be drawn
is that if the Latter-day Saint deity is different from that of the Bible, then the
Latter-day Saint deity is really no deity at all but nothing more than a mere
manufactured idol. Both the Old and New Testaments are replete with warn-
ings against idolatry. In fact, one of the Ten Commandments warns specifically
against idolatry when the Holy One of Israel demands, "Do not have other
gods besides me" (Exod 20:3).

Chapter 3

Sacred Texts

To say the doctrine of sacred texts is important would be a dramatic understatement. One's doctrine of holy writ informs many other doctrines and offers vital information concerning a person's understanding of deity, humanity, and many other theological issues. Authoritative revelation is a point of commonality among members of many religious traditions who may reside in varying places around the world. Sacred texts indeed can create community among peoples who are thousands of miles apart. Evangelical theologian Carl F. H. Henry agreed with these sentiments. He argued:

> Every culture and society exudes a certain convictional glue, an undergirding outlook on life and reality that preserves its cohesiveness. When that adhesive bond deteriorates, the sense of shared community tends to come apart at the seams. Recent modern thinkers define this bond of conceptualities or value-constellations as myth, that is, man's representation of the transcendent or divine in human or earthly terms.[1]

In commenting further on the concept of myth, he noted:

> If myth is broadly defined as any representation of the transcendent "in human or earthly terms," the fact that human thought and language are the only means of interpersonal communication available to human beings can hardly be made a definitive basis for settling the issue. If myth is any form of representing God, then conceptual

---

[1] Carl F. H. Henry, *God, Revelation, and Authority* (Wheaton, IL: Crossway, 1999), 1:44.

language is myth, and conceptual thought likewise. To emphasize in the interest of the inescapability of mythology the obvious fact that human language is composed of symbols would hardly disadvantage religious language in any special way, since language about anything and everything falls under the same restriction. . . . The precise definition of myth is therefore crucial if we are to answer the indicated questions intelligently. Decisive for the evaluation of myth are how one relates myth to objective truth and to external history, and what religious significance one attaches to rational truth and historical events. The basic issues reduce really to two alternatives: either man himself projects upon the world and its history a supernatural reality and activity that disallows objectively valid cognitive statements on the basis of divine disclosure, or a transcendent divine reality through intelligible revelation establishes the fact that God is actually at work in the sphere of nature and human affairs.[2]

He concludes, then, "The most critical question in the history of thought is whether all the convictional frameworks through which different peoples arrive at the meaning and worth of human life are by nature mythical, or whether perhaps at least one of these perspectives stems from divine revelation and has objective cognitive validity."[3] Thus, we embark on the study now of Latter-day Saint sacred texts. Specifically, what do Latter-day Saints believe about sacred texts? What constitutes holy writ? Is it revelation from heaven? If it is revelation from heaven, has it ceased or does it continue? If it continues, through what person(s) or medium does it find its continuance? And, though some will no doubt disagree with how Latter-day Saints characterize and define holy writ, we must keep in mind that for Latter-day Saints, their sacred texts are indeed truth for the world. Henry is again helpful here. He notes, "We must keep in mind that myths in all cases are championed by their proponents not as imaginative representations but as accounts of some actual divine incursion or participation in the affairs of man and the world."[4]

---

[2] Henry, 45.
[3] Henry, 44.
[4] Henry, 46.

The Bible

People often wonder how Latter-day Saints regard the Bible, especially considering, as we will see later in this chapter, their regard for additional books as authoritative revelation. The first section of Article of Faith 8 reads as follows: "We believe the Bible to be the word of God as far as it is translated correctly." Although this statement, specifically the second portion of this quoted section, sounds as though Latter-day Saints would hold something less than utmost respect for the Bible, that is not necessarily the case. Elder M. Russell Ballard, a member of the Quorum of the Twelve Apostles, said during the LDS General Conference in April 2007:

> My brothers and sisters, the Holy Bible is a miracle! It is a miracle that the Bible's 4,000 years of sacred and secular history were recorded and preserved by the prophets, apostles, and inspired churchmen. . . . It is a miracle that the Bible literally contains within its pages the converting, healing Spirit of Christ, which has turned men's hearts for centuries, leading them to pray, to choose right paths, and to search to find their Savior.[5]

He continued, "The Holy Bible is well named. It is holy because it teaches truth, holy because it warms us with its spirit, holy because it teaches us to know God and understand His dealings with men, and holy because it testifies throughout its pages of the Lord Jesus Christ."[6] He noted further:

> Honest, diligent study of the Bible does make us better and better, and we must ever remember the countless martyrs who knew of its power and who gave their lives that we may be able to find within its words the path to the eternal happiness and the peace of our Heavenly Father's Kindgom. . . . Tens of millions of individuals have come to a faith in God and in Jesus Christ through seeking truth in the Holy Bible. Countless numbers of them had nothing *but* the Bible to feed and guide their faith. . . . I love the Bible, its teachings, its lessons, and its spirit. I love the Old Testament's compelling, profound stories and its great prophets testifying of the coming of Christ. I love the New Testament's apostolic travels and miracles and the letters of Paul. Most of

---

[5] M. Russell Ballard, "The Miracle of the Holy Bible," *Ensign*, May 2007, 80.
[6] Ballard, 80.

all, I love its eyewitness accounts of the words and the example and the Atonement of our Savior Jesus Christ. I love the perspective and peace that come from reading the Bible.[7]

He concluded by saying, "My brothers and sisters, we must help all people, including our own members, understand the power and importance of the Holy Bible. The Bible is scripture that leads us and all mankind to accept Jesus Christ as our Savior."[8]

Similarly, Elder Bruce R. McConkie, a former member of the Quorum of the Twelve Apostles, in his work *A New Witness for the Articles of Faith*, explained:

> The holy Bible—as of now—is the most influential book ever written in the entire history of the world. As presently constituted, it contains those portions of the sacred writings of Judaism and of Christianity which have come down to us in relative purity. In its pure and primeval state it was composed of divine revelations and inspired writings. In substance and thought content, the word of the Lord thus written by the apostles and prophets and inspired men of old has been preserved for us by the transcribers and translators through whose hands it has passed. It is thus a divine library, a heaven-sent volume of holy scripture, a voice from the past that contains the mind and will and law of the Lord. It is a partial and fragmentary record of God's dealings with his ancient covenant people, a people who had either the fulness of the everlasting gospel or were being schooled by the preparatory gospel as time and circumstances dictated.[9]

Continuing in this line of thought, McConkie wrote of the Bible, "It is the book of books, accepted by believers of every hue and tone and in every sect and church as the source of their doctrine, their ethical standards, and their very way of life. Salvation itself, so they suppose, is dependent upon belief in and an understanding of the sacred sayings found in this canonized volume."[10] Similarly, he noted, "[The Bible] has done more, with greater numbers

---

[7] Ballard, 81.

[8] Ballard, 81.

[9] Bruce R. McConkie, *A New Witness for the Articles of Faith* (Salt Lake City: Deseret, 1985), 391.

[10] McConkie, 392.

of people, to preserve Christian culture, uphold gospel ethics, and teach true doctrine than any other book ever written, many times over. Nations have been born and have died, continents have been conquered, and hemispheres settled because of biblical influence. There is no way to overstate the worth and blessings of the Bible for mankind."[11]

Probably the best summary for the positive view Latter-day Saints take of the Bible comes from Robert L. Millet, former professor and dean of religious education at Brigham Young University. He wrote, "I love the Bible. I treasure its teachings and delight in the spirit of worship that accompanies its prayerful study. My belief in additional scripture does not in any way detract from what I feel toward and learn from the Holy Bible. Studying the Bible lifts my spirits, lightens my burdens, enlightens my mind, and motivates me to seek to live a life of holiness."[12]

One could conclude, based on the statements and writings of the surveyed Latter-day leaders and scholars, that the Bible indeed holds a special place of prominence among the Latter-day Saint canon. And in reading very positive statements like these, one may even conclude that Latter-day Saints view the Bible as the most helpful and trustworthy book within their collection of holy writ. However, there are nuances that must be explored concerning a full and complete understanding of the Bible from an LDS perspective. Specifically, what does Article of Faith 8 mean, referring to the Bible, when it says Latter-day Saints believe the Bible "as far as it is translated correctly"?

First Nephi 13 begins this nuanced understanding and offers added explanation as to the Latter-day Saint perception of the Bible:

> And it came to pass that I saw among the nations of the Gentiles the formation of a great church. And the angel said unto me: Behold the formation of a church which is most abominable above all other churches, which slayeth the saints of God, yea, and tortureth them and bindeth them down, and yoketh them with a yoke of iron, and bringeth them down into captivity. And it came to pass that I beheld this great and abominable church; and I saw the devil that he was the founder of it. (vv. 4–6)

Later in the same chapter, the storyline continues:

---

[11] McConkie, 393.
[12] Robert L. Millet, "A Latter-day Saint Perspective on Biblical Inerrancy," in Millet, *No Weapon Shall Prosper*, 138 (see chap. 2, n. 98).

And after they go forth by the hand of the twelve apostles of the Lamb, from the Jews unto the Gentiles, thou seest the formation of that great and abominable church, which is most abominable above all other churches; for behold, they have taken away from the gospel of the Lamb many parts which are plain and precious; and also many covenants of the Lord have they taken away. And all this have they done that they might pervert the right ways of the Lord, that they might blind the eyes and harden the hearts of the children of men. Wherefore, thou seest that after the book hath gone forth through the hands of the great and abominable church, that there are many plain and precious things taken away from the book, which is the book of the Lamb of God. And after these plain and precious things were taken away it goeth forth unto all nations of the Gentiles; and after it goeth forth unto all nations of the Gentiles, yea, even across the many waters which thou hast seen with the Gentiles which have gone forth out of captivity, thou seest—because of the many plain and precious things which have been taken out of the book, which were plain unto the understanding of the children of men, according to the plainness which is in the Lamb of God—because of these things which are taken away out of the gospel of the Lamb, an exceedingly great many do stumble, yea, insomuch that Satan hath great power over them. (vv. 26–29)

These plain and precious things, according to Latter-day Saint leaders and scholars, are those doctrines in Mormonism not plainly elucidated within the biblical text. This purportedly occurred due to information being removed from the Bible, which resulted from an apostasy that took place shortly after the death of the last New Testament apostle.[13] Again, McConkie is helpful here. He explained:

As long as inspired men are the keepers of holy writ; as long as prophets and apostles are present to identify and perfect the scriptures by revelation; as long as scriptural translations are made by the gift and power of God—all will be well with the written word. But when the gospel sun sets and apostate darkness shrouds the minds of men, the scriptural word is in jeopardy. From Adam to Malachi, the ancient

---

[13] The Latter-day Saint understanding of and belief in an apostasy from true Christianity will be discussed later in this work.

biblical word was in prophetic hands. For the next three or four centuries, uninspired men kept the records, adding and deleting as they chose and for their own purposes. During these dark days, apocryphal and pseudepigraphic writings—intermingling as they do the truths of heaven with the heresies from beneath—arise in great numbers. And there were no prophetic voices either to condemn or to canonize them. History repeated itself in New Testament times. The inspired word flowed from Spirit-guided pens; inspired men kept the records; and true believers rejoiced in the truths that thus were theirs. True, there were apostates and traitors even while the apostles lived, but at least there was divine guidance that identified the true word and kept the faithful from following every false and evil wind of doctrine. But after the passing of those who held the keys by which the mind and will of the Lord can be gained; after the holy apostles mingled their blood with that of the prophets who were before them; after the age of inspiration ceased—all was no longer well with the written word. Wolves scattered the flock and tore the flesh of the saints; false teachers led the church into apostate darkness; the post-apostolic fathers wrote their own views—and there was no way to distinguish with divine certainty the light from above the darkness that soon covered the earth.[14]

An immediate question comes to mind, namely, what doctrines were removed or lost from the biblical text? When these wolves, to use McConkie's analogy, tore the flesh from the early saints, which original doctrines did they remove so as to cause such pain, agony, and heartache? McConkie responds:

And what then happened to the Bible? "Behold, they have taken away from the gospel of the Lamb many parts which are plain and most precious," saith the angel, "and also many covenants of the Lord have they taken away" (1 Nephi 13:20–26). What effect did this have upon true worship? The answer to this question becomes apparent by asking such other questions as these: What happened to celestial marriage, to baptism for the dead, and to those holy ordinances by which mortals are endowed with power from on high? Where do we find churches that lay on hands for the present conferral of the gift of the Holy Ghost? How is it that the churches of Christendom do not have

---

[14] McConkie, *A New Witness for the Articles of Faith,* 402–4.

apostles, prophets, high priests, seventies, and all of the New Testament offices and callings? Has baptism by immersion for the remission of sins been replaced by infant baptism or discarded entirely, as the case may be? Indeed, how did infant baptism find its way into the churches of the day? Is the sacrament of the Lord's Supper the same simple ceremony that it once was? Whence came the numerous ordinances and performances, so common in Christendom, that have no biblical precedent? How does modern Christianity compare with that of the primitive saints? Have we lost the simplicity that was in Christ?[15]

Similarly, Joseph Fielding McConkie and Robert L. Millet, two former professors at Brigham Young University, commented:

As early as 1820 young Joseph Smith recognized that salvation was not to be found within the covers of the Bible alone; confusion and uncertainty were the obvious results of unillumined minds and undirected study, even when the object of that study was the Holy Bible. Seeking for both personal fulfillment and the one system of religious practice which would lead him back to the divine presence, Joseph Smith discovered that not all of the answers were to be found within the Bible.[16]

A second avenue worth exploration concerning the Latter-day Saint understanding of the Bible is found in 2 Nephi 29:3–10. The text reads:

And because my words shall hiss forth—many of the Gentiles shall say: A Bible! A Bible! We have got a Bible, and there cannot be any more Bible. But thus saith the Lord God: O fools, they shall have a Bible; and it shall proceed forth from the Jews, mine ancient covenant people. And what thank they the Jews for the Bible which they receive from them? Yea, what do the Gentiles mean? Do they remember the travails, and the labors, and the pains of the Jews, and their diligence unto me, in bringing forth salvation unto the Gentiles? O ye Gentiles, have ye remembered the Jews, mine ancient covenant people? Nay;

---

[15] McConkie, 409.
[16] Joseph Fielding McConkie and Robert L. Millet, *Doctrinal Commentary on the Book of Mormon* (Salt Lake City: Bookcraft, 1987), 1:94–95.

but ye have cursed them, and have hated them, and have not sought to recover them. But behold, I will return all these things upon your own heads; for I the Lord have not forgotten my people. Thou fool, that shall say: A Bible, we have got a Bible, and we need no more Bible. Have ye obtained a Bible save it were by the Jews? Know ye not that there are more nations than one? Know ye not that I, the Lord your God, have created all men, and that I remember those who are upon the isles of the sea; and that I rule in the heavens above and in the earth beneath; and I bring forth my word unto the children of men, yea, even upon all the nations of the earth? Wherefore murmur ye, because that ye shall receive more of my word? Know ye not that the testimony of two nations is a witness unto you that I am God, that I remember one nation like unto another? Wherefore, I speak the same words unto one nation like unto another. And when the two nations shall run together the testimony of the two nations shall run together also. And I do this that I may prove unto many that I am the same yesterday, today, and forever; and that I speak forth my words according to mine own plea-sure. And because that I have spoken one word ye need not suppose that I cannot speak another; for my work is not yet finished; neither shall it be until the end of man, neither from that time henceforth and forever. Wherefore, because that ye have a Bible ye need not suppose that it contains all my words; neither need ye suppose that I have not caused more to be written.

Put in a more concise way, the idea that the Bible alone is sufficient for all things is simply not a Latter-day Saint idea. Millet summarizes the point quite well in writing, "As to the Bible's sufficiency, to state that the Bible is the final word of God—more specifically, the final written word of God—is to claim more for the Bible than it claims for itself."[17] We can now turn to Latter-day Saint officially published works, leaders, and scholars to obtain a fuller picture of what they claim is wrong with, or missing from, the Bible.

The officially published manual *Gospel Principles* contains a short section on the Bible. It states:

The Bible is a collection of sacred writings containing God's reve-lations to man. These writings cover many centuries, from the time

---

[17] Millet, "A Latter-day Saint Perspective on Biblical Inerrancy," 124.

of Adam through the time when the Apostles of Jesus Christ lived. They were written by many prophets who lived at various times in the history of the world. . . . Through the Prophet Joseph Smith, the Lord has expanded our understanding of some passages in the Bible. The Lord inspired the Prophet Joseph to restore truths to the Bible text that had been lost or changed since the original words were written. These inspired corrections are called the Joseph Smith Translation of the Bible. In the Latter-day Saint edition of the King James Version of the Bible, selected passages from the Joseph Smith Translation are found on pages 797–813 and in many footnotes.[18]

Thus, from *Gospel Principles*, we can understand Latter-day Saints to believe the Bible to be the Word of God, but we also learn they believe some truths were lost from the Bible and were restored via the writing of Joseph Smith. Interestingly, even though Joseph Smith completed a great deal of revision work on the Bible, the Salt Lake City branch of the Church of Jesus Christ of Latter-day Saints does not use the full version. Instead, they use the King James Version of the Bible and only a very small percentage of Joseph Smith's revisions.[19]

Elder Bruce McConkie noted, "When the Bible is read under the guidance of the Spirit, and in harmony with the many Latter-day revelations which interpret and make plain its more mysterious parts, it becomes one of the most priceless volumes known to man."[20] Thus, for Latter-day Saints to understand the Bible in its proper context, it must be interpreted according to the guidance of the Holy Spirit and in light of additional writings and teachings believed by Latter-day Saints to be revelations from heaven. Then, and only then, does it become, as McConkie noted, "one of the most priceless volumes known to man." In light of McConkie's mention of additional revelatory information needed for biblical interpretation, he also argued, "One of the great heresies of modern Christendom is the unfounded assumption that the Bible contains all of the inspired teachings now extant among men."[21] Therefore, as McConkie would likely maintain, Latter-day Saints believe the Bible to be one part of revelation, but not the entire corpus of authoritative revelation from heaven. And

---

[18] Church of Jesus Christ of Latter-day Saints, *Gospel Principles*, 45–46 (see chap. 1, n. 69).
[19] For a discussion on this topic, see McConkie, *Mormon Doctrine*, 383–85 (see chap. 2, n. 11).
[20] McConkie, *Mormon Doctrine*, 82.
[21] McConkie, 83.

when reading the Bible, one needs modern-day revelation and modern-day interpretation to read the text properly.

Before turning to other books recognized by Latter-day Saints as holy writ, we can say a few points in summary concerning the Latter-day Saint understanding of the Bible. First, the Bible is revelation from heaven. Second, although the Bible is God's word to humanity, it is not the final word from heaven. Third, although the Bible is God's word to humanity, it is not inerrant or infallible. Fourth, truths have been removed from the Bible that must be restored if humanity is to know the proper way to salvation. To use Francis Schaeffer's phrase, how should we then live?[22] Do Latter-day Saints believe there is further revelation from heaven that can, and does, give these truths back to humanity which have been allegedly removed from the text of the Bible? Robert Millet declared, "The Book of Mormon was given to us to set things straight, to make things right, to bring our thinking into conformity with truth, to bring back or restore to propriety, and to counteract ideas or teachings or practices that are harmful."[23] With that, we now turn our attention to the Book of Mormon.

The Book of Mormon

The second part of the eighth Article of Faith reads, "We also believe the Book of Mormon to be the word of God." As Millet noted, Latter-day Saints believe the Book of Mormon was given in order to set humanity back on the right path. Indeed, on Sunday, November 28, 1841, Joseph Smith met with his Quorum of Twelve Apostles at the home of Brigham Young, Smith's counselor. He recorded the events of that meeting in his somewhat autobiographical history of the LDS Church and remembered, famously:

> I spent the day in the council with the Twelve Apostles at the house of President Young, conversing with them upon a variety of subjects. Brother Joseph Fielding was present, having been absent four years on a mission to England. I told the brethren that the Book of Mormon was the most correct book on earth, and the keystone of our religion,

---

[22] This phrase is the title of a book originally published by Schaeffer in 1976 and has been used and attributed to him time and again.
[23] Robert L. Millet, *Restored and Restoring* (Salt Lake City: Eborn, 2014), 36.

and a man would get nearer to God by abiding by its precepts, than by any other book.[24]

Likewise, the introduction to the current edition (2013) of the Book of Mormon reads, "The Book of Mormon is a volume of holy scripture comparable to the Bible. It is a record of God's dealings with ancient inhabitants of the Americas and contains the fulness of the everlasting gospel."[25]

Gospel Principles offers a concise, helpful explanation of the Book of Mormon. "The Book of Mormon is a sacred record of some of the people who lived on the American continents between about 2000 B.C. and A.D. 400. It contains the fulness of the gospel of Jesus Christ. The Book of Mormon tells of the visit Jesus Christ made to the people in the Americas soon after His Resurrection."[26] Likewise, *Preach My Gospel* notes, "The Book of Mormon is powerful evidence of the divinity of Christ. It is also proof of the Restoration through the Prophet Joseph Smith. An essential part of conversion is receiving a witness from the Holy Ghost that the Book of Mormon is true."[27]

History of the Book of Mormon

The Book of Mormon is indeed a fascinating piece of literature, and its history even more so. Concerning the Book of Mormon, Grant Hardy, professor at the University of North Carolina, argues:

> Yet the Book of Mormon remains a curious text—easily dismissible as a nineteenth-century hoax or delusion, yet still capable of inspiring reverence among some fifteen million believers almost two hundred years later; a classic of American religious history that many find nearly impossible to read all the way through; the core scripture of a modern faith whose most distinctive beliefs and practices (including temples, eternal families, premortal existence, multiple heavens, deification, polygamy, and a health code) are hardly mentioned therein; and a book that insists on its authenticity as an ancient record, miraculously preserved and translated, which is nevertheless notably

---

[24] Joseph Smith Jr., *History of the Church* (Salt Lake City: Deseret, 1978), 4:461.
[25] Church of Jesus Christ of Latter-day Saints, *Introduction to the Book of Mormon* (Salt Lake City: Church of Jesus Christ of Latter-day Saints, 2013).
[26] Church of Jesus Christ of Latter-day Saints, *Gospel Principles*, 46.
[27] Church of Jesus Christ of Latter-day Saints, *Preach My Gospel* (Salt Lake City: Church of Jesus Christ of Latter-day Saints, 2004), 103.

lacking in standard archaeological support. For students of Mormonism, American history, religious studies, or world scripture, it is hard to know where to begin with this strange, influential, puzzling work.[28]

The best place to begin with the Book of Mormon is with its unveiling to Joseph Smith, or, at least, his reporting of its unveiling. In a somewhat lengthy, but very helpful, passage, Smith recounts the initial visit from the angel Moroni concerning the golden plates:

I continued to pursue my common vocation in life until the twenty-first of September, one thousand eight hundred and twenty-three, all the time suffering severe persecution at the hands of all classes of men, both religious and irreligious, because I continued to affirm that I had seen a vision. . . . In consequence of these things, I often felt condemned for my weakness and imperfections; when, on the evening of the above-mentioned twenty-first of September, after I had retired to my bed for the night, I betook myself to prayer and supplication to Almighty God for forgiveness of all my sins and follies, and also for a manifestation to me, that I might know of my state and standing before Him; for I had full confidence in obtaining a divine manifestation, as I previously had done. While I was thus in the act of calling upon God, I discovered a light appearing in my room, which continued to increase until the room was lighter than at noonday, when immediately a personage appeared at my bed side, standing in the air, for his feet did not touch the floor. He had on a loose robe of most exquisite whiteness. It was a whiteness beyond anything earthly I had ever seen; nor do I believe that any earthly thing could be made to appear so exceedingly white and brilliant. His hands were naked and his arms also, a little above the wrist, so, also were his feet naked, as were his legs, a little above the ankles. His head and neck were also bare. I could discover that he had no other clothing on but this robe, as it was open, so that I could see into his bosom. Not only was his robe exceedingly white, but his whole person was glorious beyond description, and his countenance truly like lightning. The room was exceedingly light, but not so very bright as immediately around his person. When first I looked

---

[28] Grant Hardy, "The Book of Mormon," in *Oxford Handbook of Mormonism*, Terryl L. Givens and Philip L. Barlow, eds. (New York: Oxford University Press, 2015), 134.

upon him, I was afraid; but the fear soon left me. He called me by name, and said unto me that he was a messenger sent from the presence of God to me and that his name was Moroni; that God had a work for me to do; and that my name should be had for good and evil among all nations, kindreds, and tongues, or that it should be both good and evil spoken of among all people. He said there was a book deposited, written upon gold plates, giving an account of the former inhabitants of this continent, and the sources from whence they sprang. He also said that the fullness of the everlasting Gospel was contained in it, as delivered by the Savior to the ancient inhabitants; also that there were two stones in silver bows—and these stones, fastened to a breastplate, constituted what is called the Urim and Thummim—deposited with the plates; and the possession and use of these stones were what constituted "Seers" in ancient or former times; and that God had prepared them for the purpose of translating the book.[29]

Eminent Latter-day Saint historian Terryl L. Givens sums up the entire saga with Moroni's visit quite well. He writes:

Now on the night of September 21, 1823, the 17-year-old Smith was once again engaged in a private spiritual quest. Nothing in particular seems to have been the catalyst behind his petition that night, other than a sense that the absolution of sin granted him as a youth of 14 was in need of renewal. He was merely seeking once again "forgiveness of all my sins and follies," in his words. And yet, Smith at the same time recorded that he prayed this night with "full confidence in obtaining a divine manifestation, as I previously had one." His expectation was fully satisfied when his room erupted with brilliant light and an angel who identified himself as Moroni appeared at Joseph's bedside. And this time, before the night was over, the young man would no longer be able to doubt that he was caught up in events of world-shaking importance.[30]

Concerning Moroni's message to Smith, Givens notes, "This book 'written upon golden plates' would forever alter the life and reputation of the young

---

[29] Joseph Smith, *History of the Church*, 1:9–12.
[30] Terryl L. Givens, *By the Hand of Mormon: The American Scripture that Launched a New World Religion* (New York: Oxford University Press, 2002), 11.

farmboy, and would serve as the principal catalyst behind the rise of a world-wide church. More than any other factor, it would come to ground Joseph's reputation as seer and charlatan, beloved prophet and reviled blasphemer, as distributer of the peace and empire builder."[31] Givens's synopsis continues:

> Smith learned that the actual "time that [the plates] should be obtained was not yet fulfilled," although "the vision was opened to my mind that I could see the place where the plates were deposited." He was warned that the plates were not to be shown to any person, and then the angel, "ascended till he entirely disappeared, and the room was left as it had been before." Shortly thereafter the angel reappeared, rehearsed the entire message with additional words of "great judgments which were coming upon the earth," and disappeared as before. Then, yet a third time the scene was repeated. . . . The morning after the heavenly messenger's three visits, he appeared a fourth time. In a field where the fatigued Smith fainted while returning home early from chores, Moroni rehearsed the entirety of his teachings, warnings, and commands, and then instructed Joseph to relate all that he had experienced to his father. Joseph immediately did so, and his father encouraged him to visit the hill to see the miraculous artifacts.[32]

After Joseph had these experiences, he determined it would be best to visit the Hill Cumorah, where the plates were purportedly buried, and see if he could unearth them. Upon attempting to do so, the angel Moroni appeared, chastised Joseph for attempting to remove the plates early, and told him to return to the hill every year on the same date. Givens notes, "What followed Smith's first visit to the hill was in effect an imposed probation of four years. During that interim, Smith was required to report to the same place on each yearly anniversary, to be tutored by the angel Moroni in the mission he was charged to perform."[33] Finally, in 1827, Smith was allowed to retrieve the plates and, along with the plates, he also discovered other objects with the plates in a large wooden box. Talmage writes:

> The plates of the Book of Mormon as delivered by the angel Moroni to Joseph Smith, according to the description given by the modern

---

[31] Givens, 11.
[32] Givens, 13–14.
[33] Givens, 15.

prophet, were of gold, of uniform size, each about seven inches wide by eight inches long; in thickness, a little less than ordinary sheet tin; they were fastened together by three rings running through the plates near one edge; together they formed a book nearly six inches in thickness.[34]

In the wooden box along with the plates were artifacts described by Smith as a breastplate and, as the angel Moroni had promised, two stones in silver bows, explained as the Urim and Thummim. These additional artifacts would later prove to be some tools used for the translation of the plates.

Translation of the Book of Mormon

Our question must now turn toward how the allegedly ancient plates were translated. If these plates were indeed God's revelation to humanity, they would need to be translated from their original language into English in order for Smith to understand them and teach their principles. Talmage is again helpful. He comments:

> The translation of the Book of Mormon was effected through the power of God manifested in the bestowal of the gift of revelation. The book professes not to be dependent upon the wisdom or learning of man; its translator was not versed in linguistics; his qualifications were of a different and of a far more efficient order. With the plates, Joseph Smith received from the angel other sacred treasures, including a breastplate, to which were attached the Urim and Thummim, called by the Nephites, *Interpreters*; and by the use of these he was enabled to render the ancient records in our modern tongue. The details of the work of translation have not been recorded, beyond the statement that the translator examined the engraved characters by means of the sacred instruments, and then dictated to the scribe the English sentences.[35]

Fortunately for us, more information is to be found concerning the translation of the information on the plates.

David Whitmer, one of the original three witnesses for the golden plates listed in the frontispiece to the Book of Mormon, composed a work entitled *An Address to All Believers in Christ*. Within this work, he defended the Book of

---

[34] Talmage, *The Articles of Faith*, 268 (see chap. 2, n. 10).
[35] Talmage, 273.

Mormon and offered more detailed explanations about the process by which Joseph Smith translated the golden plates:

> I will now give you a description of the manner in which the Book of Mormon was translated. Joseph Smith would put the seer stone into a hat, and put his face in the hat, drawing it closely around his face to exclude the light; and in the darkness the spiritual light would shine. A piece of something resembling parchment would appear, and on that appeared the writing. One character at a time would appear, and under it was the interpretation in English. Brother Joseph would read off the English to Oliver Cowdry, who was his principal scribe, and when it was written down and repeated to Brother Joseph to see if it was correct, then it would disappear, and another character with the interpretation would appear. Thus the Book of Mormon was translated by the gift and power of God, and not by any power of man.[36]

David Whitmer, though, was not the only eyewitness who made the claim concerning seer stones and a hat. James Lancaster recounts an interview of Joseph Smith's wife, Emma:

> Smith's wife, Emma Smith Bidamon, was interviewed late in her life by her son Joseph Smith III about her knowledge of the early church. This interview took place in February 1879 in the presence of Lewis C. Bidamon, her husband. At one point Emma stated the following: "In writing for your father I frequently wrote day after day, often sitting at the table close by him, he sitting with his face buried in his hat, with the stone in it, and dictating hour after hour with nothing between us . . . He had neither manuscript nor book to read from . . . If he had anything of the kind, he could not have concealed it from me . . . The plates often lay on the table without any attempt at concealment, wrapped in a small linen tablecloth, which I had given him to fold them in . . . Oliver Cowdry and your father wrote in the room where I was at work." According to his wife, Smith translated the Book of Mormon sitting with his face in a hat with a stone in the hat as well.

---

[36] David Whitmer, *An Address to All Believers in Christ* (Richmond, MO: David Whitmer, 1887), 12.

He did not look at the plates which were nearby, wrapped in a small tablecloth.[37]

We can conclude, therefore, for the purposes of the actual creation of the Book of Mormon, that the golden plates were not used and, to some degree, are a moot point in the history of the English version of the work.

Contents of the Book of Mormon

The Book of Mormon is likely the piece of scripture most people recognize as distinctively Latter-day Saint. Without question, it is the most important piece of scripture within the Mormon canon, thereby making the contents extremely important. *Preach My Gospel* declares:

> The Prophet Joseph Smith taught that the Book of Mormon is "the keystone of our religion." On another occasion, he stated: "Take away the Book of Mormon and the revelations, and where is our religion? We have none." An arch is a strong architectural structure made from wedge-shaped pieces that lean against each other. The middle piece, or keystone, is usually larger than the other wedges and locks the other stones in place. When Joseph Smith called the Book of Mormon "the keystone of our religion," he taught that the Book of Mormon holds our religion together.[38]

If this book is indeed the keystone of faith for Mormonism, then what are its contents?

First, the Book of Mormon is about Jesus.

> A central purpose of the Book of Mormon is to convince all people that Jesus is the Christ. It testifies of Christ by affirming the reality of His life, mission, and power. It teaches true doctrine concerning the Atonement—the foundation for the plan of salvation. . . . Those who know little or nothing about the Savior will come to know Him by reading, pondering, and praying about the Book of Mormon. The testimony of the Book of Mormon confirms the testimony of the Bible that Jesus is the Only Begotten Son of God and the Savior of the world.[39]

---

[37] James E. Lancaster, "The Translation of the Book of Mormon" in *The Word of God*, ed. Dan Vogel (Salt Lake City: Signature, 1990), 98–99.
[38] Church of Jesus Christ of Latter-day Saints, *Preach My Gospel*, 103–4.
[39] Church of Jesus Christ of Latter-day Saints, 105.

Second, the Book of Mormon is about a group of people who migrated from the ancient world to the Americas and contains information about their history, struggles, and beliefs. *Gospel Principles* summarizes nicely in noting, "The Book of Mormon is a sacred record of some of the people who lived on the American continents between about 2000 B.C. and A.D. 400. It contains the fulness of the gospel of Jesus Christ. The Book of Mormon tells of the visit Jesus Christ made to the people in the Americas soon after His Resurrection."[40]

In a lengthy section from his work *The Articles of Faith*, former LDS apostle James Talmage offers his own summary of the entirety of the Book of Mormon:

> From the title page, we learn that in the Book of Mormon we have to deal with the histories of two nations, who flourished in America as the descendants of small colonies brought hither from the eastern continent by divine direction. Of these we may conveniently speak as the Nephites and the Jaredites. The Nephite Nation was the later, and in point of the fulness of the records, the more important. The progenitors of this people were led from Jerusalem in the year 600 B.C., by Lehi, a Jewish prophet of the tribe of Manasseh. His immediate family, at the time of their departure from Jerusalem, comprised his wife Sariah, and their sons Laman, Lemuel, Sam, and Nephi; at a later stage of the history daughters are mentioned, but whether any of these were born before the family exodus we are not told. Beside his own household, the colony of Lehi included Zoram and Ishmael, the latter an Israelite of the tribe of Ephraim. Ishmael, with his family, joined Lehi's company in the wilderness, and his descendants were numbered with the nation of whom we are speaking. It appears that the company journeyed somewhat east of south, keeping near the borders of the Red Sea; then, changing their course to the eastward, crossed the peninsula of Arabia; and there, on the shores of the Arabian Sea, built and provisioned a vessel in which they committed themselves to divine care upon the waters. It is believed that their voyage must have carried them eastward across the Indian Ocean, then over the Pacific to the western coast of America, whereon they landed about 590 B.C. The landing place is not described in the book itself with such detail as to warrant definite conclusions.

---

[40] Church of Jesus Christ of Latter-day Saints, *Gospel Principles*, 46.

The people established themselves on what was the land of promise; many children were born, and in the course of a few generations a numerous posterity held possession of the land. After the death of Lehi a division occurred, some of the people accepting as their leader, Nephi, who had been duly appointed to the prophetic office; while the rest proclaimed Laman, the eldest of Lehi's sons, as their chief. Thenceforth the divided people were known as the Nephites and the Lamanites respectively. At times they observed toward each other a semblance of friendly relations; but generally they were opposed, the Lamanites manifesting implacable hatred and hostility toward their Nephite kindred. The Nephites advanced in the arts of civilization, built large cities, and established prosperous commonwealths; yet they often fell into transgression, and the Lord chastened them by permitting their hereditary enemies to be victorious. It is traditionally believed that they spread northward, occupying a considerable area in Central America, and then expanded eastward and northward over part of what is now the United States of America. The Lamanites, while increasing in numbers, fell under the curse of divine displeasure; they became dark in skin and benighted in spirit, forgot the God of their fathers, lived a wild nomadic life, and degenerated into the fallen state in which the American Indians—their lineal descendants—were found by those who rediscovered the western continent in later times.

The final struggles between Nephites and Lamanites were waged in the vicinity of the Hill Cumorah, in what is now the State of New York, resulting in the destruction of the Nephites as a nation, about 400 A.D. The last Nephite representative was Moroni, who, wandering for safety from place to place, daily expecting death from the victorious Lamanites, wrote the concluding parts of the Book of Mormon, and hid the record in Cumorah. It was this same Moroni who, as a resurrected being, gave the records into the hands of Joseph Smith in the present dispensation.

Of the two nations whose histories constitute the Book of Mormon, the first in order of time consisted of the people of Jared, who followed their leader from the Tower of Babel at the time of the confusion of tongues. Their history was written on twenty-four plates of gold by Ether, the last of their prophets, who, foreseeing the destruction of his people because of their wickedness, hid away the historic plates. They were afterward found, about B.C. 122, by an expedition sent out by King Limhi, a Nephite ruler. The record engraved on these plates was subsequently abridged by Moroni, and the condensed account was attached by him to the Book of Mormon record; it appears in the modern translation under the name the Book of Ether.

The first and chief prophet of the Jaredites is not specified by name in the record as we have it; he is known only as the brother of Jared. Of his people we learn that, amidst the confusion of Babel, Jared and his brother importuned the Lord that they and their associates be spared from the impending disruption. Their prayer was heard, and the Lord led them with a considerable company, who, like themselves, were free from the taint of idolatry, away from their homes, promising to conduct them to a land choice above all other lands. Their course of travel is not given with exactness; we learn only that they reached the ocean and there constructed eight vessels, called barges, in which they set out upon the waters. These vessels were small and dark within; but the Lord made certain stones luminous, and these gave light to the imprisoned voyagers. After a passage of three hundred and forty-four days, the colony landed on the western shore of North America, probably at a place south of the Gulf of California, and north of the Isthmus of Panama.

Here they became a flourishing nation; but, giving way in time to internal dissensions, they divided into factions, which warred with one another until the people were totally destroyed. This destruction, which occurred near the Hill Ramah, afterward known among the Nephites as Cumorah, probably took place at about the time of Lehi's landing, near 590 B.C. The last representative of the ill-fated race was Coriantumr, the king, concerning whom Ether had prophesied that he should survive all his subjects and live to see another people in possession of the land. This prediction was fulfilled in that the king, whose people had been exterminated, came, in the course of his solitary wanderings, to a region occupied by the people of Mulek, who are to be mentioned here as the third ancient colony of emigrants from the eastern continent.

Mulek was the son of Zedekiah, king of Judah, an infant at the time of his brothers' violent deaths and his father's cruel torture at the hands of the king of Babylon. Eleven years after Lehi's departure from

Jerusalem, another colony was led from the city, amongst whom was Mulek. The colony took his name, probably on account of his recognized rights of leadership by virtue of lineage. The Book of Mormon record concerning Mulek and his people is scant; we learn, however, that the colony was brought across the waters to a landing, probably on the northern part of the American continent. The descendants of this colony were discovered by the Nephites under Mosiah; they had grown numerous, but, having had no scriptures for their guidance had fallen into a condition of spiritual darkness. They joined the Nephites and their history is merged into that of the greater nation. The Nephites gave to a part of North America the name Land of Mulek.[41]

With this extensive summary from Talmage, then, we can conclude that the Book of Mormon is mainly concerned with the history of two people groups, the Nephites and the Jaredites, specifically, with their dealings with each other, with their religious beliefs, and with their encounter with the resurrected Jesus. This work, then, as Joseph Smith declared, is the keystone of the faith of Latter-day Saints. Without it, there is indeed no Mormonism. There are, however, additional scriptures that offer more information to Latter-day Saints. With that in mind, we now turn our attention to the Doctrine and Covenants.

The Doctrine and Covenants

Put simply, the Doctrine and Covenants is understood by Latter-day Saints to be modern scripture. *Gospel Principles* states, very concisely, "The Doctrine and Covenants is a collection of modern revelations."[42] Joseph Fielding McConkie, a former professor at Brigham Young University, and a former mission president, stake president, and LDS Institute Director, notes:

[Joseph Smith] described our dispensation as the "complete and perfect union," the "welding together" of all the rights, keys, honors, majesty, glory, power, and priesthood of past dispensations. Thus the story of the Restoration as it unfolds in the compilation of revelations found in the Doctrine and Covenants constitutes a great Urim and Thummim through which we can view and understand events and doctrines in the Old and New Testaments. It is for us both map and compass to the

---

[41] Talmage, *The Articles of Faith*, 264–68.
[42] Church of Jesus Christ of Latter-day Saints, *Gospel Principles*, 47.

rich treasures of the past. It gives perspective, direction, meaning, and understanding to our study of the Bible that is in many instances light years ahead of that which we can gain from sectarian commentaries, archaeological digs, and such finds as the Dead Sea Scrolls and the Ebla Tablets. To attempt to study the Bible without the aid of the Doctrine and Covenants and other revelations of the restoration would be a serious mistake in gospel scholarship.[43]

Gospel Principles adds further insight:

This book contains the revelations regarding the Church of Jesus Christ as it has been restored in these last days. Several sections of the book explain the organization of the Church and define the offices of the priesthood and their functions. Other sections . . . contain glorious truths that were lost to the world for hundreds of years. Still others . . . shed light on teachings in the Bible. In addition, some sections . . . contain prophecies of events to come.[44]

Bruce McConkie offers additional summary information. Concerning the Doctrine and Covenants, he writes:

That volume of Latter-day scripture which contains selections from the revelations given to Joseph Smith and his successors in the Presidency of the Church is called the Doctrine and Covenants. Certain parts of these revelations were published in Independence, Missouri, in 1833 under the title Book of Commandments, but mob violence destroyed the printing press and stopped the work at that time. By 1835, however, a new and enlarged selection of revelations had been made by the Prophet, and the first edition of the Doctrine and Covenants came off the press. Thereafter, of course, written revelations continued to be received. After the saints came west, Elder Orson Pratt was commissioned and directed by the First Presidency to prepare an up-to-date edition of the Doctrine and Covenants for publication. This volume, the one now in use, containing additional revelations and being divided into sections and verses, was first published in 1876.[45]

---

[43] Joseph Fielding McConkie, *The Spirit of Revelation* (Salt Lake City: Deseret, 1984), 107.
[44] Church of Jesus Christ of Latter-day Saints, *Gospel Principles*, 47.
[45] McConkie, *Mormon Doctrine*, 205–6.

He continues:

> As now constituted the Doctrine and Covenants contains 136 sections
> or chapters to which are appended an Official Declaration commonly
> called the Manifesto. Most of these sections came to Joseph Smith
> by direct revelation, the recorded words being those of the Lord Je-
> sus Christ himself. The power of the Holy Ghost was manifest in the
> receipt of all the revelations. Some came by the whisperings of the
> Spirit to the Prophet (D&C 20); some were received by means of the
> Urim and Thummim (D&C 3); others are the recorded words of an-
> gelic ministrants (D&C 2); others are accounts of visions (D&C 76);
> a few are inspired epistles of the Prophet (D&C 128); a few others
> contain inspired items of instruction (D&C 131); one is an article set-
> ting forth church beliefs relative to governments and laws in general
> (D&C 134); one is an inspired announcement of the martyrdom of the
> Prophet and patriarch (D&C 135); and, since its adoption in 1890, the
> Official Declaration (or Manifesto) of President Wilford Woodruff has
> been published in the Doctrine and Covenants.[46]

For the year 2017, the scripture study emphasis for the Church of Jesus
Christ of Latter-day Saints was on the Doctrine and Covenants. Because of
this emphasis, the LDS Church released new information and study guides
to help its members work through the highlighted book of scripture. In late
2016, a small study guide to the Doctrine and Covenants, entitled *Revelations
in Context: The Stories Behind the Sections of the Doctrine and Covenants*,
was released. In the preface, there is a short summary of the LDS view of the
Doctrine and Covenants. The authors note:

> Latter-day Saints believe in a loving God who speaks to His children
> "in these times as in times of old, and as well in times of old as in
> times to come" (1 Nephi 10:19). This fundamental principle of the
> restored gospel is reflected in Latter-day Saint scripture, which con-
> tains records of God's dealings with His children in the remote past, as
> well as His words to Joseph Smith and other Latter-day prophets. The
> book of Doctrine and Covenants is a witness of this outpouring of con-
> tinuing revelation. Each section answers pressing questions, reveals

---

[46] McConkie, 206.

important truths, or gives practical guidance. These revelations are the fruit of an ongoing dialogue between the Lord and His people. But in many cases, the Doctrine and Covenants contains only half of the dialogue—the Lord's revealed responses. In this way, it is unique among Latter-day Saints books of scripture. In the Bible, Book of Mormon, and Pearl of Great Price, gospel teaching is often couched in narrative. The narrative gives us clues that help us interpret the teachings and see how they influenced the lives of men and women of the scriptures. But the Doctrine and Covenants does not contain the stories behind the revelations.[47]

McConkie offers a great summary position concerning the Doctrine and Covenants. He writes, "Perhaps no other book is of such great worth to the saints as is the Doctrine and Covenants. It is their book, the voice of God in their day. The revelations therein are true, and men are commanded to search them. (D&C 1:37-39)."[48]

Pearl of Great Price

The Pearl of Great Price is the smallest of the Latter-day Saint sacred texts, yet it may be the most controversial and hold the greatest amount of unique information. Split into two larger sections and two smaller sections, the Pearl of Great Price contains various works considered by Latter-day Saints to be holy writ. *Gospel Principles* notes, "The Pearl of Great Price contains the book of Moses, the book of Abraham, and some inspired writings of Joseph Smith. The book of Moses contains an account of some of the visions and writings of Moses, revealed to the Prophet Joseph Smith. It clarifies doctrines and teachings that were lost from the Bible and gives added information concerning the Creation of the earth."[49] With reference to the specific works within the Pearl of Great Price, *Gospel Principles* states, "The book of Abraham was translated by the Prophet Joseph Smith from a papyrus scroll taken from the Egyptian catacombs. This book contains valuable information about the Creation, the gospel, the nature of God, and the priesthood. The writings of Joseph Smith

---

[47] Church of Jesus Christ of Latter-day Saints, *Revelations in Context* (Salt Lake City: Church of Jesus Christ of Latter-day Saints, 2016), vii.
[48] McConkie, *Mormon Doctrine*, 206.
[49] Church of Jesus Christ of Latter-day Saints, *Gospel Principles*, 48.

include part of Joseph Smith's inspired translation of the Bible, selections from his *History of the Church*, and the Articles of Faith."[50]

Former member of the First Quorum of Seventy Milton R. Hunter gave an entire conference talk in October 1955 on the unique scriptures of Latter-day Saints. He included a very helpful section on the Pearl of Great Price. Hunter said:

> The third great treasure which I hold in my hand is the Pearl of Great Price, a pearl indeed. It is composed of two revelations given to Moses and revealed to Joseph Smith; the book of Abraham, written by the great patriarch and translated by the Prophet Joseph; the twenty-fourth chapter of Matthew; some of the early visions beheld by the Prophet; some of his teachings; and the Articles of Faith. They are compacted in approximately sixty pages, but every page is dynamic and powerful. It is a wonderful book.[51]

He continued:

> The Pearl of Great Price also contains revelations on certain subjects superior to any other scriptures or writings on those subjects found in the world; for example, Abraham's vision of pre-mortal life in which he learned of the eternal nature of things; of the grand council in heaven; and of the plan of salvation as presented there constitutes one of the greatest of God's revelations to his holy prophets. And the knowledge obtained by Moses in his vision of Lucifer and the part he played at the grand council, added to Abraham's vision, gives us the most complete understanding found in any literature regarding man's pre-mortal life and God's purposes for the good of man.[52]

The Book of Moses

McConkie takes his summary much further and is more helpful than the purposefully concise *Gospel Principles*. Concerning the book of Moses, he explains:

---

[50] Church of Jesus Christ of Latter-day Saints, 48.
[51] Milton R. Hunter, discourse in *Conference Report* (Salt Lake City: Church of Jesus Christ of Latter-day Saints, October 1955), 67.
[52] Hunter, 67.

Contrary to the false notions of the higher critics, Moses personally is the author of the Pentateuch or the first five books of the Old Testament. In their present form, however, these five books no longer contain many of the teachings and doctrines originally placed in them by the great lawgiver of ancient Israel. But by direct revelation in modern times the Lord has restored through the Prophet many of the great truths lost from the early Mosaic scriptures.[53]

He continues:

The Book of Moses, a work containing eight chapters and covering the same general period and events as are found in the first six chapters of Genesis, contains much of this restored truth. The 1st and 7th chapters of Moses are entirely new revelations having no counterpart in Genesis. The other chapters in Moses cover the same events recorded in the first six chapters of Genesis, but the account revealed in Latter-days has been so enlarged, contains so much new material, and so radically changes the whole perspective of the Lord's dealings with Adam and the early patriarchs that for all practical purposes it may be considered as entirely new matter. The whole view of the creation of all things; of pre-existence and the purpose of life; of Adam and his fall; of the primeval revelation of the gospel to man; of the terms and conditions in accordance with which salvation is offered to the living and the dead; of Enoch, his ministry and his establishment of Zion; and of Noah, his priesthood and ministry—the whole view and perspective relative to all these things is radically changed by the new revelations in the Book of Moses. This book which is also contained in the Prophet's Inspired Version of the Bible, is one of the most important documents the Lord has ever revealed.[54]

Thus, we can say the book of Moses, though it generally presents the same type of information given in the first few chapters of Genesis, is nonetheless a significant change from those chapters. In the end, then, the book of Moses, as McConkie noted, is fundamentally new material.

---

[53] McConkie, *Mormon Doctrine*, 563.
[54] McConkie, 563.

The Book of Abraham

The second large section of the Pearl of Great Price is the book of Abraham. To rehearse the already quoted material from *Gospel Principles*, the book of Abraham "was translated by the Prophet Joseph Smith from a papyrus scroll taken from the Egyptian catacombs. This book contains valuable information about the Creation, the gospel, the nature of God, and the priesthood."[55] Likewise, McConkie writes, "This work was translated by the Prophet from a papyrus record taken from the catacombs of Egypt, a record preserved by the Lord to come forth in this day of restoration. Abraham was the original author, and the scriptural account contains priceless information about the gospel, pre-existence, the nature of Deity, the creation, and priesthood, information which is not otherwise available in any other revelation now extant."[56]

Throughout the years, the book of Abraham has garnered a great deal of attention due to the issue of the translation of the Egyptian papyrus obtained by Joseph Smith. Indeed, an article titled "Gospel Topic Essay" and published at www.lds.org in 2016 explained more about the LDS Church's understanding of the book of Abraham and its translation.[57] The essay states, "The book originated with Egyptian papyri that Joseph Smith translated beginning in 1835. Many people saw the papyri, but no eyewitness account of the translation survives, making it impossible to reconstruct the process. Only small fragments of the long papyrus scrolls once in Joseph Smith's possession exist today. The relationship between those fragments and the text we have today is largely a matter of conjecture." The essay continues:

> Some evidence suggests that Joseph studied the characters on the Egyptian papyri and attempted to learn the Egyptian language. His history reports that, in July 1835, he was "continually engaged in translating an alphabet to the Book of Abraham, and arranging a grammar of the Egyptian language as practiced by the ancients." This "grammar," as it was called, consisted of columns of hieroglyphic characters followed by English translations recorded in a large notebook by Joseph's scribe,

---

[55] Church of Jesus Christ of Latter-day Saints, *Gospel Principles*, 48.

[56] McConkie, *Mormon Doctrine*, 564.

[57] The remainder of the quotes in this section are taken from Church of Jesus Christ of Latter-day Saints, "Translation and the Historicity of the Book of Abraham," LDS.org, accessed April 5, 2017, https://www.lds.org/topics/translation-and-historicity-of-the-book-of-abraham?lang=eng&old=true.

William W. Phelps. Another manuscript, written by Joseph Smith and Oliver Cowdry, has Egyptian characters followed by explanations.

There is at least, then, some evidence to suggest Smith grappled with the text and tried to translate the text from the papyrus directly. This, however, would prove to be significantly problematic.

Concerning this attempt at translation, the essay states, "The relationship of these documents to the book of Abraham is not fully understood. Neither the rules nor the translations in the grammar book correspond to those recognized by Egyptologists today."

The essay continues, "Ten papyrus fragments once in Joseph Smith's possession ended up in the Metropolitan Museum of Art in New York City. In 1967, the museum transferred these fragments to the Church, which subsequently published them in the Church's magazine, the *Improvement Era.*"

The authors of the article then move to yet a more interesting discussion. They state:

> The discovery of the papyrus fragments renewed debate about Joseph Smith's translation. The fragments include one vignette, or illustration, that appears in the book of Abraham as facsimile 1. Long before the fragments were published by the Church, some Egyptologists had said that Joseph Smith's explanations of the various elements of these facsimiles did not match their own interpretations of these drawings. Joseph Smith had published the facsimiles as freestanding drawings, cut off from the hieroglyphs or hieratic characters that originally surrounded the vignettes. The discovery of the fragments meant that readers could now see the hieroglyphs and characters immediately surrounding the vignette that became facsimile 1.

They conclude:

> None of the characters on the papyrus fragments mentioned Abraham's name or any of the events recorded in the book of Abraham. Mormon and non-Mormon Egyptologists agree that the characters on the fragments do not match the translation given in the book of Abraham, though there is not unanimity, even among non-Mormon scholars, about the proper interpretation of the vignettes on these fragments. Scholars have identified the papyrus fragments as parts of standard funerary texts that were deposited with mummified bodies.

These fragments date to between the third century B.C.E. and the first century C.E., long after Abraham lived.

How, considering this information released by the LDS Church, could the book of Abraham be trusted by Latter-day Saints? The essay states:

Of course, the fragments do not have to be as old as Abraham for the book of Abraham and its illustrations to be authentic. Ancient records are often transmitted as copies or as copies of copies. The record of Abraham could have been edited or redacted by later writers much as the Book of Mormon prophet-historians Mormon and Moroni revised the writings of earlier peoples. Moreover, documents initially composed for one context can be repackaged for another context or purpose. Illustrations once connected with Abraham could have either drifted or been dislodged from their original context and reinterpreted hundreds of years later in terms of burial practices in a later period of Egyptian history. The opposite could also be true: illustrations with no clear connection to Abraham anciently could, by revelation, shed light on the life and teachings of this prophetic figure.

Therefore, Latter-day Saints are told they can trust the book of Abraham because, regardless of the connection of the book to the ancient papyri, Joseph Smith received the information via revelation from heaven. The essay explains further:

Alternatively, Joseph's study of the papyri may have led to a revelation about key events and teachings in the life of Abraham, much as he had earlier received a revelation about the life of Moses while studying the Bible. This view assumes a broader definition of the words *translator* and *translation*. According to this view, Joseph's translation was not a literal rendering of the papyri as a conventional translation would be. Rather, the physical artifacts provided an occasion for meditation, reflection, and revelation. They catalyzed a process whereby God gave to Joseph Smith a revelation about the life of Abraham, even if that revelation did not directly correlate to the characters on the papyri.

In conclusion, the essay argues:

The veracity and value of the book of Abraham cannot be settled by scholarly debate concerning the book's translation and historicity. The book's status as scripture lies in the eternal truths it teaches and the powerful spirit it conveys. The book of Abraham imparts profound truths about the nature of God, His relationship to us as His children, and the purpose of this mortal life. The truth of the book of Abraham is ultimately found through careful study of its teachings, sincere prayer, and the confirmation of the Spirit.

Thus, it can be said that Latter-day Saints believe in four books of scripture: the Bible, the Book of Mormon, the Doctrine and Covenants, and the Pearl of Great Price. All four books hold a special place in the Latter-day Saint canon and the individual member's heart. It can also be said that all four books are unique, functioning as individual, stand-alone books, yet all four support each other as the four legs of a table support the weight of the tabletop and anything sitting on the table.

Though there are four written books within the Latter-day Saint canon, there is a fifth, unwritten "book," another aspect of scripture which is critical to Latter-day Saints, possibly even more important than the four written texts. That fifth, unwritten "book" is continuing revelation, something issued for the entire Church by members of the First Presidency and the Quorum of Twelve Apostles, and usually during the Annual General Conference or the Semi-Annual General Conference.

Continuing Revelation

In a letter to I. Daniel Rupp, Joseph Smith articulated clearly the LDS belief in continuing revelation. He wrote, "We believe all that God has revealed, all that He does now reveal, and we believe that He will yet reveal many great and important things pertaining to the Kingdom of God."[58] James Talmage defined the idea that God continues to communicate with humanity: "In a theological sense, the term *revelation* signifies the making known of Divine truth by communication from heaven."[59] One Latter-day Saint scholar even differentiated between varying types of continuing revelation. Joseph Fielding McConkie

---

[58] Articles of Faith 1:9 (see chap. 2, n. 9).
[59] Talmage, *The Articles of Faith*, 308.

argued for the existence of four specific types of revelation: institutional, stewardship, shared, and personal.[60] He explained:

> By *institutional revelation*, we mean the canon of scripture known to Latter-day Saints as the standard works. By *stewardship revelation*, we mean those inspired promptings, in their multitude of forms, that are granted to sustain and direct us in our various offices and callings as we labor in the Lord's vineyard. The phrase *shared revelation* is used to describe experiences had in company with others. By *personal revelation* is meant those spiritual directions intended for us individually or for our families.[61]

Put simply, Latter-day Saints believe that God has communicated to humanity by means of the Bible, the Book of Mormon, the Doctrine and Covenants, and the Pearl of Great Price. They also believe that God continues to communicate to humanity by means of revelations given to the president of the Church. Those revelations given to the president become scripture and may be added to the current LDS standard works. *Gospel Principles* declares, "In addition to [the standard works], the inspired words of our living prophets become scripture to us. Their words come to us through conferences, Church publications, and instructions to local priesthood leaders."[62]

Historical Foundations

Historically speaking, Joseph Smith formed a desire for more revelations from God at an early age. He wrote of these thoughts in his work *Joseph Smith— History*, a section of which is included within the Pearl of Great Price. During his childhood, Smith was overwhelmed by religious questions. Yet each time he inquired of different ministers, he received varying answers. This lack of unity between various Christian denominations caused young Smith great consternation. He recalled:

> In the midst of this war of words and tumult of opinions, I often said to myself: What is to be done? Who of all these parties are right; or, are they all wrong together? If anyone of them be right, which is it, and how shall I know it? While I was laboring under the extreme

---

[60] Joseph Fielding McConkie, *The Spirit of Revelation*, 10.
[61] McConkie, 10.
[62] Church of Jesus Christ of Latter-day Saints, *Gospel Principles*, 55.

difficulties caused by the contests of these parties of religionists, I was one day reading the Epistle of James, first chapter and fifth verse, which reads: *If any of you lack wisdom, let him ask of God, that giveth to all men liberally, and upbraideth not; and it shall be given him.* Never did any passage of scripture come with more power to the heart of man than this did at this time to mine. It seemed to enter with great force into every feeling of my heart. I reflected on it again and again, knowing that if any person needed wisdom from God, I did; for how to act I did not know; for the teachers of religion of the different sects understood the same passage of scripture so differently as to destroy all confidence in settling the question by an appeal to the Bible. At length I came to the conclusion that I must either remain in darkness and confusion, or else I must do as James directs, that is, ask of God. I at length came to the determination to "ask of God," concluding that if he gave wisdom to them that lacked wisdom, and would give liberally, and not upbraid, I might venture.[63]

Commenting on this passage, Millet wrote, "Joseph Smith did not believe, however, that the Bible was complete or that all religious difficulties could necessarily be handled by turning to the Old or New Testaments for help."[64] Thus, early in his life, Smith had already formed his view that God would indeed continue to pour forth revelations from heaven.

Scriptural Foundation

Similar ideas are found within the Book of Mormon and the Doctrine and Covenants. The most often-quoted passage in the Book of Mormon with reference to continuing revelation is 2 Nephi 28:26–30. The passage reads,

Yea, wo be unto him that hearkeneth unto the precepts of men, and denieth the power of God, and the gift of the Holy Ghost! Yea, wo be unto him that saith: We have received, and we need no more! And in fine, wo unto all those who tremble, and are angry because of the truth of God! For behold, he that is built upon the rock receiveth it with gladness; and he that is built upon a sandy foundation trembleth

---

[63] Joseph Smith, *Joseph Smith—History*, 1:10–13.
[64] Robert L. Millet and Noel B. Reynolds, eds., *Latter-day Christianity: 10 Basic Issues* (Provo, UT: Foundation for Ancient Research and Mormon Studies and Religious Studies Center, Brigham Young University, 1998), 19.

lest he shall fall. Wo be unto him that shall say: We have received the word of God, and we need no more of the word of God, for we have enough! For behold, thus saith the Lord God: I will give unto the children of men line upon line, precept upon precept, here a little and there a little; and blessed are those who hearken unto my precepts, and lend an ear unto my counsel, for they shall learn wisdom; for unto him that receiveth I will give more; and from them that shall say, We have enough, from them shall be taken away even that which they have.

Similarly, 2 Nephi 29:10 reads, "Wherefore, because that ye have a Bible ye need not suppose that it contains all my words; neither need ye suppose that I have not caused more to be written." Joseph Fielding McConkie and Robert Millet explained, "Among the worst of sectarian heresies is the idea that the Bible contains all the word of God. . . . The word of God cannot be confined to books, let alone to a single book."[65] In an earlier work, they declared, "We cannot rely solely on the thunderings of Sinai or even on the sublime utterances of the Sermon on the Mount; we are desperately in need of our Palmyras, our Kirtlands, our Nauvoos, and our Salt Lake Cities—living fruit from the living tree of life."[66]

The Doctrine and Covenants also houses declarations stating that continuing revelation will indeed take place. Section 76:7 reads, "And to them will I reveal all mysteries, yea, all the hidden mysteries of my kingdom from days of old, and for ages to come, will I make known unto them the good pleasure of my will concerning all things pertaining to my kingdom." Likewise, section 121:26 declares, "God shall give unto you knowledge by his Holy Spirit, yea, by the unspeakable gift of the Holy Ghost, that has not been revealed since the world was until now." Also, Doctrine and Covenants 124:41 states, "For I design to reveal unto my church things which have been kept hid from before the foundation of the world, things that pertain to the dispensation of the fulness of times." These passages clearly show a God who has revealed, does reveal, and will continue to reveal new revelations to humanity.

---

[65] Joseph Fielding McConkie and Robert L. Millet, *Doctrinal Commentary on the Book of Mormon*, 1:351.

[66] Joseph Fielding McConkie and Robert L. Millet, *Sustaining and Defending the Saints* (Salt Lake City: Bookcraft, 1985), 34.

Theological Foundation

Latter-day Saints hold a number of theological positions that require God to continue to reveal truths to humanity. First, the LDS believe the Bible to be incomplete. Bruce McConkie declared, "One of the great heresies of modern Christendom is the unfounded assumption that the Bible contains all of the inspired teachings now extant among men."[67] Similarly, Robert Millet wrote, "I for one believe we ought to be especially careful about claiming for scripture what it does not claim for itself. For example, there is the matter of biblical sufficiency—whether the Bible is the final and complete word of God, the 'seal of the prophets' to borrow a phrase from our Muslim friends. Do we really know that God has chosen not to reveal himself beyond the Bible?"[68]

Second, Latter-day Saints believe the canon of scripture to be open. Elder Neal A. Maxwell of the Quorum of the Twelve Apostles argued, "Many more scriptural writings will yet come to us." He continued, "Today we carry convenient quadruple combinations of the scriptures, but one day, since more scriptures are coming, we may need to pull little red wagons brimful with books."[69] Another member of the Quorum of the Twelve Apostles, M. Russell Ballard, agrees. He wrote:

> But perhaps the most important thing that young Joseph learned that day in what is now referred to by Church members as the Sacred Grove is this significant eternal truth: the heavens are *not* sealed. God is *not* limited. Certainly He isn't bound by the limitations with which some churches try to restrict Him. To those who say that all revelation ended with the death of Christ's original apostles and that we already have all of the instruction from God we will ever need, Joseph Smith's story stands as solemn testimony that God hasn't shut the door on His children. He loves us today just as much as He loved those who lived anciently, and He is just as concerned about us as He was about them. What comfort that sweet assurance provides in a world filled with confusion and discouragement! What peace and security comes to the heart that understands there is a God in heaven who is our Father, who knows us and cares about us—individually and collectively—and who

---

[67] Bruce McConkie, *Mormon Doctrine*, 83.

[68] Millet and McDermott, *Claiming Christ*, 35 (see chap. 1, n. 68).

[69] Neal A. Maxwell, *Wonderful Flood of Light* (Salt Lake City: Bookcraft, 1990), 18.

will communicate with us, either directly or through His living prophets, according to our needs.[70]

Robert Millet offered a succinct statement concerning the openness of the
canon when, in answering a questioning professor, he said, "Well, I suppose
you could say that the Mormons believe the canon of scripture is *open, flexible,*
and *expanding!*"[71] Likewise, Joseph Fielding McConkie explained, "It is expected that we do more than read of spiritual feasts that were eaten anciently;
we too much approach the table and feed our souls. The tree of life continues
to bring forth living fruit. To have one revelation is to have the seedlings of yet
others."[72] James Talmage wrote, "The canon of scripture is still open; many
lines, many precepts, are yet to be added."[73]

Third, Latter-day Saints deem contemporary revelation from God necessary. McConkie and Millet argued, "The Church of Jesus Christ is dynamic in
the sense that it is dependent on current revelation for its daily operation—living fruit from the living tree of life. We honor and reverence the names and
works of those who have gone before. But their revelations are not sufficient
to save this generation."[74] James Talmage commented, "We have no record of
a period of time during which an authorized minister of Christ has dwelt on
earth, when the Lord did not make known to that servant the Divine will concerning the people."[75] He explained further:

> The scriptures are conclusive as to the fact, that from Adam to John
> the Revelator, God directed the affairs of His people by personal com-
> munication through chosen servants. As the written word—the record
> of revelation previously given—grew with time, that became a law
> unto the people; but in no period was that deemed sufficient. While
> the revelations of the past have ever been indispensable as guides to
> the people, showing forth as they do, the plan and purpose of God's
> dealings under particular conditions, they may not be universally and
> directly applicable to the circumstances of succeeding times.[76]

---

[70] M. Russell Ballard, *Our Search for Happiness* (Salt Lake City: Deseret, 1993), 41–42.
[71] Millet and McDermott, *Claiming Christ,* 37.
[72] Joseph Fielding McConkie, *The Spirit of Revelation,* 47.
[73] Talmage, *The Articles of Faith,* 323.
[74] McConkie and Millet, *Sustaining and Defending the Faith,* 67.
[75] Talmage, *The Articles of Faith,* 310.
[76] Talmage, 314.

Former Latter-day Saint president Spencer W. Kimball wrote, "Continuous revelation is indeed the very lifeblood of the gospel of the living Lord and Savior, Jesus Christ."[77] He continued, "How absurd it would be to think that the Lord would give to a small handful of people in Palestine and the Old World his precious direction through revelation and now, in our extremity, close the heavens."[78] Former president John Taylor argued:

> We require a living tree—a living fountain—living intelligence, proceeding from the living priesthood in heaven, through the living priesthood on earth. And from the time that Adam first received a communication from God, to the time that John, on the Isle of Patmos, received his communication, or Joseph Smith had the heavens opened to him, it always required new revelations, adapted to the peculiar circumstances in which the churches or individuals were placed. Adam's revelation did not instruct Noah to build his ark; nor did Noah's revelation tell Lot to forsake Sodom; nor did either of these speak of the departure of the children of Israel from Egypt. These all had revelations for themselves, and so had Isaiah, Jeremiah, Ezekiel, Jesus, Peter, Paul, John, and Joseph. And so must we, or we shall make a shipwreck.[79]

To review, then, there are three theological reasons, from a Latter-day Saint perspective, for continuing revelation. First, the Bible is believed to be incomplete. Second, the scriptural canon is believed to be open. Third, Latter-day Saints believe it is necessary to continue to hear from God.

The Nature of Continuing Revelation

Finally, an inquiry into the nature of continuing revelation is needed in order to understand fully this doctrine. If revelation continues to be offered, how does modern revelation impact or affect previous revelations? Are modern revelations more important than past revelations? How do Latter-day Saints view currently accepted revelations in light of the possibility of future revelations that may or may not supersede presently accepted truth statements? Spencer J. Condie offered a wonderfully concise, yet insightful, statement concerning

---

[77] Spencer W. Kimball, "Revelation," *Ensign,* May 1977, 76.
[78] Kimball, 77.
[79] G. Homer Durham, ed., *The Gospel Kingdom: Selections from the Writings and Discourses of John Taylor* (Salt Lake City: Improvement Era, 1941), 34.

continuing revelation. He wrote, "For some members of the Church it is easy to accept and sustain the notion of continuous *revelation*; they just have a problem accepting *change*. But change is an inevitable consequence of continuous revelation."[80] Condie also offered a word of warning to Latter-day Saints:

> Our quest to remain steadfast may, if we are not introspective, lead to an undue concern with exactness and the letter of the law. It is well to remind ourselves of Paul's concern that the "letter killeth" as we become more concerned with following the rule than with understanding the purpose of the rule as leading our lives to a higher plane. On the other hand, when we become too flexible, too open-minded, too creative, and too willing to uncritically accept new ideas, there is always a danger of losing sight of eternal objectives as absolutes. And we are in danger of abandoning absolute values altogether as we begin to consider eternal principles in light of the changing values of the world in which we live.[81]

In discussing the nature of revelations given to humanity, Condie wrote, "*The light never moves*. Only our perceptions of the light change."[82] Talmage explained, "Revelation, surpassing in importance and glorious fulness any that has been recorded, will yet be given to the Church, and be declared to the world."[83] So the question becomes, then, does revelation change our perspective on eternally true principles, as Condie argued, or do we gain new principles that surpass in importance older, previous principles, as Talmage wrote? This question must be answered because, as Spencer Kimball declared, continuing revelation will never stop: "The foreverness of this kingdom and the revelations which it brought into existence are absolute realities. Never again will the sun go down; never again will all men prove totally unworthy of communication with their Maker. Never again will God be hidden from his children on the earth. Revelation is here to remain."[84] President Joseph F. Smith, along with counselors John R. Winder and Anthon H. Lund, declared, "Truth has but one source, and all revelations from heaven are harmonious with each

---

[80] Spencer J. Condie, *In Perfect Balance* (Salt Lake City: Bookcraft, 1993), 106.
[81] Condie, 111-12.
[82] Condie, 112.
[83] Talmage, *The Articles of Faith*, 323.
[84] Kimball, "Revelation," 78.

other."[85] Likewise, President Joseph F. Smith, along with counselors Anthon H. Lund and Charles W. Penrose, argued:

> When visions, dreams, tongues, prophecy, impressions, or an extraordinary gift of inspiration conveys something out of harmony with the accepted revelations of the Church or contrary to the decisions of its constituted authorities, Latter-day Saints may know that it is not of God, no matter how plausible it may appear. Also, they should understand that directions for guidance of the Church will come by revelation, through the head.[86]

According to these sources, then, any revelation offered by God to the leadership of the Church will necessarily agree with previous revelations. As Presidents Smith, Lund, and Penrose wrote, if a revelation is in disagreement with a previously accepted truth statement, that new revelation must be considered false.

To summarize, the LDS believe these changes to be essential to their faith. Millet expressed the essential nature of continuing revelation when he wrote, "The Doctrine and Covenants speaks of the Church as both *true* and *living* (D&C 1:30). It is not, as someone has suggested, a fossilized faith but rather a kinetic kingdom. The Latter-day Saints believe that change is a part of growth and development, a vital sign that God continues to reveal his mind and will to his people."[87] Continuing revelation is understood to be fundamental to the LDS Church. The question now becomes whether or not this doctrine has ever caused Latter-day Saint presidents to issue new revelations seemingly contrary to previously held revelations. In the history of the LDS Church, two examples come to the forefront. Specifically, in the cases of plural marriage and the priesthood, new revelations were offered by Church presidents that altered previously held beliefs. Both of these historical examples will now be explored.

Plural Marriage

At present, the LDS Church does not endorse the concept of plural marriage. In fact, before 1841, LDS scripture forbade plural marriage. The pre-1876

---

[85] James R. Clark, comp., *Messages of the First Presidency of the Church of Jesus Christ of Latter-day Saints* (Salt Lake City: Bookcraft, 1971), 4:199.
[86] Clark, 4:285.
[87] Millet, *The Mormon Faith*, 173.

editions of the Doctrine and Covenants included the following passage: "In-asmuch as the Church of Christ has reproached with the crime of fornication and polygamy, we declare that we believe that one man should have one wife, and one woman but one husband, except in the case of death, when either is at liberty to marry again."[88] Also, D&C 49:16, given by Joseph Smith in 1831, reads, "Wherefore, it is lawful that he should have one wife, and they twain shall be one flesh, and all this that the earth might answer the end of its cre-ation." Similarly, Jacob 2:27, in the Book of Mormon, instructs, "Wherefore, my brethren, hear me, and hearken to the word of the Lord: For there shall not any man among you have save it be one wife; and concubines he shall have none." Thus, before the revelation concerning plural marriage in 1843, the practice of plural marriage was officially forbidden among the Saints. Not only did LDS scripture forbid the practice of plural marriage; Illinois, the state in which plural marriage was begun, made plural marriages illegal. February 12, 1833, saw the enacting of a state law that banned bigamy. Those convicted of the crime faced a fine up to $1,000 and up to two years in prison.[89]

Joseph Smith and Plural Marriage

Those items found in holy writ and state law did not stop early Latter-day Saints from entering into plural marriages. Beginning as early as April 5, 1841, Joseph Smith began entering into plural marriages in Nauvoo, Illinois. Ac-cording to one demographic study, Smith eventually entered into forty-two plural marriages (not including his first marriage to Emma Hale) and fathered at least five children before his death on June 27, 1844.[90] Smith was not the only Latter-day Saint who had more than one wife. According to the same

---

[88] Joseph Smith, *History of the Church of Jesus Christ of Latter-day Saints* (Salt Lake City: Church of Jesus Christ of Latter-day Saints, 1948), 2:257.

[89] "Bigamy consists in the having of two wives or two husbands at one and the same time, knowing that the former husband or wife is still alive. If any person or persons within the State, being married, or who shall hereafter marry, do at any time marry any person or persons, the former husband or wife being alive, the person so offended shall, on conviction thereof, be punished by a fine, not exceeding one thousand dollars, and imprisoned in the penitentiary, not exceeding two years." *Revised Laws of Illinois* (Vandalia: Greiner and Sherman, 1833), 198–99.

[90] George D. Smith, "Nauvoo Roots of Mormon Polygamy, 1841–46: A Preliminary Demo-graphic Report," *Dialogue* 27 (1994): 123–58, https://www.dialoguejournal.com/wp-content/uploads/sbi/articles/Dialogue_V34N0102_135.pdf: 138. These are the avenues through which one could enter into a plural marriage: A couple could be married for time only, meaning their time spent together on earth. A couple could also be married for eternity only, meaning their time spent together in the afterlife. Or, a couple could be married for time and eternity, the current practice of the LDS Church's monogamous system.

demographic report, 153 families were involved in plural marriage in Nauvoo, which increased to more than 4,000 families during the westward trek, climaxing in approximately 50,000 families in the late 1800s in Salt Lake City.[91]

Interestingly, Smith began his venture into plural marriages more than two years before issuing the revelation allowing the practice. Again, Smith entered his first plural relationship on April 5, 1841, but the revelation was not issued until July 12, 1843. Was this idea of plural marriage Smith's invention, or were others around Nauvoo engaging in the practice during the Saints' time in Illinois? Richard S. Van Wagoner stated that LDS plural marriages resulted from the influence of "restoration Protestant sectarianism" and "flourishing contemporary social experiments."[92] Historian George D. Smith noted, "In 1837, when Mormon headquarters was located in Kirtland, Ohio, a Cleveland newspaper fifteen miles away printed a letter which argued for polygamy as a remedy for the 'distress' of 'so many old maids.'"[93] So the practice was already taking place around the early Saints and was not purely an invention of Smith's, but an adaptation.

After two years of debates, public outcry, and threats, Joseph Smith issued a revelation on July 12, 1843, that made plural marriage a religious practice of the early Saints. McConkie commented, "In the early days of this dispensation, as part of the promised restitution of all things, the Lord revealed the principle of *plural marriage* to the Prophet."[94] This revelation is still contained with the Doctrine and Covenants. Section 132:61 reads, "And again, as pertaining to the law of the priesthood—if any man espouse a virgin, and desire to espouse another, and the first give her consent, and if he espouse the second, and they are virgins, and have vowed to no other man, then is he justified; he cannot commit adultery for they are given unto him; for he cannot commit adultery with that that belongeth unto him and to no one else." Thus, all previous revelations banning the practice of plural marriage were nullified.

[91] Smith, 158.
[92] Richard S. Van Wagoner, "Mormon Polyandry in Nauvoo," *Dialogue* 18 (1985): 67. Van Wagoner noted that Smith was probably influenced by the communitarianism of the Shakers of Ann Lee, the Harmonists of George Rapp, and Robert Owen, the teacher of Joseph Smith's closest friend, Sidney Rigdon. This communitarian understanding of material possessions also included the communitarian sharing of wives.
[93] George Smith, "Nauvoo Roots of Mormon Polygamy, 1841–46," 126.
[94] Bruce McConkie, *Mormon Doctrine*, 578.

Theology of Plural Marriage

President Brigham Young first discussed the doctrine of plural marriage, initially practiced by Joseph Smith in the early 1830s, publicly in 1852. In August 1852, Young chose Apostle Orson Pratt to offer the first theological defense of the practice. Pratt, speaking to the gathered congregation of Latter-day Saints in the Tabernacle in Salt Lake City, made an impassioned plea not only for the constitutionality of the practice, but also for the strict religious nature of the practice. Pratt's defense served as a foundation for all subsequent apologetic attempts.

First, Pratt argued that plural marriage had indeed been given by revelation from God. Pratt said, recalling the questioning of some nonmembers, "But, says one, how have you obtained this information [concerning plural marriage]? By new revelation."[95] With reference to the reasoning behind plural marriage, historians Leonard J. Arrington and Davis Bitton noted, "The motivation behind the introduction of a practice shocking to Gentiles and Mormons alike can scarcely have been as trivial as the usual anti-Mormon explanation suggests—Smith's personal lust. The standard Mormon explanation is simply that God chose to introduce the practice, as he had in ancient Israel, and he therefore made his will known to his spokesman on earth."[96] They commented further, "In short, there were practical, sociological, and theological predisposing tendencies within the new movement that required only a word from God, a revelation, to initiate the practice of plural marriage."[97] Likewise, while some nonmembers have argued that Smith's personal sexual desires inspired his want for a system of plural marriage, Arrington and Bitton argued, "It is far from likely that [Smith's] personal sex drive was the motivation. If he had been unprincipled, motivated solely by a desire for sexual gratification, there were tried and proven ways of satisfying such desires in American society without the burden of providing for additional families. Whatever the ultimate explanation of the reinstitution of polygamy, if Smith's religious sincerity is conceded, then he would naturally see the whole idea in religious terms."[98]

---

[95] Orson Pratt, "Celestial Marriage," in *Journal of Discourses*, comp. G. D. Watt (London: Latter-day Saints' Book Depot, 1854), 1:64.
[96] Leonard J. Arrington and Davis Bitton, *The Mormon Experience: A History of the Latter-day Saints* (New York: Alfred A. Knopf, 1979), 195.
[97] Arrington and Bitton, 196.
[98] Arrington and Bitton, 197.

Second, Pratt argued that plural marriage was necessary for exaltation in the highest realm of the celestial kingdom. He said, "In reply we will show you that [plural marriage] is incorporated as a part of our religion, and necessary for our exaltation to the fullness of the Lord's glory in the eternal world."[99] Of who would reject the doctrine of plural marriage, Pratt said:

> Now, let us enquire, what will become of those individuals who have this law taught unto them in plainness, if they reject it? I will tell you: they will be damned, saith the Lord God Almighty, in the revelation He has given. Why? Because where much is given, much is required; where there is great knowledge unfolded for the exaltation, glory, and happiness of the sons and daughters of God, if they close up their hearts, if they reject the testimony of His word, and will not give heed to the principles He has ordained for their good, they are worthy of damnation, and the Lord has said they shall be damned."[100]

Pratt further explained that those who refused to accept and practice plural marriage, after hearing of the doctrine, would have no chance of exaltation in the celestial kingdom. He argued:

> Let us inquire after those who are to be damned, admitting that they will be redeemed, which they will be, unless they have sinned against the Holy Ghost. They will be redeemed, but what will it be to? Will it be to exaltation, and to a fulness of glory? Will it be to become the sons of God, or Gods to reign upon thrones, and multiply their poster-ity, and reign over them as kings? No, it will not. They have lost that exalted privilege forever.[101]

Pratt concluded that those who were upstanding Latter-day Saints, but who also refused to accept and practice plural marriage, would be the eternal servants of those who did accept the practice. He contended, "What will be their condition? The Lord has told us. He says these are angels; because they

---

[99] Pratt, "Celestial Marriage," 54.

[100] Pratt, 64.

[101] Pratt, 64. A few paragraphs later, Pratt returned to this same line of thinking: "There will be many who will not hearken; there will be the foolish among the wise, who will not receive the new and everlasting covenant in its fulness; and they never will attain to their exaltation." Pratt, 65.

keep not this law, they shall be ministering servants unto those who are worthy of obtaining a more exceeding and eternal weight of glory."[102]

Third, Pratt argued that plural marriage was not a new doctrine; it was a reintroduction of the Old Testament way of life in latter days. He said:

> Why not look upon Abraham's blessings as your own, for the Lord blessed him with a promise of seed as numerous as the sand upon the seashore; so will you be blessed, or else you will not inherit the blessings of Abraham. How did Abraham manage to get a foundation laid for this mighty kingdom? Was he to accomplish it all through one wife? No. Sarah gave a certain woman to him whose name was Hagar, and by her a seed was to be raised up unto him. Is this all? No. We read of his wife Keturah, and also of a plurality of wives and concubines, which he had, from whom he raised up many sons.[103]

Pratt also believed the blessings of Abraham would be removed from any person not participating in the practice of plural marriage. He alleged:

> I think there is only about one-fifth of the population of the globe, that believe in the one-wife system; the other four-fifths believe in the doctrine of a plurality of wives. They have had it handed down from time immemorial, and are not half so narrow and contracted in their minds as some of the nations of Europe and America, who have done away with the promises, and deprived themselves of the blessings of Abraham, Isaac, and Jacob.[104]

Fourth, Pratt underscored the need for plural marriage because of the necessity of bringing more of God the Father's spirit children to earth. According to Pratt, the spirit children brought to earth through a plural marriage had been reserved for just such a relationship. Those spirits deemed most noble and intelligent by God the Father were reserved for plural marriages. It is worth quoting Pratt at length here:

> Very well; if this be the case, that the righteous are gathering out, and are still being gathered from among the nations, and being planted by themselves, one thing is certain—that that people are better calculated

[102] Pratt, 65.
[103] Pratt, 60.
[104] Pratt, 60–61.

to bring up children in the right way, than any other under the whole heavens. If you are under the influence, power, and guidance of the Almighty, you must be the best people under heaven, to dictate the young mind . . . I have already told you that among them are many spirits that are more noble, more intelligent than others, that were called the great and mighty ones, reserved until the dispensation of the fullness of times, to come forth upon the face of the earth, through a noble parentage that shall train their young and tender minds in the truths of eternity, that they may grow up in the Lord, and be strong in the power of His might, be clothed upon with His glory, be filled with exceeding great faith; that the visions of eternity may be opened to their minds; that they may be Prophets, Priests, and Kings to the Most High God. Do you believe, says one, that they are reserved until the last dispensation, for such a noble purpose? yes; and among the Saints is the most likely place for these spirits to take their tabernacles, through a just and righteous parentage. They are to be sent to that people that are the most righteous of any other people upon the earth.[105]

He argued further:

The Lord has not kept [intelligent and noble spirits] in store for five or six thousand years past, and kept them waiting for their bodies all this time to send them among the Hottentots, the African negroes, the idolatrous Hindoos, or any other of the fallen nations that dwell upon the face of this earth. They are not kept in reserve in order to come forth to receive such a degraded parentage upon the earth; no, the Lord is not such a being; His justice, goodness, and mercy will be magnified towards those who were chosen before they were born; and they long to come, and they will come among the Saints of the living God; this would be their highest pleasure and joy, to know that they could have the privilege of being born of such noble parentage.[106]

There was, then, a set of extremely complex theological justifications offered for the practice of plural marriage. First, the practice was based on a revelation given to Joseph Smith by God. Second, plural marriage was believed to be a parallel of plural marriages in the Old Testament. Third, for a person

---

[105] Pratt, 62–63.
[106] Pratt, 63.

to achieve exaltation in the celestial kingdom, practicing plural marriage was necessary. Fourth, the need was great to provide physical bodies for the most noble and intelligent of God's spirit children. Although intelligent Latter-day Saints, such as Orson Pratt, staunchly defended this doctrine, cultural and political circumstances were not dictated by their arguments. The groundwork would be laid over the next four decades for the issuing of the manifesto by Wilford Woodruff in September 1890.

Plural Marriage after Joseph Smith

The practice of plural marriage continued after Smith was murdered on June 27, 1844, and the Saints took the idea with them through Missouri, on to the Idaho territory, and eventually to the Great Salt Lake basin, currently known as Salt Lake City, Utah. Arriving in the Salt Lake valley during 1847, the Saints began to rebuild their lives and continue their religious practices, including plural marriage. The year 1847, though, marked the beginning of the downfall of one of the most infamous religious teachings in American history, namely, Latter-day Saint plural marriage.

The years 1847 to 1850 proved substantial for the politics of the Utah territory. The LDS pioneers formed a territorial legislature, installed Brigham Young as governor, suggested the area be granted statehood, and requested the name Deseret for the state.[107] Though the name request was rejected and the name Utah was given to the territory, the LDS played a vital role in the formation of the territory's laws.

From 1850 to 1861, the Salt Lake Saints fought battle after battle over the issue of plural marriage. While all other territories of the United States adopted American common law, Brigham Young denounced it, saying, "Those who attempted to fasten their peculiar dogmas upon all succeeding generations although thought to be men of legal learning, were instead profound ignoramuses" and that the United States would not "shine forth in her true colors until they should divest themselves of tradition and ignorance."[108] Put simply, the acceptance of common law by the territory of Utah would have outlawed

---

[107] Michael W. Homer, "The Judiciary and the Common Law in Utah Territory, 1850–61," *Dialogue* 21 (1988): 97–108. The word *deseret* reportedly means "honey bee" in the language of the Jaredites, a people group in the Book of Mormon. The Saints have always viewed themselves as honey bees, workers who never rest. Hence, the Saints requested the name of the new state to reflect their religious heritage and work ethic. Interestingly, local LDS bookstores are called the Beehive.

[108] Homer, 97.

plural marriage; therefore, Young rejected every attempt by the federal government to enforce it in the territory.

The year 1854 also held profound significance for the practice of plural marriage. Homer noted:

> On 14 January 1854, the legislature obediently passed a measure, unprecedented elsewhere in the United States, which provided that "no laws nor parts of laws shall be read, argued, cited, or adopted in any court . . . except those enacted by the Governor and Legislative Assembly." Thus the Mormons hoped to finally establish by statute their long-argued position that the common law, both criminal and civil, did not apply in Utah and that the judiciary could not apply common-law precepts. In so doing, they arguably overrode the provision of the Organic Act, by which Congress created Utah Territory, providing that the Supreme Court and district courts of the territory "shall possess chancery as well as common law jurisdiction." The First Presidency urged the Saints to carry on all of their activities.[109]

With that action, Latter-day Saints offered their disapproval of the federal government and continued their practice of plural marriage, though the federal government attempted to stop them through every available avenue, unofficially.[110] It was not until the Utah War of 1858–59 that the federal government, under the leadership of President James Buchanan, would officially interfere in the government of Utah by replacing sitting governor Brigham Young with Buchanan's handpicked alternate, Alfred Cumming.[111]

The next few decades, the 1860s through the 1890s, saw the rise and fall of the United States Civil War (1861–65), Reconstruction in the eastern United States, and the fall of plural marriage in the western United States. In 1862, the United States Congress passed the Morrill Anti-Bigamy Act, making bigamy a crime in the territories, punishable by a fine of up to $500 and up to five years in prison. This action angered the people of the Utah territory and eventually led to a court trial, climaxing in the case of *Reynolds v. the United States*, an 1879 United States Supreme Court case. George Reynolds, personal secretary to Brigham Young, and an advocate of plural marriage, was

---

[109] Homer, 102.
[110] Kenneth W. Godfrey, "The Coming of the Manifesto," *Dialogue* 5 (1970): 12.
[111] Richard D. Poll, "The Utah War," *Utah Historical Quarterly*, 1994, https://heritage.utah.gov/history/uhg-ut-war.

the voluntary defendant for the test case "to determine the constitutionality of the Anti-Bigamy Law of 1862, in which case he was found guilty in a lower court."[112] The Supreme Court upheld the anti-bigamy law, and Reynolds was forced to pay a $500 fine and spent two years in prison. Three years later, in 1882, the United States Congress passed the Edmunds Act, making plural marriage a felony, disenfranchising polygamists of their right to vote, banning polygamists from holding public office and from jury duty, removing their civil rights, and declaring open all representative and elected offices in the territory of Utah.[113] As the tension continued to build in the Utah territory and continued calls for statehood were made to the federal government by the Latter-day Saints, the practice of plural marriage continued, and Church president John Taylor, and later Wilford Woodruff, purportedly received numerous revelations stating God would protect the institution of plural marriage from the federal government.[114]

Seeing that the Edmunds Act was not stringent enough, the United States Congress passed a tougher law, the Edmunds–Tucker Act of 1887. This act unincorporated the LDS Church and the LDS Perpetual Emigration Fund because the two entities encouraged plural marriage.[115] The Edmunds–Tucker Act also authorized the federal government to seize Church real estate (valued at approximately $800,000) and freeze Church assets. The federal government then leased the property and assets back to the LDS at a substantially higher cost. Also, because the Morrill Act imposed a fine of $500 on any convicted person engaged in plural marriage, the federal government imposed a $50,000 fine on the Church for the more than 1,300 convictions of LDS men.[116] Leaders of the Church became extremely frustrated with this strict law and, three years after the act was passed, took the United States government to court again in the case of *The Late Corporation of the Mormon Church v. the United States*. As had happened in the previous case, the Supreme Court upheld the Edmunds–Tucker Act and called for the Church to ban plural marriage.

---

[112] Perry Porter, "A Chronology of Federal Legislation on Polygamy," xmission.com, January 4, 1998, http://www.xmission.com/~plporter/lds/chron.htm.

[113] Porter, "A Chronology."

[114] Godfrey, "The Coming of the Manifesto," 15.

[115] The Perpetual Emigration Fund was started in 1849 as a monetary source to help Latter-day Saints move from Nauvoo, Illinois, and Great Britain to the Salt Lake basin. See James B. Allen and Glen M. Leonard, *The Story of the Latter-day Saints* (Salt Lake City: Deseret, 1976), 282; and Arrington and Bitton, *The Mormon Experience*, 130–32.

[116] Porter, "A Chronology of Federal Legislation on Polygamy." Why the federal government did not impose the full fine of at least $650,000 on the Church is unknown.

Finally, after years of battle with the federal government, Church leaders began to give up their defense of plural marriage. Godfrey noted, "By 1886 it was becoming more obvious that something would have to be done regarding either the law or plural marriage, or both, or the Saints would have to leave the United States."[117] Thus, "because of such stringent law which sought to circumscribe the Saints, President Woodruff, as early as 1889, secretly ceased giving permission for plural marriages to be solemnized."[118] Also, "as pressure from the United States government continued in some quarters, at least a few of the Saints argued that if plural marriages had in fact been discontinued in secret that a public declaration of such a policy should indeed be given so that the effects could be fully utilized."[119] Feeling the pressure building to an insurmountable level, President Woodruff, on September 24, 1890, issued an official declaration of a new revelation from God, a declaration known as the Manifesto. This declaration "confirmed that it was right to prohibit the further contracting, publicly at least, of plural marriages."[120] Concerning the issuing of the Manifesto, Woodruff wrote in his personal diary:

> I have arrived at a point in the History of my life as the President of the Church of Jesus Christ of Latter Day Saints whare [*sic*] I am under the necessity of acting for the Temporal Salvation of the Church. The United States Government has taken a Stand & passed Laws to destroy the Latter day Saints upon the Subject of poligamy [*sic*] or Patriarchal order of Marriage. And after Praying to the Lord & feeling inspired by his spirit I have issued . . . [a] Proclamation which is sustained by my Councillors and the 12 Apostles.[121]

Thus, the practice of plural marriage was officially declared anathema in September 1890. Six years later, the territory of Utah was granted statehood on January 4, 1896.

---

[117] Godfrey, "The Coming of the Manifesto," 14–15.
[118] Godfrey, 18.
[119] Godfrey, 19.
[120] Godfrey, 20.
[121] Thomas G. Alexander, "The Odyssey of a Latter-day Prophet: Wilford Woodruff and the Manifesto of 1890," *Journal of Mormon History* 17 (1991): 170.

Contradiction of Previously Received Revelation?

Some Latter-day Saints saw Woodruff's Manifesto as nothing more than a politically motivated move. The Utah territory had requested statehood on a number of occasions, but the practice of plural marriage kept statehood at bay. Before the Manifesto was issued, another bill, the Cullom–Struble Bill, was introduced on the floor of the United States House of Representatives. This bill, upon passage, would have disenfranchised all members of the LDS Church in order to take all political power within the Utah territory away from the Church. Church leaders dispatched a delegation from Salt Lake City to Washington to lobby against the passage of the bill. Historians James B. Allen and Glen M. Leonard noted, "The Utah delegation to Washington met with little encouragement, and returned to Salt Lake City confident that nothing short of a declaration by the Church that plural marriage had ended would prevent approval of the Cullom–Strobble [sic] Bill or assure statehood for Utah."[122] The issuing of the Manifesto prompted some Latter-day Saints to see it as nothing more than a political move. However, Allen and Leonard commented:

> The Manifesto was not simply a political document. In many ways it represented other deep-rooted religious principles, some of which were much more important to the Saints than the principle of plural marriage. One of these was millennialism. The Latter-day Saints firmly believed that through Joseph Smith the Kingdom of God had been established in preparation for the second coming of Christ and the establishment of the Millennium. In preparation for that event, they had tried to establish a political as well as an ecclesiastical kingdom. The political kingdom was no longer functioning, but to allow the spiritual kingdom, the Church, to be destroyed would be, in President Woodruff's opinion, the great failure of all. Obviously, the Church must be preserved to meet the Savior when he came, even if it meant withdrawing approval of plural marriage. In this sense, preparation for the Millennium was a factor in producing the Manifesto.[123]

Although the Saints were given continual reminders that President Woodruff had received the idea for the Manifesto from God, "a few members could not accept [the Manifesto] as revelation, for it seemed to contradict an earlier

---

[122] Allen and Leonard, *The Mormon Experience*, 413.
[123] Allen and Leonard, 413.

command."[124] Church leaders attempted to salve the situation by arguing that God would not have the Saints keep His commands in the event of cultural and political problems. Allen and Leonard recorded, "These few were not even persuaded by President Cannon's powerful sermon on October 6 reminding them that the Lord had said through Joseph Smith that He would not require the Saints to fulfill a command that became impossible because of persecution from their enemies."[125] Similarly, President Woodruff, speaking to a group of Latter-day Saints in Utah in 1891, said:

> The Lord showed me by vision and revelation exactly what would take place if we did not stop this practice. He has told me exactly what to do, and what the result would be if we did not do it. I have been called upon by friends outside of the Church and urged to take some steps with regard to this matter. They knew the course which the government was determined to take. I saw exactly what would come to pass if there was not something done. I have had this spirit upon me for a long time. But I want to say this: I should have let all the temples go out of our hands; I should have gone to prison myself, and let every other man go there, had not the God of heaven commanded me to do what I did do; and when the hour came that I was commanded to do that, it was all clear to me.[126]

The Priesthood

Before 1978, the LDS Church did not allow all worthy male members of the Church to be ordained into the priesthood. However, with a revelation issued by Spencer W. Kimball, N. Eldon Tanner, and Marion G. Romney on June 8, 1978, and that revelation being sustained by a vote of the General Conference on September 30, 1978, all worthy male members of the LDS Church, including males with dark skin, were allowed to be ordained as members of the priesthood. As with plural marriage, a change was made to Latter-day Saint doctrine. A discussion of the origin and resolution of the issue of males with dark skin and the priesthood is necessary to understand the issue and to show

---

[124] Allen and Leonard, 415.
[125] Allen and Leonard, 415.
[126] Allen and Leonard, 416.

by way of a second historical example that the Latter-day Saint God has indeed changed doctrine.

History of the Priesthood Doctrine with Reference to the Seed of Cain

The foundation for the Latter-day Saint belief that dark-skinned males could not hold the priesthood is found in Genesis 4. In that chapter, Cain murders his brother, Abel, and is cursed for it. Verse 15 is the text on which Latter-day Saints focus due to the sign, or mark, being placed on Cain for the heinous crime he committed. Latter-day Saints believe the sign placed on Cain was dark skin.[127] This mark was passed on to all generations following in Cain's line; hence, the nomenclature of the seed of Cain.[128]

Cain's crime, however, is not the singular foundation for people being given dark skin. Another foundation is found in the spirit world, a world in which all humans lived before the formation of the universe. In this world, God the Father's spirit children lived in paradise and were given the choice to follow either Jehovah or Lucifer. Those following Jehovah would be blessed with light skin in their earthly life; those following Lucifer would be cursed with dark skin in their earthly life. In the 1966 edition of *Mormon Doctrine*, Bruce McConkie wrote, "Though he was a rebel and an associate of Lucifer in pre-existence, Cain managed to attain the privilege of mortal birth. As a result of his rebellion, Cain was cursed with a dark skin; he became the father of the Negroes, and those spirits who are not worthy to receive the priesthood are born through his lineage."[129] Brigham Young is also helpful in understanding the doctrine of the priesthood and the seed of Cain. In 1859, Young declared:

> You see some classes of the human family that are black, uncouth, uncomely, disagreeable and low in their habits, wild, and seemingly deprived of nearly all the blessings of the intelligence that is general- ly bestowed upon mankind. The first man that committed the odious crime of killing one of his brethren will be cursed the longest of any one of the children of Adam. Cain slew his brother. Cain might have

---

[127] McConkie, *Mormon Doctrine*, 109.
[128] Some Latter-day Saints believe Cain's line was continued through the flood through the wife of Noah's son Ham. Then Apostle Joseph Fielding Smith argued that Ham was given that particular name because of a cognate of "Ham" in Egyptian meaning "black." For an extended discussion of this, see Joseph Fielding Smith, *Answers to Gospel Questions* (Salt Lake City: Deseret, 1958), 2:173–78.
[129] McConkie, *Mormon Doctrine*, 108–9.

been killed, and that would have put a termination to that line of human beings. This was not to be, and the Lord put a mark upon him, which is the flat nose and black skin. Trace mankind down to after the flood, and then another curse is pronounced upon the same race—that they should be the "servants of servants;" and they will be, until that curse is removed; and the Abolitionists cannot help it, nor in the least alter that decree.[130]

More than seventy years later, Latter-day Saint president Joseph Fielding Smith agreed with Young's appraisal of the seed of Cain. He wrote:

Not only was Cain called upon to suffer, but because of his wickedness he became the father of an inferior race. A curse was placed upon him and that curse has been continued through his lineage and must do so while time endures. Millions of souls have come into this world cursed with a black skin and have been denied the privilege of priesthood and the fullness of the blessings of the Gospel. These are the descendants of Cain. Moreover, they have been made to feel their inferiority and have been separated from the rest of mankind from the beginning. Enoch saw the people of Canaan, descendants of Cain, and he says, "and there was a blackness came upon all the children of Canaan, that they were despised among all people."[131]

As mentioned above, the dark skin given to Cain and his descendants is ultimately grounded in those individuals' actions in the preexistent spirit realm. While addressing the Convention of Teachers of Religion in 1954, Elder Mark E. Peterson delivered an insightful speech entitled "Race Problems—as They Affect the Church." In this speech, Peterson offered a well-known and oft-quoted evaluation of the situation regarding African-Americans within the LDS Church. Peterson also discussed his understanding of why African-Americans had dark skin and why those with dark skin could not hold the priesthood:

We can account in no other way for the birth of some of the children of God in darkest Africa, or in floodridden China, or among the starving hordes of India, while some of the rest of us are born in the United

---

[130] Brigham Young, "Intelligence, Etc.," in *Journal of Discourses*, comp. G. D. Watt, J. V. Long, et al. (London: Latter-day Saints' Book Depot, 1860), 7:290.
[131] Joseph Fielding Smith, *The Way to Perfection* (Salt Lake City: Genealogical Society of Utah, 1949), 101–02.

States? [*sic*] We cannot escape the conclusion that because of per-
formance in our pre-existence some of us are born as Chinese, some
as Japanese, some as Indians, some as Negroes, some as Americans,
some as Latter-day Saints. There are rewards and punishments, fully
in harmony with His established policy in dealing with sinners and
saints, regarding all according to their deeds.[132]

Peterson continued:

Who placed the Negroes originally in darkest Africa? Was it some
man, or was it God? And when He placed them there, He segregated
them. Who placed the Chinese in China? The Lord did. It was an act
of segregation. When He placed only some of His chosen people in the
tribe of Judah, the royal tribe, wasn't that an act of segregation? And
when He gave the birthright only to Ephraim, wasn't that an act of segregation? The Lord segregated the people both as to blood and place
of residence, at least in the bases of the Lamanites and the Negroes we
have the definite word of the Lord himself that He placed a dark skin
upon them as a curse—as a sign to all others. He forbade intermarriage
with them under threat of extension of the curse (2 Nephi 5:21). And
He certainly segregated the descendants of Cain when He cursed the
Negro as to the Priesthood, and drew an absolute line. You may even
say He dropped an iron curtain there. The Negro was cursed as to the
Priesthood, and therefore, was cursed as to the blessings of the Priesthood. Certainly God made a segregation there.[133]

He concluded:

Think of the Negro, cursed as to the Priesthood. Are we prejudiced
against him? Unjustly, sometimes we're accused of having such a
prejudice. But what does the mercy of God have for him? This Negro,
who in the pre-existence life lived the type of life which justified the
Lord in sending him to the earth in the lineage of Cain with a black
skin, and possibly being born in darkest Africa—if that negro is willing when he hears the gospel to accept it, he may have many of the

---

[132] Mark E. Peterson, "Race Problems—as They Affect the Church" (address, Convention of
Teachers of Religion on the College Level, Provo, UT, August 27, 1954).
[133] Peterson.

blessings of the gospel. In spirit of all he did in the pre-existent life, the Lord is willing, if the Negro accepts the gospel with real, sincere faith, and is really converted, to give him the blessings of baptism and the gift of the Holy Ghost. If that Negro is faithful all his days, he can and will enter the Celestial Kingdom. He will go there as a servant, but he will get a Celestial resurrection.[134]

Peterson, then, understood the dark skin of African-Americans as a curse levied upon them because of their actions and attitudes in the preexistent spirit realm. This curse, given by God, not only darkened the skin of some; it likewise removed the possibility of their being ordained into the priesthood.[135]

Spencer W. Kimball and the Priesthood

In June 1978, President Spencer W. Kimball issued a revelation changing the beliefs of the LDS Church regarding the priesthood. Indeed, Gottlieb and Wiley described the revelation as "the most significant change in the church belief system in the twentieth century."[136] The year 1978, however, was not the first time Kimball began considering this issue.

As early as 1963, Kimball began thinking about the issue of the priesthood. He wrote:

The things of God cannot be understood by the spirit of men. It is impossible to always measure and weigh all spiritual things by man's yardstick or scales. Admittedly, our direct and positive information is limited. I have wished for the Lord had given [*sic*] us a little more clarity in the matter. But for me, it is enough. The prophets for 133 years of the existence of the Church have maintained the position of the prophet of the Restoration that the Negro could not hold the priesthood nor have the temple ordinances which are preparatory for exaltation. I believe in the living prophets as much or almost more than the

---

[134] Peterson.

[135] The priesthood is vital within Latter-day Saint life. Bruce McConkie explained, "As pertaining to eternity, priesthood is the eternal power and authority of Deity by which they are created, governed, and controlled; by which the universe and worlds without number have come rolling into existence; by which the great plan of creation, redemption, and exaltation operates throughout immensity. It is the power of God." Bruce McConkie, *Mormon Doctrine*, 2nd ed., 594. Being ordained into the priesthood is absolutely necessary to reach the highest level of the celestial kingdom; therefore, dark-skinned individuals before 1978 were consigned to lower levels and not given the possibility of exaltation.

[136] Gottlieb and Wiley, *America's Saints*, 177 (see chap. 1, n. 55).

dead ones. They are here to clarify and reaffirm. I have served with
and under three of them. The doctrine or policy has not varied in my
memory. I know it could. I know the Lord could change his policy and
release the ban and forgive the possible error which brought about the
deprivation. If the time comes, that he will do, I am sure. These smart
members who would force the issue, and there are many of them,
cheapen the issue and certainly bring into contempt the sacred principle of revelation and divine authority.[137]

Similarly, immediately after being sustained as the twelfth president of the
Church in 1973, Kimball held a press conference. During the press conference
one of the reporters asked Kimball about his views concerning dark-skinned
males, the priesthood, and the possibility of the moratorium being lifted. Kimball responded, "Blacks and the priesthood: I am not sure that there will be
change, although there could be. We are under the dictates of our Heavenly
Father, and this is not my policy or the Church's policy. It is the policy of the
Lord who has established it, and I know of no change, although we are subject
to revelations of the Lord in case he should ever wish to make a change."[138]
For Kimball, the possibility of changing the long-held belief of ordaining only
light-skinned people was indeed open. Kimball realized the priesthood ban
was a significant problem, especially in light of international missionary efforts, efforts Kimball himself wanted to increase. The most significant pressure put on Kimball did not come from converts within the United States, but
from international converts, especially in Brazil.

Gottlieb and Wiley note:

In Brazil, more than any other country, the race factor was critical. The church was established there in the late 1920s among the
German-speaking communities of southern Brazil. Many of the early members of the church were pro-Nazi, and the church was noted
for its anti-Latin, prowhite [sic] attitudes. Shortly before the out-
break of World War II, the Brazilian government became wary of its
German-speaking citizens, including the Mormons, because of the
growth of pro-Nazi sentiment. Subsequently, the government banned
German-language meetings and finally shut down the German branch

---

[137] Edward L. Kimball, ed., *The Teachings of Spencer W. Kimball* (Salt Lake City: Bookcraft, 1982), 448.
[138] Kimball, 449.

of the church for seven months. When the church reopened, the missionaries shifted their focus to the darker-skinned Portuguese-speaking community.[139]

This shift in focus would prove disastrous for the Church, both publicly and privately. Gottlieb and Wiley continued:

From the outset, the missionaries, who were particularly concerned about the racial origins of their new recruits, experienced enormous difficulties in sorting out "pure-blooded" descendants of the Portuguese from "mixed-bloods," who were the products of intermarriage with Brazil's former slave population. In order to bar those with African ancestry, the church issued instruction sheets for missionaries, describing methods for determining lineage. Missionaries were told to get potential converts to look through their family photo albums in their presence, to carefully question family members, and to be particularly sensitive to skin shading. At times, baptisms did not happen because of a convert's Negroid appearance.[140]

Latter-day Saint mission president W. Grant Bangerter recognized the problems in Brazil as well. When asked about it, he said, "If there was any question you could not get the priesthood. [So] many Brazilians [were] not either black or white but a shade of brown, and it would be impossible to distinguish clearly between those who have Negro blood and those who don't."[141]

Problems in Brazil, though, did not stop simply with increased missionary efforts. Because missionaries began focusing more on the dark-skinned Portuguese community, new member numbers from that community began to rise. The increase in number eventually led President Kimball, in 1974, to announce plans for constructing a new temple in Brazil. Gottlieb and Wiley noted:

This new temple would compound the existing difficulties involved in preserving the church's racial criterion for priesthood. Since the focus had largely shifted from lineage determination to skin coloration as the main criterion for evaluating potential members, it was apparent that a number of light-skinned blacks or mulattoes would eventually,

---

[139] Gottlieb and Wiley, *America's Saints*, 182–83.
[140] Gottlieb and Wiley, 183.
[141] Quoted in Gottlieb and Wiley, 183.

or had already, been granted the priesthood. Once the temple was built, these nonwhite members would then enter that most holy of Mormon places.[142]

LeGrand Richards, a member of the Quorum of Twelve Apostles during this time, recognized a significant problem with the temple construction. He said, "All those people with negro blood in them have been raising money to build the temple, and then if we don't change, then they can't even use it after they've got it."[143]

As problems continued to mount in Brazil, and in the United States, the Church was being led down the path of having to reconsider its position on the priesthood.

> By 1978, as the temple neared completion, it had become clear that the policy had reached a crisis point. James E. Faust, the General Authority in charge of Brazil, began to be called the Apostle for the Blacks. More and more information about the Brazilian situation began to reach the pages of church publications, and a well-orchestrated public relations buildup seemed under way. The groundwork was being laid for a change of policy that would hopefully rid the church of one of its most embarrassing features.[144]

Besides the problems in Brazil, Richard Abanes's extremely helpful work, *One Nation under Gods*, lists at least six problems within the United States faced by the Church, problems ranging from Brigham Young University basketball game disruptions to discrimination charges brought against the Church.[145]

Upon realizing that the priesthood situation would need to be rectified, President Kimball began asking friends, and God, for guidance. The Ostlings noted:

> Kimball had been mulling the policy with American black friends, and when the cornerstone was laid for the São Paulo temple, he met a prominent black Brazilian believer, Helvecio Martins. Martins had

---

[142] Gottlieb and Wiley, 184.
[143] Quoted in Gottlieb and Wiley, 184. Richards made this statement in August of 1978, two months after the revelation had been issued.
[144] Gottlieb and Wiley, 184.
[145] Richard Abanes, *One Nation under Gods* (New York: Four Walls Eight Windows, 2002), 368–69.

faithfully saved funds to send his son on a mission, only to learn that the lad could not serve because of his race and consequent lack of priesthood. By one account, Kimball privately advised Martins that he should prepare himself to receive the priesthood.[146]

Kimball also started seriously praying about the issue and seeking guidance from God and other leaders in the Church:

Around that time Kimball began a systematic personal plan of prayer and fasting, asking God for change. In the weeks leading up to the revelation Kimball faithfully went to the Salt Lake Temple each day to pray alone. Meanwhile, Kimball and his two counselors in the First Presidency discussed the issue over several weeks, then informed the Twelve Apostles about their deliberations and asked them to pray over the matter. Apostles provided Kimball with written materials giving their thoughts and background on the policy, and Kimball talked with a number of them individually.[147]

Finally, June 1, 1978, arrived, and a regular meeting had been scheduled for the Quorum of Twelve to meet on that day. After the regular business of the group was conducted, "Kimball asked the first and second counselors and the apostles to remain behind (two apostles were absent). The thirteen men discussed the priesthood problem for more than two hours."[148] At the conclusion of the discussion, Kimball led the group of thirteen in prayer, and the purported revelation ending the ban within the priesthood was received. "On June 7 Kimball told his two counselors he had decided to announce the elimination of the ban and asked three apostles to draft a public statement. At the regular weekly temple meeting on June 8 the First Presidency and the Twelve reaffirmed the inspiration they had received on June 1 and agreed on the wording of the official statement."[149] With the public announcement of the revelation and the vote of the General Conference four months later, the revelation was added to the end of the Doctrine and Covenants and the restriction on the priesthood was ended.

---

[146] Ostling and Ostling, *Mormon America*, 96–97 (see chap. 1, n. 33).
[147] Ostling and Ostling, 97.
[148] Ostling and Ostling, 97.
[149] Ostling and Ostling, 98.

Conclusion

A significant and surely weighty issue, the Latter-day Saint doctrine of sacred texts is anything but simple or simplistic. It is assuredly complex, multifaceted, and in places, riddled with questions and difficulties. Inquiries often arise around the issue of an older, printed canon of text versus an unprinted, contemporary canon of text, specifically, which is to be followed and how the two relate. Some Latter-day Saints will turn to the pages of the Bible, the Book of Mormon, the Doctrine and Covenants, and/or the Pearl of Great Price before looking to continuing revelation. Others do the opposite, looking to continuing revelation before consulting the printed, four-part canon. Still others try to combine all five pieces into one harmonious collaboration of prophets and soothsayers, poetry and prose. However the individual Latter-day Saint chooses to read his or her sacred texts, the opinion of Latter-day Saint leadership is clear: both past and present revelation are binding and authoritative. Bruce McConkie writes:

> The books, writings, explanations, expositions, views, and theories of even the wisest and greatest of men, either in or out of the Church, do not rank with the standard works. Even the writings, teachings, and opinions of the prophets of God are acceptable only to the extent they are in harmony with what God has revealed and what is recorded in the standard works. When the living oracles speak in the name of the Lord or as moved upon by the Holy Ghost, however, their utterances are then binding upon all who hear, and whatever is said will without any exception be found to be in harmony with the standard works. The Lord's house is a house of order, and one truth never contradicts another.[150]

Seemingly on the other side of the same issue, former President Harold B. Lee explains, "Sometimes we get the notion that [something] being written in a book makes it more true than if it is spoken in the last general conference. Just because it is written in a book does not give it more authority to guide us."[151] An early member of the Quorum of Twelve Apostles, George Q. Cannon offered his own advice:

[150] McConkie, *Mormon Doctrine*, 764.
[151] Harold B. Lee, "The Place of the Living Prophet, Seer, and Revelator," in *Charge to Religious Educators*, 2nd ed., Church of Jesus Christ of Latter-day Saints, ed, (Salt Lake City:

As Latter-day Saints, we need constantly the guidance of Jehovah. We have the Bible, the Book of Mormon, and the Book of Doctrine and Covenants; but all these books, without the living oracles and a constant stream of revelation from the Lord, would not lead any people into the Celestial Kingdom of God. This may seem a strange declaration to make, but strange as it may sound, it is nevertheless true. Of course, these records are all of infinite value. They cannot be too highly prized, nor can they be too closely studied. But in and of themselves, with all the light that they give, they are insufficient to guide the children of men and to lead them into the presence of God. To be thus led requires a living Priesthood and constant revelation from God to the people according to the circumstances in which they may be placed.[152]

With a foundation laid for the doctrines of God and sacred texts from the Latter-day Saint perspective, we now turn our attention to another major question addressed by nearly every religion in human history. This question has plagued humans for thousands of years: namely, what must I do to be saved?

Church of Jesus Christ of Latter-day Saints, 1982), 109.

[152] George Q. Cannon, comp. Jerreld L. Newquist, *Gospel Truth: Discourses and Writings of President George Q. Cannon* (Salt Lake City: Deseret Book, 1957), 252.

Chapter 4

Salvation

T he question of salvation has plagued humanity for thousands of years. According to the Bible, one of the earliest revelations of knowledge to humans concerns the coming salvation offered to humanity. Genesis 3:14–15, often called the *proto-evangelium* by scholars, referring to Satan, reads, "Because you have done this, you are cursed more than any livestock and more than any wild animal. You will move on your belly and eat dust all the days of your life. I will put hostility between you and the woman, and between your offspring and her offspring. He will strike your head, and you will strike his heel." Scholars argue that this *proto-evangelium*, or first gospel, is God's first mention of salvation—through the offspring of a woman—found in the Bible. From that point, the Bible is filled with references to salvation. Probably the most pressing question in the Bible concerning salvation is found in Acts 16:30, when the Philippian jailer asks Paul and Silas simply, "Sirs, what must I do to be saved?" Paul and Silas answered as simply as the jailer asked: "Believe in the Lord Jesus, and you will be saved" (v. 31). Indeed, the question asked by the Philippian jailer has been asked countless times by countless people. All major living world religions have an answer to the questions of humanity's problems and the ways those problems may be solved by deity. Likewise, nearly all new religious movements and minority religions answer the same questions. Those investigating the Church of Jesus Christ of Latter-day Saints have asked the same question the jailer asked thousands of years ago: what must I do to be saved? With that, we turn our attention to the Latter-day Saint doctrine of soteriology to answer the Philippian jailer's question from an LDS perspective.

The Postmortem Spirit World

Latter-day Saints believe in a multitiered afterlife. *Gospel Principles* states, "At the Final Judgment we will inherit a place in the kingdom for which we are prepared. The scriptures teach of three kingdoms of glory—the celestial kingdom, the terrestrial kingdom, and the telestial kingdom (see D&C 88:20–32)."[1] *Gospel Principles* explains, "In Doctrine and Covenants 76, the Lord described the ways we can choose to live our mortal lives. He explained that our choices will determine which kingdom we are prepared for. We learn from this revelation that even members of the Church will inherit different kingdoms because they will not be equally faithful and valiant in their obedience to Christ."[2] With this in mind, we turn to the three kingdoms and one realm of misery in the afterlife (celestial, terrestrial, telestial, and outer darkness) to gain a foundation before discussing the answer to our original question, "What must I do to be saved?"

The Celestial Kingdom

The celestial kingdom of heaven is the highest of the four major divisions of the afterlife. James Talmage notes:

> There are some who have striven to obey all the Divine commandments, who have accepted the testimony of Christ, and received the Holy Spirit; these are they who have overcome evil by godly works, and who are therefore entitled to the highest glory; these belong to the Church of the Firstborn, unto whom the Father has given all things; they are made Kings and Priests of the Most High, after the order of Melchisedek [*sic*]; they possess celestial bodies, "whose glory is that of the sun, even the glory of God, the highest of all, whose glory the sun of the firmament is written of as being typical;" they indeed are

---

[1] Church of Jesus Christ of Latter-day Saints, *Gospel Principles*, 271 (see chap. 1, n. 69).
[2] Church of Jesus Christ of Latter-day Saints, 271. It is important to discuss these varying degrees of glory because, within Latter-day Saint belief, the term *salvation* is sometimes equivalent to a general resurrection into the afterlife and sometimes equivalent to exaltation in the celestial kingdom. For the purposes of this work, the term *salvation* will be used to reference exaltation in the celestial kingdom. However, all three degrees of the afterlife need to be explained in order that a full-orbed understanding of Latter-day Saint soteriology may be gained.

admitted to the celestial company, being crowned with the celestial glory, which makes them Gods.[3]

As can be seen from this quote from Talmage, besides the idea of deification, there is not much significant descriptive material concerning the celestial kingdom. *Gospel Principles* offers a bit more description. The manual states, "All who inherit the celestial kingdom will live with Heavenly Father and Jesus Christ forever."[4] Bruce McConkie asserts:

> By obedience to celestial law men gain *celestial bodies*, bodies which are sanctified by the Spirit (D&C 84:33; 88:16–32; Alma 13:12; 3 Ne. 27:19–21). They become new creatures of the Holy Ghost, having been born again (Alma 5). Their renewed bodies are just as different from bodies still in their carnal state as the bodies of the various animals, fowls, and fishes differ from each other (1 Cor. 15:39–42). Those who have gained celestial bodies will, in the resurrection, receive back "the same body which was a natural body" (D&C 88:28), that is their celestial bodies will be immortalized and then they will gain admission to the celestial kingdom.[5]

He explains further, "If a man obeys celestial law in this life, he obtains a celestial body and spirit. In the resurrection these are received back again quickened by a *celestial glory*, thus qualifying him to go to a celestial kingdom where alone celestial glory is found (D&C 88:16–32). Mortal man has no concept of the glory of that world."[6] He continues:

> Exaltation consists of gaining a fulness of celestial glory (D&C 132:19–20). Those so attaining will receive "a fulness of the glory of the Father" and be glorified in Christ as he is in the Father (D&C 93:16–20). The Prophet said that in the resurrection the righteous "shall rise again to dwell in everlasting burnings in immortal glory, not to sorrow, suffer, or die any more; but they shall be heirs of God and joint-heirs with Jesus Christ."[7]

---

[3] Talmage, *The Articles of Faith*, 94–95 (see chap. 2, n. 10).
[4] The Church of Jesus Christ of Latter-day Saints, *Gospel Principles*, 272.
[5] Bruce R. McConkie, *Mormon Doctrine* (see chap. 2, n. 11).
[6] McConkie, 115–16.
[7] McConkie, 116.

McConkie further affirmed:

> Highest among the kingdoms of glory hereafter is the *celestial king-dom*. It is the kingdom of God, the glory thereof being typified by the sun in the firmament. The Prophet has left us this record of a glorious occurrence that took place in the Kirtland Temple on January 21, 1836: "The heavens were opened upon us, and I beheld the celestial kingdom of God, and the glory thereof, whether in the body or out I cannot tell. I saw the transcendent beauty of the gate through which the heirs of that kingdom will enter, which was like unto circling flames of fire; also the blazing throne of God, whereon was seated the Father and the Son. I saw the beautiful streets of that kingdom, which had the appearance of being paved with gold."[8]

We can say, then, that though Latter-day Saints know little about the celestial kingdom, they believe it to be a marvelous place where both the Heavenly Father and Jesus Christ are found. However, there is more to the celestial kingdom than this.

Latter-day Saints also believe there is a tiered system of degrees within the celestial kingdom itself. *Gospel Principles* notes:

> When we lived with our Heavenly Father, He explained a plan for our progression. We could become like Him, an exalted being. The plan required that we be separated from Him and come to earth. This separation was necessary to prove whether we would obey our Father's commandments even though we were no longer in His presence. The plan provided that when earth life ended, we would be judged and rewarded according to the degree of our faith and obedience. From the scriptures we learn that there are three kingdoms of glory in heaven. . . . The celestial is the highest, and the terrestrial is second. Through Latter-day revelation we learn that the third kingdom is the telestial kingdom. We also learn that there are three heavens or degrees within the celestial kingdom.[9]

---

[8] McConkie, 116.
[9] Church of Jesus Christ of Latter-day Saints, *Gospel Principles*, 275.

Though nothing is mentioned about the lower two degrees within the celestial kingdom, there is a great deal of information concerning the highest of the three levels within the celestial kingdom, otherwise known as "exaltation." Concerning exaltation, *Gospel Principles* declares:

> Exaltation is eternal life, the kind of life God lives. He lives in great glory. He is perfect. He possesses all knowledge and all wisdom. He is the Father of spirit children. He is a creator. We can become like our Heavenly Father. This is exaltation. If we prove faithful to the Lord, we will live in the highest degree of the celestial kingdom of heaven. We will become exalted, to live with our Heavenly Father in eternal families. Exaltation is the greatest gift that Heavenly Father can give His children.[10]

The manual continues:

> Those who receive exaltation in the celestial kingdom through faith in Jesus Christ will receive spiritual blessings. . . . These are some of the blessings given to exalted people: 1. They will live eternally in the presence of Heavenly Father and Jesus Christ. 2. They will become gods. 3. They will be united eternally with their righteous family members and will be able to have eternal increase. 4. They will receive a fulness of joy. 5. They will have everything that our Heavenly Father and Jesus Christ have—all power, glory, dominion, and knowledge.[11]

Again, Bruce McConkie is helpful when he adds:

> Celestial marriage is the gate to exaltation, and exaltation consists in the continuation of the family unit in eternity. Exaltation is eternal life, the kind of life which God lives. Those who obtain it gain an inheritance in the highest of three heavens within the celestial kingdom. They have eternal increase, a continuation of the seeds forever and ever, a continuation of the lives, eternal lives; that is, they have spirit children in the resurrection, in relation to which offspring they stand in the same position that God our Father stands to us. They inherit in due course the fulness of the glory of the Father, meaning that they have all

---

[10] Church of Jesus Christ of Latter-day Saints, 275–77.
[11] Church of Jesus Christ of Latter-day Saints, 277.

power in heaven and on earth. "Then shall they be gods, because they have no end; therefore shall they be from everlasting to everlasting, because they continue; then shall they be above all, because all things are subject unto them. Then shall they be gods; because they have all power and the angels are subject unto them." Although salvation may be defined in many ways to mean many things, in its most pure and perfect definition it is a synonym for exaltation. This was the way in which the Prophet used it.[12]

The Terrestrial Kingdom

One degree of glory lower than the celestial kingdom is the terrestrial kingdom. *Gospel Principles* explains, "These are they who rejected the gospel on earth but afterward received it in the spirit world. These are the honorable people on the earth who were blinded to the gospel of Jesus Christ by the craftiness of men. These are also they who received the gospel and a testimony of Jesus but then were not valiant. They will be visited by Jesus Christ but not by our Heavenly Father."[13] McConkie concurs:

> Those attaining a terrestrial kingdom will be inheritors of *terrestrial glory* which differs from celestial glory "as that of the moon differs from the sun in the firmament." In effect they bask, as does the moon, in reflected glory, for there are restrictions and limitations placed on them. They "receive of the presence of the Son, but not of the fulness of the Father," and to all eternity they remain unmarried and without exaltation.[14]

Likewise, Talmage notes, "We read of those who receive glory of a secondary order only, differing from the highest as 'the moon differs from the sun in the firmament'; these are they, who, though honorable, were still in darkness, blinded by the craftiness of men, and unable to receive and obey the higher laws of God, they proved 'not valiant in the testimony of Jesus,' and therefore are not entitled to the fulness of glory."[15]

Concerning those who will enter the terrestrial kingdom, McConkie notes:

---

[12] McConkie, *Mormon Doctrine*, 256–57.
[13] Church of Jesus Christ of Latter-day Saints, *Gospel Principles*, 272.
[14] McConkie, *Mormon Doctrine*, 784.
[15] Talmage, *The Articles of Faith*, 95.

To the *terrestrial kingdom* will go: 1. Accountable persons who die without law (and who, of course, do not accept the gospel in the spirit world under those particular circumstances which would make them heirs of the celestial kingdom); 2. Those who reject the gospel in this life and who reverse their course and accept it in the spirit world; 3. Honorable men of the earth who are blinded by the craftiness of men and who therefore do not accept and live the gospel law; and 4. Members of The Church of Jesus Christ of Latter-day Saints who have testimonies of Christ and the divinity of the great Latter-day work and who are not valiant, but who are instead lukewarm in their devotion to the Church and to righteousness.[16]

The person who enters the terrestrial kingdom has, according to McConkie, lived his or her life to the standards of terrestrial law. This law is defined as "living an upright, honorable life but one that does not conform to the standards whereby the human soul is sanctified by the Spirit."[17] Similarly, those who gain entrance to the terrestrial kingdom are given terrestrial bodies. McConkie explains, "By obedience to terrestrial law men develop *terrestrial bodies and spirits*, thus conditioning themselves to be quickened in the resurrection with terrestrial glory, which is found in a terrestrial kingdom. As is the case with the development of celestial bodies, those who gain terrestrial ones have bodies as different from other kinds of flesh as one form of life differs from another."[18]

The Telestial Kingdom

The lowest of the three degrees of glory is the telestial kingdom. *Gospel Principles* describes this kingdom as follows:

> These people did not receive the gospel of the testimony of Jesus either on earth or in the spirit world. They will suffer for their own sins in hell until after the Millennium, when they will be resurrected. "These are they who are liars, and sorcerers, and adulterers, and whoremongers, and whosoever loves and makes a lie." These people are as numerous

---

[16] McConkie, *Mormon Doctrine*, 784.
[17] McConkie, 784.
[18] McConkie, 783–84.

as the stars in heaven and the sand on the seashore. They will be visited by the Holy Ghost but not by the Father or the Son.[19]

McConkie expounds further:

> Most of the adult people who have lived from the day of Adam to the
> present time will go to the *telestial kingdom*. The inhabitants of this
> lowest kingdom of glory will be "as innumerable as the stars in the
> firmament of heaven, or as the sand upon the seashore." They will be
> the endless hosts of people of all ages who have lived after the man-
> ner of the world; who have been carnal, sensual, and devilish; who
> have chosen the vain philosophies of the world rather than accept the
> testimony of Jesus; who have been liars and thieves, sorcerers and
> adulterers, blasphemers and murders. Their number will include "all
> the proud, yea, and all that do wickedly" (Mal. 4:1), for all such have
> lived a telestial law. "And they shall be servants of the Most High; but
> where God and Christ dwell they cannot come, worlds without end"
> (D&C 76:112).[20]

Talmage adds:

> We learn of a still lower kind of glory, differing from the higher orders
> as the stars differ from the brighter orbs of the firmament; this is given
> to those who received not the testimony of Christ, but who still did
> not deny the Holy Spirit; who have led lives exempting them from the
> heaviest punishment, yet whose redemption will be delayed till the
> last resurrection. In the telestial world there are innumerable degrees
> of glory, comparable to the varying lustre of the stars. Yet all who
> receive of any one of these orders of glory are at last saved, and upon
> them Satan will finally have no claim. Even the telestial glory, as we
> are told by those who have been permitted to gaze upon it, "surpasses
> all understanding; and no man knows it except him to whom God has
> revealed it."[21]

---

[19] Church of Jesus Christ of Latter-day Saints, *Gospel Principles*, 272.
[20] McConkie, *Mormon Doctrine*, 778.
[21] Talmage, *The Articles of Faith*, 95.

John A. Widtsoe, a former member of the Quorum of Twelve Apostles, explains:

> The [Doctrine and Covenants] explains clearly that the lowest glory to which man is assigned is so glorious as to be beyond the understanding of man. It is a doctrine fundamental in Mormonism that the meanest sinner, in the final judgment, will receive a glory which is beyond human understanding, which is so great that we are unable to describe it adequately. Those who do well will receive an even more glorious place.[22]

Those who will inherit the telestial kingdom must keep telestial law. McConkie explains:

> A telestial glory, found only in a telestial kingdom, is reserved for those who develop telestial bodies, such bodies resulting naturally from obedience to telestial law. This law is the law of the world, and worldly people are conforming to its terms and conditions. Those who refuse to worship the true and living God, who are unclean and immoral, who are proud and rebellious, who walk in paths of wickedness, who are carnal and sensual, who do not maintain standards of decency, uprightness, and integrity, are as a result conforming their lives to the provisions of telestial law. All the inhabitants of the earth are living at least a telestial law, unless, perchance, there are some who are in open rebellion against the truth, some who willfully break the law, abide not in it, but seek to become a law unto themselves, choosing to abide in sin, and altogether abiding therein. Such, of course, will be sons of perdition in eternity and will inherit "a kingdom which is not a kingdom of glory" (D&C 88:24).[23]

Outer Darkness

The final degree of the afterlife, and most abhorred by Latter-day Saints, is outer darkness. Concerning those who inherit this station in the afterlife, *Gospel Principles* explains, "These are they who had testimonies of Jesus through the Holy Ghost and knew the power of the Lord but allowed Satan to overcome them. They denied the truth and defied the power of the Lord. There is no forgiveness for them, for they denied the Holy Spirit after having received

---

[22] Church of Jesus Christ of Latter-day Saints, *Doctrine and Covenants Student Manual*, 166 (see chap. 2, n. 110).
[23] McConkie, *Mormon Doctrine*, 778–79.

it. They will not have a kingdom of glory. They will live in eternal darkness, torment, and misery with Satan and his angels forever."[24] McConkie explains:

> Hell is referred to as *outer darkness*. At death the spirits of the wicked "shall be cast out into outer darkness; there shall be weeping, and wailing, and gnashing of teeth, and this because of their own iniquity, being led captive by the will of the devil. Now this is the state of the souls of the wicked, yea, in darkness, and a state of awful, fearful looking for the fiery indignation of the wrath of God upon them; thus they remain in this state, as well as the righteous in paradise, until the time of their resurrection" (Alma 40:13–14). So complete is the darkness prevailing in the minds of these spirits, so wholly has gospel light been shut out of their consciences, that they know little or nothing of the plan of salvation, and have little hope within themselves of advancement and progression through the saving grace of Christ. Hell is literally a place of outer darkness, darkness that hates light, buries truth, and revels in iniquity.[25]

Robert L. Millet, former dean of religion at Brigham Young University, notes, "Outer darkness is also used to describe the final state of the sons of perdition, the only ones who will be subject to the second death, meaning the second spiritual death, and who will suffer over their denial, defiance, and defection for eternity."[26]

The sons of perdition, as Millet referenced, are an interesting subject within Mormonism, one that garners a great deal of attention. McConkie writes:

> Lucifer is Perdition. He became such by open rebellion against the truth, a rebellion in the face of light and knowledge. Although he knew God and had been taught the provisions of the plan of salvation, he defied the Lord and sought to enthrone himself with the Lord's power. He thus committed the unpardonable sin. In rebellion with him were one-third of the spirit hosts of heaven. These all were thus *followers* of perdition. They were denied bodies, were cast out onto the earth, and thus came the devil and his angels—a great host of *sons of perdition*.

[24] Church of Jesus Christ of Latter-day Saints, *Gospel Principles*, 273.
[25] McConkie, *Mormon Doctrine*, 551–52.
[26] Robert L. Millet, "Outer Darkness" in *LDS Beliefs*, ed. Robert L. Millet et al. (Salt Lake City: Deseret, 2011), 469–70.

Those in this life who gain a perfect knowledge of the divinity of the
gospel cause, a knowledge that comes only by revelation from the
Holy Ghost, and who then link themselves with Lucifer and come
out in open rebellion, also become sons of perdition. Their destiny,
following their resurrection, is to be cast out with the devil and his
angels, to inherit the same kingdom in a state where "the worm dieth
not, and the fire is not quenched." Joseph Smith said: "All sins shall be
forgiven, except the sin against the Holy Ghost; for Jesus will save all
except the sons of perdition."[27]

Millet agrees:

Lucifer, the father of all lies, is Perdition, meaning ruin or destruction.
It is his work, his whole purpose, to oppose, undermine, and defy the
work and glory of God and to proselyte as many to that nefarious
effort as possible. Cain became the father of Satan's lies, the devil's
earthly counterpart, or Perdition. Those who have accepted the gospel
of Jesus Christ through baptism, have received the gift of the Holy
Ghost, have had the heavens opened, have come to know God, and
who then spurn that supernatural knowledge and witness and become
an enemy to the cause of righteousness are they whom the scriptures
designate as sons of perdition. These are they about whom Jesus spoke
when he taught of sin that was unpardonable, of sin or blasphemy
against the Holy Ghost, of those who would not be forgiven in this
world or the next. . . . The ultimate fate of the sons of perdition has not
been revealed, nor will it be save to those who so qualify; we know
only that the sons of perdition who have mortal bodies will be resurrected to a kingdom of no glory. . . . They are the only ones who suffer
the second death, meaning the second spiritual death.[28]

Just a few months before his death in June 1844, Joseph Smith said:

All sins shall be forgiven, except the sin against the Holy Ghost; for
Jesus will save all except the sons of perdition. What must a man do to
commit the unpardonable sin? He must receive the Holy Ghost, have
the heavens opened unto him, and know God, and then sin against

[27] McConkie, *Mormon Doctrine*, 746.
[28] Robert L. Millet, "Perdition, Sons of" in Millet et al., *LDS Beliefs*, 488–89.

him. After a man has sinned against the Holy Ghost, there is no repentance for him. He has got to say that the sun does not shine while
he sees it; he has got to deny Jesus Christ when the heavens have
been opened unto him, and to deny the plan of salvation with his eyes
open to the truth of it; and from that time he begins to be an enemy.
This is the case with many apostates of the Church of Jesus Christ of
Latter-day Saints.[29]

In an extended passage concerning the Sons of Perdition, James Talmage
writes:

Consider the word of the Lord regarding those whose sin is the unpardonable one, whose transgression has carried them beyond the present
horizon of possible redemption; those who have sunk so low in their
wickedness as to have lost the power and even the desire to attempt
reformation. Sons of Perdition they are called. These are they who,
having learned the power of God afterward renounce it; those who
sin willfully in the light of knowledge; those who open their hearts to
the Holy Spirit and then put the Lord to a mockery and a shame by
denying it; and those who commit murder wherein they shed innocent
blood; these are they of whom the Savior has declared that it would
be better for them had they never been born. These are to share the
punishment of the devil and his angels—punishment so terrible that
the knowledge is withheld from all except those who are consigned
to this doom, though a temporary view of the picture is permitted to
some. These sinners are the only ones over whom the second death
hath power. . . . As to the duration of punishment, we may take assur-
ance that it will be graded according to the sin; and that the conception
of every sentence for misdeeds being interminable is false. Great as
is the effect of this life upon the hereafter, and certain as is the responsibility of opportunities lost for repentance, God holds the power
to pardon beyond the grave. Yet the scriptures speak of eternal and
endless punishment. Any punishment ordained of God is eternal, for
He is eternal. His is a system of endless punishment, for it will always
exist as a place or condition prepared for disobedient spirits; yet the

[29] Quoted in Church of Jesus Christ of Latter-day Saints, *Doctrine and Covenants Student
Manual*, 93.

infliction of the penalty will have an end in every case of acceptable repentance and reparation. And repentance is not impossible in the spirit world. However, as seen, there are some sins so great that their consequent punishments are not made known to man; these extreme penalties are reserved for the sons of Perdition.[30]

The sons of perdition, then, along with outer darkness, are estates inherited by those who, according to the above-quoted authors and leaders, have been given the power of the Holy Ghost but have since committed the unpardonable sin by blaspheming that power. According to the quote from Joseph Smith, the sons of perdition are made up (mostly) of those who have apostatized from their membership in the Church of Jesus Christ of Latter-day Saints. In similar fashion, former LDS Church president Joseph Fielding Smith said, while serving as a member of the Quorum of Twelve Apostles, "It is only those who have the light through the priesthood and through the power of God and through their membership in the Church who will be banished forever from his influence into outer darkness to dwell with the devil and his angels. That is a punishment that will not come to those who have never known the truth."[31]

With these things in mind, let us now turn our attention to the Latter-day Saint doctrine of soteriology. As stated earlier, because the terms *salvation* and *exaltation* are used as synonyms within LDS thought, the following explanation of LDS soteriology applies directly to exaltation within the celestial kingdom as described earlier. Sufficient information has been given for the lower degrees of glory and for outer darkness, so the terrestrial and telestial kingdoms and outer darkness will not be referenced in the following discussion.

The Doctrine of Soteriology

Soteriology, loosely defined, is the study of the doctrine of salvation. As mentioned earlier, the question, "What must I do to be saved?" has plagued humans for millennia. Answers to this question have been offered by almost all religious groups ever formed, and Latter-day Saints are no different. The third and fourth articles of faith offer, at least to some degree, the Latter-day Saint answer. They read, "(3) We believe that through the Atonement of Christ, all mankind may be saved, by obedience to the laws and ordinances of the Gospel.

---

[30] Talmage, *The Articles of Faith*, 62–63.
[31] Church of Jesus Christ of Latter-day Saints, *Conference Report* (Salt Lake City: Church of Jesus Christ of Latter-day Saints, October 1958), 21.

(4) We believe that the first principles and ordinances of the Gospel are: first, Faith in the Lord Jesus Christ; second, Repentance; third, Baptism by immersion for the remission of sins; fourth, Laying on of hands for the gift of the Holy Ghost." Doctrine and Covenants 20:25–29 offers further explanation:

> That as many as would believe and be baptized in his holy name, and endure in faith to the end, should be saved—not only those who believed after he came in the meridian of time, in the flesh, but all those from the beginning, even as many as were before he came, who believed in the words of the holy prophets, who spake as they were inspired by the gift of the Holy Ghost, who truly testified of him in all things, should have eternal life, As well as those who should come after, who should believe in the gifts and callings of God by the Holy Ghost, which beareth record of the Father and of the Son; which Father, Son, and Holy Ghost are one God, infinite and eternal, without end. Amen. And we know that all men must repent and believe on the name of Jesus Christ, and worship the Father in his name, and endure in faith on his name to the end, or they cannot be saved in the kingdom of God.

Similarly, Doctrine and Covenants 18:22 reads, "And as many as repent and are baptized in my name, which is Jesus Christ, and endure to the end, the same shall be saved."

Article of Faith 3 makes reference to "obedience to the laws and ordinances of the gospel" and Article of Faith 4 offers some further explanation, but is that all that is required? Do Latter-day Saints believe salvation, or exaltation, is gained through faith, repentance, baptism, and the laying on of hands for the gift of the Holy Ghost, or is there more? Doctrine and Covenants seems to indicate more is involved, as the phrase "endure to the end," or "endure in faith to the end," is used in four separate passages (D&C 10:69; 14:7; 18:22; 63:20, 47; 101:35). If faith, repentance, baptism, and the laying on of hands are all that is required, then either the phrase "endure to the end" must have something to do with those four items, or something further is required. McConkie offers a helpful thought:

> *Conditional or individual salvation*, that which comes by grace coupled with gospel obedience, consists in receiving an inheritance in the celestial kingdom of God. This kind of salvation follows faith, repentance, baptism, receipt of the Holy Ghost, and continued righteousness

to the end of one's mortal probation. . . . Salvation in its true and full meaning is synonymous with *exaltation* or *eternal life* and consists in gaining an inheritance in the highest of the three heavens within the celestial kingdom. With few exceptions this is the salvation of which the scriptures speak. It is the salvation which the saints seek. . . . This full salvation is obtained in and through the continuation of the family unit in eternity, and those who obtain it are gods. . . . If it had not been for Joseph Smith and the restoration, there would be no salvation. There is no salvation outside The Church of Jesus Christ of Latter-day Saints.[32]

Brent L. Top, current dean of religious education at Brigham Young University, argues, "The Prophet Joseph Smith called exaltation 'the fullness of salvation' which is obtained only by abiding the celestial law and 'going through with all those ordinances [of the temple].'"[33] With a new concept, celestial law, introduced by Top, we now need to focus attention, at least briefly, on what this is exactly and how it impacts salvation.

Celestial law is, basically, the law that must be kept in order to gain entrance into the celestial kingdom. Doctrine and Covenants 88:22 reads, "For he who is not able to abide the law of a celestial kingdom cannot abide a celestial glory." McConkie notes, "That law by obedience to which men gain an inheritance in the kingdom of God in eternity is called *celestial law.*"[34] In another work, McConkie argues:

Celestial law is the law of the gospel; it is the law of Christ. It calls upon men to forsake the world and rise above every carnal and evil thing. It calls upon men to repent and be baptized and receive the sanctifying power of the Holy Spirit of God. It requires that they become new creatures of the Holy Ghost. Only those who so live acquire thereby celestial bodies; only such bodies can stand celestial glory, and this glory is found only in a celestial kingdom.[35]

Likewise, Talmage writes:

---

[32] McConkie, *Mormon Doctrine*, 669–70.
[33] Brent L. Top, "Exaltation" in Millet et al., *LDS Beliefs*, 199.
[34] McConkie, *Mormon Doctrine*, 117.
[35] Bruce R. McConkie, *Millennial Messiah: The Second Coming of the Son of Man* (Salt Lake City: Deseret, 1982), 697.

There are some who have striven to obey all the divine commandments, who have accepted the testimony of Christ, obeyed "the laws
and ordinances of the Gospel," and received the Holy Spirit; these
are they who have overcome evil by godly works and who are therefore entitled to the highest glory; these belong to the Church of the
Firstborn, unto whom the Father has given all things; they are made
kings and priests of the Most High, after the order of Melchizedek;
they possess celestial bodies, "whose glory is that of the sun, even the
glory of God, the highest of all, whose glory the sun of the firmament
is written of as being typical"; they are admitted to the glorified company, crowned with exaltation in the celestial kingdom.[36]

With these things in mind, we now turn attention away from the appetizers
and to the main course of Latter-day Saint soteriology, namely, answering our
original question, "What must I do to be saved?" To answer this question with
as much official information as possible, we will follow the outline in *Gospel
Principles* and address each area of that outline individually. Though not mentioning it specifically in this way, according to *Gospel Principles*, there are a
number of areas implied within celestial law. Those areas are faith, repentance,
baptism, the gift of the Holy Ghost, the gifts of the Holy Spirit, the sacrament,
the Sabbath day, fasting, sacrifice, work and personal responsibility, service,
the Lord's law of health, charity, honesty, tithes and offerings, missionary
work, developing our talents, obedience, the family, eternal marriage, the law
of chastity, temple work, and family history. Let us first address the topic of
faith.

Faith

As quoted earlier, the fourth Article of Faith makes clear that faith is one of
the first principles and ordinances of the gospel. *Gospel Principles* states, very
clearly, "Faith in the Lord Jesus Christ is the first principle of the gospel. It
is a spiritual gift, and it is necessary to our salvation."[37] The manual explains
further:

> To have faith in Jesus Christ means to have such a trust in Him that we
> obey whatever He commands. As we place our faith in Jesus Christ,

---

[36] Talmage, *The Articles of Faith*, 94–95.
[37] Church of Jesus Christ of Latter-day Saints, *Gospel Principles*, 101.

becoming His obedient disciples, Heavenly Father will forgive our sins and prepare us to return to Him. . . . We cannot have faith in Jesus Christ without also having faith in our Heavenly Father. If we have faith in Them, we will also have faith that the Holy Ghost, whom They send, will teach us all truth and will comfort us.[38]

This faith is not stagnant; it must always grow. *Gospel Principles* asks, "How can we increase our faith?" then goes on to explain:

The same way we increase or develop any other skill. How do we develop skills in woodcarving, weaving, painting, cooking, making pottery, or playing a musical instrument? We study and practice and work at it. As we do so, we improve. So it is with faith. If we want to increase our faith in Jesus Christ, we must work at it. . . . So we can increase our faith in God by acting on our *desire* to have faith in Him. We can also increase our faith by praying to Heavenly Father about our hopes, desires, and needs. But we must not suppose that all we have to do is ask. . . . Faith involves doing all we can to bring about the things we hope and pray for. . . . An important way to increase our faith is to hear and study the word of the Lord. We hear the word of the Lord at our Church meetings. We can study His word in the scriptures.[39]

Similar to *Gospel Principles*, James Talmage also offers significant information concerning the nature of faith. He writes, "Inasmuch as salvation is attainable only through the mediation and atonement of Christ, and since this is made applicable to individual sin only in the cases of those who obey the laws of righteousness, faith in Jesus Christ is indispensable to salvation. But no one can believe in Jesus Christ, and at the same time doubt the existence and authority of either the Father or the Holy Ghost; therefore faith in the entire Godhead is essential to salvation."[40] He continues:

Though within reach of all who diligently strive to gain it, faith is nevertheless a Divine gift, and can be obtained only from God. As is fitting for so priceless a pearl, it is given to those only who show by their sincerity that they are worthy of it, and who give promise of

---

[38] Church of Jesus Christ of Latter-day Saints, 103.
[39] Church of Jesus Christ of Latter-day Saints, 104–5.
[40] Talmage, *The Articles of Faith*, 110.

abiding by its dictates. Although faith is called the first principle of the gospel of Christ, though it be in fact the foundation of all religion, yet, even faith is preceded by sincerity of disposition, and humility of soul, whereby the word of God may make an impression upon the heart. No compulsion is used in bringing men to a knowledge of God; yet, as fast as we open our hearts to the influences of righteousness, the faith that leads to life eternal will be given us of our Father.[41]

Concerning the relationship of faith and works, Talmage argues:

Faith in a passive sense, that is, as mere belief, is inefficient as a means of salvation. This truth was clearly set forth both by Christ and the apostles, and the vigor with which it was declared may be an indication of the early development of a most pernicious doctrine, that of justification by belief alone. The Savior taught that works were essential to the validity of profession and the efficacy of faith. . . . To these teachings may be added many inspired utterances, from Nephite scriptures and from modern revelation, all affirming the necessity of works, and denying the saving efficacy of mere belief.[42]

Bruce McConkie agrees. He writes:

Faith bringeth salvation; miracles are wrought by faith; by faith the worlds were made. God is God because faith dwells in him independently; and faith is power, the very power of God himself. Any man who has faith in the Lord Jesus Christ, in the full and true sense, will sit down with him on his throne in the kingdom of his Father. All who do not gain this saving faith will fall short of that inheritance which might have been theirs had they believed and obeyed the word of faith.[43]

According to McConkie, even God the Father has faith: "God the Father, in the ultimate and final sense, is the Creator of all things. He is the creator of spirit men, or mortal men, and of immortal men. He created life and death and immortality and eternal life. He made the laws whereby spirit men gain mortality, and mortal men gain immortality, and faithful men gain eternal life. The

---

[41] Talmage, 111.
[42] Talmage, 112–13.
[43] McConkie, *A New Witness for the Articles of Faith*, 163–64 (see chap. 3, n. 9).

power he uses in these and in all things is faith. Faith is power, and the power of God is the faith of God."[44] He continues:

> God the Father is an eternal being. The very name of the kind of life he lives is eternal life, and thus eternal life consists in living and being as he is. In other words, eternal life is to gain the power of God, which power is faith, and thus to be able to do what he does and to live as he lives. And the great and eternal plan of salvation that he has ordained and established consists of those laws, ordinances, and powers whereby faith is acquired and perfected until it is possessed in the same degree and to the same extent that it exists in Deity. Faith will thus dwell independently in every person who gains eternal life.[45]

Although faith is an absolute necessity for salvation according to Latter-day Saints, works also have their part. The specific works will be discussed in the following material, but two former leaders are helpful here in summary. Before becoming president of the LDS Church, then elder Joseph Fielding Smith, a member of the Quorum of Twelve Apostles, in discussing faith, wrote:

> Unless a man will adhere to the doctrine and walk in faith, accepting the truth and observing the commandments as they have been given, it will be impossible for him to receive eternal life, no matter how much he may confess with his lips that Jesus is the Christ, or believe that his Father sent him into the world for the redemption of man. So James is right when he says the devils "believe and tremble," but they do not repent. So it is necessary, not merely that we believe, but that we repent, and in faith perform good works until the end; and then shall we receive the reward of the faithful and a place in the celestial kingdom of God.[46]

Similarly, President Heber J. Grant notes:

> Of what good are our faith, our repentance, our baptism, and all the sacred ordinances of the gospel by which we have been made ready to receive the blessings of the Lord, if we fail, on our part, to keep the commandments? All that we expect, or all that we are promised, is

---

[44] McConkie, 168.
[45] McConkie, 169.
[46] Joseph Fielding Smith, *Doctrines of Salvation* (Salt Lake City: Deseret, 1955), 2:311.

predicated on our own actions, and if we fail to act, or to do the work which God has required of us, we are little better than those who have not received the principles and ordinances of the gospel. We have only started, and when we rest there, we are not following our faith by our works, and are under condemnation; our salvation is not attained.[47]

Repentance

Like faith, repentance is mentioned in the fourth Article of Faith as one of the first principles of the gospel. McConkie argues for a very close, if not inseparable, relationship between faith and repentance: "Thus repentance follows faith. It is born of faith; it is the child of faith; and it operates only in the lives of those who have faith—faith in the Lord Jesus Christ. Faith comes first and repentance second; one is the first principle of the gospel, the other the second."[48] *Gospel Principles* declares:

Faith in Jesus Christ naturally leads to repentance. There has been need for repentance in the world from the time of Adam to the present day. . . . We come to earth for the purpose of growing and progressing. This is a lifelong process. During this time we all sin. We all have need to repent. Sometimes we sin because of ignorance, sometimes because of our weaknesses, and sometimes because of willful disobedience. . . . Except for Jesus Christ, who lived a perfect life, everyone who has lived upon the earth has sinned. Our Heavenly Father in His great love has provided us this opportunity to repent of our sins.[49]

Further, *Gospel Principles* states:

Repentance is the way provided for us to become free from our sins and receive forgiveness for them. Sins slow our spiritual progression and can even stop it. Repentance makes it possible for us to grow and develop spiritually again. The privilege of repenting is made possible through the Atonement of Jesus Christ. . . . Repentance sometimes

---

[47] Heber J. Grant and G. Homer Durham, *Gospel Standards: Selections from the Sermons and Writings of Heber J. Grant* (Salt Lake City: Deseret, 1941), 6.
[48] McConkie, *A New Witness for the Articles of Faith*, 217.
[49] Church of Jesus Christ of Latter-day Saints, *Gospel Principles*, 107.

requires great courage, much strength, many tears, unceasing prayers, and untiring efforts to live the commandments of the Lord.[50]

Gospel Principles also offers the steps that move the Latter-day Saint toward repentance and ensure its realization:[51] First, "we must admit to ourselves that we have sinned. If we do not admit this, we cannot repent." Second, "in addition to recognizing our sins, we must feel sincere sorrow for what we have done. We must feel that our sins are terrible. We must want to unload and abandon them." Third, "our sincere sorrow should lead us to forsake (stop) our sins. If we have stolen something, we will steal no more. If we have lied, we will lie no more. If we have committed adultery, we will stop." Fourth,

confessing our sins is very important. The Lord has commanded us to confess our sins. Confession relieves a heavy burden from the sinner. . . . We must confess our sins to the Lord. In addition, we must confess serious sins—such as adultery, fornication, homosexual relations, spouse or child abuse, and the sale or use of illegal drugs—which might affect our standing in the Church, to the proper priesthood authority. If we have sinned against another person, we should confess to the person we have injured. Some less serious sins involve no one but ourselves and the Lord. These may be confessed privately to the Lord.

Fifth, "Part of repentance is to make restitution. This means that as much as possible we must make right any wrong that we have done." Sixth, "a vital part of repentance is to forgive those who have sinned against us. The Lord will not forgive us unless our hearts are fully cleansed of all hate, bitterness, and bad feelings against other people." Seventh, "to make our repentance complete we must keep the commandments of the Lord. We are not fully repentant if we do not pay tithes or keep the Sabbath day holy or obey the Word of Wisdom. We are not repentant if we do not sustain the authorities of the Church and do not love the Lord and our fellowmen. If we do not pray and are unkind to others, we are surely not repentant. When we repent, our life changes." Finally, *Gospel Principles* declares:

We should repent now, every day. When we get up in the morning, we should examine ourselves to see whether the Spirit of God is with us. At night before we go to sleep, we should review our acts and words

---

[50] Church of Jesus Christ of Latter-day Saints, 109.
[51] Church of Jesus Christ of Latter-day Saints, 110–13.

of the day and ask the Lord to help us recognize the things for which we need to repent. By repenting every day and having the Lord forgive our sins, we will experience the daily process of becoming perfect.

Talmage is helpful for our understanding of repentance as well. He notes:

The term repentance is used in the scriptures with several different meanings, but, as representing the duty required of all who would obtain forgiveness for transgression, it indicates a godly sorrow for sin, producing a reformation of life, and embodies, (1) a conviction of guilt; (2) a desire to escape the hurtful effects of sin; and (3) an earnest determination to forsake sin and to accomplish good. Repentance is a result of contrition of soul, which springs from a deep sense of humility, and this in turn is dependent upon the exercise of an abiding faith in God. Repentance therefore properly ranks as the second principle of the gospel, closely associated with and immediately following faith.[52]

Talmage also offers his understanding of the steps necessary to make repentance a real effect and gain forgiveness:

(1) Confession of sins is essential, for without it repentance is incomplete. . . . (2) The sinner must be willing to forgive others, if he hopes to obtain forgiveness. Surely his repentance is but superficial if his heart be not softened to the degree of tolerance for the weaknesses of his fellows. . . . (3) Confidence in Christ's atoning sacrifice constitutes the third essential condition in obtaining remission of sins. The name of Christ is the only name under heaven whereby men may be saved, and we are taught to offer our petitions to the Father in the name of His Son. Adam received this instruction from the mouth of an angel, and the Savior personally instructed the Nephites to the same effect. But no person can truthfully profess faith in Christ, and refuse to obey His commandments; therefore obedience is essential to remission of sin; and the repentant sinner will eagerly seek to learn what is further required of him.[53]

Likewise, McConkie offers a similar understanding of repentance, though with varying nuances:

---

[52] Talmage, *The Articles of Faith*, 113.
[53] Talmage, 114–16.

Because all accountable men are stained by sin, and because no unclean thing can enter into the kingdom of heaven, a merciful God has ordained the *law of repentance* whereby the human soul may be cleansed and conditioned for eternal life in his everlasting presence. Repentance is the process whereby a mortal soul—unclean and stained with the guilt of sin—is enabled to cast off the burden of guilt, wash away the filth of iniquity, and become clean every whit, entirely free from the bondage of sin.[54]

He continues:

To gain forgiveness through repentance a person must have a conviction of guilt, a godly sorrow for sin, and a contrite spirit. He must desire to be relieved of the burden of sin, have a fixed determination to forsake his evil ways, be willing to confess his sins, and forgive those who have trespassed against him; he must accept the cleansing power of the blood of Christ as such is offered through the waters of baptism and the conferral of the Holy Ghost.[55]

McConkie states, with no question, "Repentance is essential to salvation; without it no accountable person can be saved in the kingdom of God. It is a prerequisite to baptism and hence to membership in the kingdom of God on earth."[56] Concerning some of the specifics of repentance for different persons, he writes:

Repentance is easy or difficult of attainment by various people, depending upon their own attitude and conduct, and upon the seriousness of the sins they have committed. Through rebellion men sometimes place themselves in a position in which the Lord's Spirit will no longer strive with them, and when this occurs there is little hope for them. For those who have once basked in the light and who thereafter come out in open rebellion, there is no repentance whatever.[57]

When reading through various authors, one common thread is found concerning repentance, namely, the idea of one's own conduct being intimately

---

[54] McConkie, *Mormon Doctrine*, 630.
[55] McConkie, 630.
[56] McConkie, 630.
[57] McConkie, 631.

connected to repentance and the efficacy of that repentance. Concerning repentance and one's works, McConkie states simply, "Good works precede and are a part of repentance."[58] The immediate question then centers around what these good works are. He clarifies, "Thus contrition and humility, penitence and godly sorrow, confession and conformity, desires for righteousness and a determination to make amends for past sins and to live better in the future—all these precede and are part of repentance. To gain a remission of sins by repentance, men must not only forsake sin itself, but they must also forgive others their trespasses and affirmatively turn to righteousness in all things."[59] McConkie then concludes:

> Those who truly repent forsake the world; they flee unto Christ; they assemble with the saints and worship the Father in spirit and in truth. They die as to carnal and evil things and become alive in Christ, choosing thereby to walk in a newness of life. They repent of their evil deeds and of their false doctrines. A truly repentant person believes the gospel, rejects all heretical views, and goes forward along the course leading to eternal life. Repentance, thus, is not an isolated principle, standing alone by itself; it is part and portion of the plan of salvation, and it is interwoven with the whole gospel scheme of things.[60]

Baptism

Alongside faith and repentance, baptism is mentioned as necessary for salvation in the fourth Article of Faith and, like the relationship between the first two steps discussed, baptism is inextricably linked to faith and repentance. McConkie notes:

> Thus repentance prepares men for that baptism by immersion which is for the remission of sins. It precedes baptism, and to be efficacious it must be followed by baptism. There is no salvation in repentance alone, and in the gospel sense, repentance dies aborning unless the repentant soul is also baptized. Sins are washed away, as it were, in the

---

[58] McConkie, *A New Witness for the Articles of Faith*, 218.
[59] McConkie, 218.
[60] McConkie, 218.

waters of baptism; they do not simply die and cease because unbaptized persons reform their lives.[61]

Similarly, *Gospel Principles* declares, "Today, as in the days of Jesus, there are certain principles and ordinances of the gospel that we must learn and obey. A gospel principle is a true belief or teaching. An ordinance is a rite or ceremony. The first two principles of the gospel are faith in the Lord Jesus Christ and repentance. Baptism is the first ordinance of the gospel."[62]

When considering baptism, one must ask why baptism is necessary and if a particular mode of baptism is prescribed. *Gospel Principles* notes, "When we place our faith in Jesus Christ, repent, and are baptized, our sins are forgiven through the Atonement of Jesus Christ."[63] The manual also points readers to Doctrine and Covenants 20:37 in explaining that membership in the Church of Jesus Christ of Latter-day Saints has baptism as one of its prerequisites. The text reads:

> *And again, by way of commandment to the church concerning the manner of baptism*—All those who humble themselves before God, and desire to be baptized, and come forth with broken hearts and contrite spirits, and witness before the church that they have truly repented of all their sins, and are willing to take upon them the name of Jesus Christ, having a determination to serve him to the end, and truly manifest by their works that they have received of the Spirit of Christ unto the remission of their sins, shall be received by baptism into his church.

Further, *Gospel Principles* also lists five specific items baptism accomplishes: the remission of sins, admission as a member of the LDS Church, reception of the Holy Ghost, a demonstration of obedience, and access to the celestial kingdom.[64] Concerning the last of these, the manual maintains, "Baptism is the gateway through which we enter the path to the celestial kingdom."[65] But baptism by what method? *Gospel Principles* states:

---

[61] McConkie, 217.
[62] Church of Jesus Christ of Latter-day Saints, *Gospel Principles*, 115.
[63] Church of Jesus Christ of Latter-day Saints, 115.
[64] Church of Jesus Christ of Latter-day Saints, 115–16.
[65] Church of Jesus Christ of Latter-day Saints, 116.

There is only one correct mode of baptism. Jesus revealed to the
Prophet Joseph Smith that a person having the proper priesthood authority to baptize "shall go down into the water with the person who
has presented himself or herself for baptism. . . . Then shall he im-
merse him or her in the water, and come forth again out of the water"
(D&C 20:73–74). Immersion is necessary. . . . Baptism by immersion
by a person having the proper authority is the only acceptable way of
being baptized.[66]

Baptism is likewise prescribed for certain persons and not for others: "Every person who has reached eight years of age and is accountable (responsible) for his or her actions should be baptized. Some churches teach that little
children should be baptized. This is not in keeping with the teachings of the
Savior."[67] Further, "The prophet Mormon said that it is a mockery before God
to baptize little children, because they are not capable of sinning. Likewise,
baptism is not required of people who are mentally incapable of knowing right
and wrong. All other people are to be baptized. We must receive the ordinance
of baptism and remain true to the covenants we make at that time."[68]

What are these covenants mentioned by *Gospel Principles*?

Many scriptures teach about baptism. In one of these scriptures, the
prophet Alma taught that faith and repentance are steps that prepare us
for baptism. He taught that when we are baptized we make a covenant
with the Lord. We promise to do certain things, and God promises to
bless us in return. Alma explained that we must want to be called the
people of God. We must be willing to help and comfort each other. We
must stand as witnesses of God at all times and in all things and in all
places. As we do these things and are baptized, God will forgive our
sins.[69]

What are "these things"? The authors explain:

Alma taught that when we are baptized we make covenants with the
Lord to: 1. Come into the fold of God. 2. Bear one another's burdens.
3. Stand as witnesses of God at all times and in all places. 4. Serve

[66] Church of Jesus Christ of Latter-day Saints, 116–17.
[67] Church of Jesus Christ of Latter-day Saints, 117.
[68] Church of Jesus Christ of Latter-day Saints, 117.
[69] Church of Jesus Christ of Latter-day Saints, 117–18.

God and keep His commandments. When we are baptized and keep the covenants of baptism, the Lord promises to: 1. Forgive our sins. 2. Pour out His Spirit more abundantly upon us. 3. Give us daily guidance and the help of the Holy Ghost. 4. Let us come forth in the First Resurrection. 5. Give us eternal life.[70]

McConkie similarly explains:

> The gospel is the new and everlasting covenant by means of which God, on his own terms, offers salvation to man. Baptism is the formally appointed means and ordinance which the Lord has provided so that man can signify his personal acceptance of all of the terms and conditions of the eternal gospel covenant. Thus in baptism, which as part of the gospel is itself a new and an everlasting covenant, man covenants to abide by all of the laws and requirements of the whole gospel.[71]

In an interesting twist, Latter-day Saints also believe baptism to be available for those who have passed on from this life to the next. Using 1 Cor 15:29 as a New Testament "proof text" and numerous texts within the Doctrine and Covenants (especially sections 127 and 128), Latter-day Saints regularly practice this ordinance within their temples. Camille Fronk Olson, a professor at Brigham Young University, argues:

> In his mercy the Lord is also mindful of those who die without receiving a testimony of Christ and his gospel. During the three days his spirit was in the postmortal spirit world, Jesus Christ prepared the way for the gospel to be preached "to those who had died in their sins, without a knowledge of the truth, or in transgression, having rejected the prophets" (D&C 138:32; 1 Peter 3:18–21; 4:6). Authorization was then given to his representatives on earth to perform baptisms for the dead in temples, sacred edifices appropriate for this ordinance (D&C 124:29–30; 1 Corinthians 15:29).[72]

---

[70] Church of Jesus Christ of Latter-day Saints, 118.
[71] McConkie, *Mormon Doctrine*, 70.
[72] Camille Fronk Olson, "Baptism" in Millet et al., *LDS Beliefs*, 64–65.

The Gift of the Holy Ghost

With the first and second principles of the gospel (faith and repentance) and the first ordinance of the gospel (baptism), the final specific action mentioned in the fourth Article of Faith is the gift of the Holy Ghost. Put simply, for Latter-day Saints, the gift of the Holy Ghost is that continual "still small voice," prompting them to continue in their faith. *Gospel Principles* explains, "The gift of the Holy Ghost is the privilege—given to people who have placed their faith in Jesus Christ, been baptized, and been confirmed as members of the Church—to receive continual guidance and inspiration of the Holy Ghost."[73] Further, "A person may be temporarily guided by the Holy Ghost without receiving the gift of the Holy Ghost. However, this guidance will not be continuous unless the person is baptized and receives the laying on of hands for the gift of the Holy Ghost."[74]

In passing, the authors of *Gospel Principles* mention the action required to receive the gift of the Holy Ghost as the laying on of hands. Likewise, the fourth Article of Faith offers the same condition. *Gospel Principles* clarifies further:

> After people are baptized, they are confirmed members of the Church and given the gift of the Holy Ghost by the laying on of hands. . . . Every worthy elder of the Church, when authorized, may give the gift of the Holy Ghost to another person. However, there is no guarantee that the person will receive inspiration and guidance from the Holy Ghost just because the elders have laid their hands on his or her head. Each person must "receive the Holy Ghost." This means that the Holy Ghost will come to us only when we are faithful and desire help from this heavenly messenger. To be worthy to have the help of the Holy Ghost, we must seek earnestly to obey the commandments of God. We must keep our thoughts and actions pure.[75]

McConkie is also helpful here: "The gift of the Holy Ghost . . . is the right, based on faithfulness, to the constant companionship of that member of the

---

[73] Church of Jesus Christ of Latter-day Saints, *Gospel Principles*, 122.
[74] Church of Jesus Christ of Latter-day Saints, 122.
[75] Church of Jesus Christ of Latter-day Saints, 122–23.

Godhead. It is the right to receive revelation, guidance, light, and truth from the Spirit."[76] He continues:

> Further, the fact that a person has had hands laid on his head and a legal administrator has declared, "Receive the Holy Ghost," does not guarantee that the gift itself has actually been enjoyed. The gift of the Holy Ghost is the *right* to have the constant companionship of the Spirit; the actual *enjoyment* of the gift, the *actual receipt of the companionship* of the Spirit, is based on personal righteousness; it does not come unless and until the person is worthy to receive it. The Spirit will not dwell in an unclean tabernacle.[77]

In 1909, in the *Improvement Era* magazine, then president Joseph F. Smith offered his understanding of those who actually confer the right to the Holy Ghost:

> Every elder of the Church who has received the Holy Ghost by the laying on of hands, by one having authority, has power to confer that gift upon another; it does not follow that a man who has received the presentation or gift of the Holy Ghost shall always receive the recognition and witness and presence of the Holy Ghost himself, or he may receive all these, and yet the Holy Ghost not tarry with him, but visit him from time to time; and neither does it follow that a man must have the Holy Ghost present with him when he confers the Holy Ghost upon another, but he possesses the gift of the Holy Ghost, and it will depend upon the worthiness of him unto whom the gift is bestowed whether he receive the Holy Ghost or not.[78]

Therefore, we can deduce from this quote from Joseph F. Smith, combined with the information from *Gospel Principles* and Bruce McConkie, that a person who has received the right to the gift of the Holy Ghost can, through the laying on of hands, bestow that same right to another person, yet be without the actual presence of the Holy Ghost at the time when he confers the right to another.

---

[76] McConkie, *Mormon Doctrine*, 312.
[77] McConkie, 313.
[78] Joseph F. Smith, "Holy Ghost, Holy Spirit, Comforter," *Improvement Era,* 12, no. 5 (March 1909), 390.

Thus ends the four specific items mentioned in the fourth Article of Faith. From this point forward, there is no official word given on the actual commandments necessary to gain entrance into the celestial kingdom; there is no authoritative breakdown of celestial law. Therefore, we will now rely solely on the list found in *Gospel Principles* to determine that which may be classified as aspects of celestial law. Some Latter-day Saints see these as natural outworkings of faith, repentance, baptism, and the gift of the Holy Ghost. Others see them as continued necessary works to gain exaltation in the celestial kingdom. Although those two roads, theologically, are extremely divergent, the list in *Gospel Principles* is nonetheless critical and provides a good understanding of the daily lives of Latter-day Saints.

The Gifts of the Spirit

The first of the mentions in *Gospel Principles* after the gift of the Holy Ghost is the gifts of the Spirit. Article of Faith 7 alludes to many of these gifts. It reads, "We believe in the gift of tongues, prophecy, revelation, visions, healings, the interpretation of tongues, and so forth." Seemingly, the gifts mentioned as those bestowed by the Spirit are not salvific, but function as proofs of the gift of the Holy Ghost. However, *Gospel Principles* declares, "[The gifts of the Spirit] help us know and teach the truths of the gospel. They will help us bless others. They will guide us back to our Heavenly Father."[79] The gifts specifically mentioned by *Gospel Principles* are tongues, the interpretation of tongues, translation, wisdom, knowledge, teaching wisdom and knowledge, knowing that Jesus Christ is the Son of God, believing the testimony of others, prophecy, healing, working miracles, and faith.[80] We will now work through a few of these gifts individually to gain a better understanding.

Of the gifts of tongues and interpretation of tongues, *Gospel Principles* states, "Sometimes it is necessary to communicate the gospel in a language that is unfamiliar to us. When this happens, the Lord can bless us with the ability to speak that language."[81] Similarly, the gift of the interpretation of tongues "is sometimes given to us when we do not understand a language and we need to receive an important message from God."[82] McConkie writes:

---

[79] Church of Jesus Christ of Latter-day Saints, *Gospel Principles*, 125.
[80] Church of Jesus Christ of Latter-day Saints, 125–30.
[81] Church of Jesus Christ of Latter-day Saints, 125.
[82] Church of Jesus Christ of Latter-day Saints, 126.

Tongues and their interpretation are classified among the signs and miracles which always attend the faithful and which stand as evidences of the divinity of the Lord's work. . . . Frequently these gifts are manifest where the ordinary languages of the day are concerned in that the Lord's missionaries learn to speak and interpret foreign languages with ease, thus furthering the spread of the message of the restoration.[83]

Interestingly, he also notes, "Tongues and their interpretation are given for special purposes under special circumstances. There are a host of gifts that are far more important and in the use of which there is less chance of deception."[84]

Of the gift of prophecy, *Gospel Principles* explains:

Those who receive true revelations about the past, present, or future have the gift of prophecy. Prophets have this gift, but we too can have it to help us govern our own lives. We may receive revelations from God for ourselves and our own callings, but never for the Church or its leaders. It is contrary to the order of heaven for a person to receive revelation for someone over whom he or she does not preside. If we truly have the gift of prophecy, we will not receive any revelation that does not agree with what the Lord has said in the scriptures.[85]

Then Quorum of Twelve Apostles member Joseph Fielding Smith wrote, "All members of the Church should seek for the gift of prophecy, for their own guidance, which is the spirit by which the word of the Lord is understood and his purpose made known."[86] McConkie adds, "Belief in and the manifestations of the spirit of prophecy are two of the great evidences of the divinity of the great Latter-day work in which the saints are engaged. . . . Every member of the Church—acting in submission to the laws and system which the Lord has ordained—is expected to have the gift of prophecy. It is by this gift that a testimony of the truth comes."[87]

---

[83] McConkie, *Mormon Doctrine*, 799–800.
[84] McConkie, 800.
[85] Church of Jesus Christ of Latter-day Saints, *Gospel Principles*, 129.
[86] Joseph Fielding Smith, *Church History and Modern Revelation* (Salt Lake City: Church of Jesus Christ of Latter-day Saints, 1953), 1:201.
[87] McConkie, *Mormon Doctrine*, 603.

Addressing the gift of healing, *Gospel Principles* states, "Some have the faith to heal, and others have the faith to be healed. We can all exercise the faith to be healed when we are ill. Many who hold the priesthood have the gift of healing the sick. Others may be given a knowledge of how to cure illnesses."[88] McConkie explains further:

Miracles whereby diseases are cured and whereby physical and mental health are conferred by divine power are called *healings.* . . . Healings come because of faith. They are gifts of the Spirit, some persons having "faith to be healed," others being endowed with "faith to heal" (D&C 46:19–20). Healings are among the signs that follow true believers, and the faithful elders have power to perform healings whenever it is required of them by those who have faith to be healed. As with other signs and miracles, if there are no healings among church members, such people are not the saints of God. And as with certain other miracles, the devil has power to perform some acts in imitation of the Lord's power.[89]

With respect to the gift of working miracles, *Gospel Principles* notes, "The Lord has blessed His people many times in miraculous ways. When the Utah pioneers planted their first crops, a plague of locusts nearly destroyed them. The pioneers prayed that the Lord would save their crops, and He sent seagulls to devour the locusts. When we need help and ask in faith, if it is for our good the Lord will work miracles for us."[90] McConkie adds further:

Healing and being healed and raising the dead are only the beginning of miracles. Properly gifted persons control the elements, move mountains, turn rivers out of their course, walk on water, quench the violence of fire, are carried by the power of the Spirit from one congregation to another, are translated and taken up into heaven, or—and this above all—gain for themselves an eternal inheritance in the presence of Him who is Eternal. Miracles are now, have always been, and always will be part and portion of the true gospel of that God who is a God of miracles. They are gifts of the Spirit.[91]

---

[88] Church of Jesus Christ of Latter-day Saints, *Gospel Principles*, 129.
[89] McConkie, *Mormon Doctrine*, 345.
[90] Church of Jesus Christ of Latter-day Saints, *Gospel Principles*, 130–31.
[91] McConkie, *A New Witness for the Articles of Faith*, 373.

Second president of the LDS Church, Brigham Young, declared, "Miracles, or these extraordinary manifestations of the power of God, are not for the unbeliever; they are to console the Saints, and to strengthen and confirm the faith of those who love, fear, and serve God, and not for outsiders."[92]

Gospel Principles also notes that Latter-day Saints should "find out which gifts we have. We do this by praying and fasting. We should seek after the best gifts. Sometimes patriarchal blessings will help us know which gifts we have been given."[93] Likewise, the manual warns:

Satan can imitate the gifts of tongues, prophecy, visions, healings, and other miracles. Moses had to compete with Satan's imitations in Pharaoh's court. Satan wants us to believe in his false prophets, false healers, and false miracle workers. They may appear to be so real to us that the only way to know is to ask God for the gift of discernment. The devil himself can appear as an angel of light. Satan wants to blind us to the truth and keep us from seeking the true gifts of the Spirit. Mediums, astrologers, fortune tellers, and sorcerers are inspired by Satan even if they claim to follow God. Their works are abominable to the Lord. We should avoid all associations with the powers of Satan.[94]

The Sacrament

The sacrament, or Lord's Supper, is a weekly experience shared by all worthy Latter-day Saints. Though it is a small part of the actual time during Sunday meetings, the one-hour corporate worship time for Latter-day Saints is often referred to as "sacrament meeting," thereby indicating the importance of this time of remembrance and renewal. Latter-day Saints believe Jesus "wants us to remember His great atoning sacrifice and keep His commandments. To help us do this, He has commanded us to meet often and partake of the sacrament."[95] The purpose of the sacrament each week is for Latter-day Saints to "renew sacred covenants with our Heavenly Father."[96] McConkie explains, "By partaking of the sacrament, worthy saints renew the covenant previously made by them in the waters of baptism; unbaptized children, being without sin, are

[92] Widtsoe, *Discourses of Brigham Young*, 341 (see chap. 2, n. 43).
[93] Church of Jesus Christ of Latter-day Saints, *Gospel Principles*, 130.
[94] Church of Jesus Christ of Latter-day Saints, 131.
[95] Church of Jesus Christ of Latter-day Saints, 133.
[96] Church of Jesus Christ of Latter-day Saints, 133.

entitled and expected to partake of the sacrament to prefigure the covenant they will take upon themselves when they arrive at the years of accountability. Worthy partakers of the sacrament put themselves in perfect harmony with the Lord."[97] Likewise, Talmage notes, "Partaking of the sacrament worthily may be regarded therefore as a means of renewing our covenants before the Lord, of acknowledgement of mutual fellowship among the members, and of solemnly witnessing our claim and profession of membership in the Church of Christ."[98]

From *Gospel Principles*, McConkie, and Talmage, we see that there is indeed an understood covenant-renewing aspect of the sacrament. Our immediate question should focus on the nature of the covenants that are renewed during the sacrament. Put differently and more directly, which covenants are renewed? McConkie answers this directly:

> Those who partake of the sacrament worthily thereby put themselves under covenant with the Lord: 1. To always remember the broken body and spilled blood of Him who was crucified for the sins of the world; 2. To take upon themselves the name of Christ and always remember him; and 3. To keep the commandments of God, that is, to "live by every word that proceedeth forth from the mouth of God" (D&C 84:44).[99]

Gospel Principles also addresses this covenant renewal. The authors declare:

> Each time we partake of the sacrament, we renew covenants with the Lord. A covenant is a sacred promise between the Lord and His children. . . . We covenant that we are willing to take upon ourselves the name of Jesus Christ. By this we show we are willing to be identified with Him and His Church. We commit to serve Him and our fellowman. We promise that we will not bring shame or reproach upon that name. We covenant to always remember Jesus Christ. All our thoughts, feeling, and actions will be influenced by Him and His mission. We promise to keep His commandments. We take these obligations upon ourselves when we are baptized. Thus, when we partake

---

[97] McConkie, *Mormon Doctrine*, 660.
[98] Talmage, *The Articles of Faith*, 175.
[99] McConkie, *Mormon Doctrine*, 660.

of the sacrament, we renew the covenants we made when we were baptized.[100]

Next, our question should focus on the result of this covenant renewal. Is there a dispensation of grace because of this renewal; is this truly a sacrament? Is this nothing more than a remembrance for which no means of grace are given? Or is there a middle ground? *Gospel Principles* states, "The Lord promises that if we keep our covenants, we will always have His Spirit to be with us. A person guided by the Spirit will have the knowledge, faith, power, and righteousness to gain eternal life."[101] McConkie writes:

> Few ordinances or performances in the church act as a greater incentive to personal righteousness than worthy partaking of the sacrament. Those who partake of the sacramental emblems—having a comprehension of the covenant involved—are marking for themselves a course which will result in obedience, holiness, and sanctification. Such persons—having placed themselves in the spirit of prayer, humility, and worship which attend sacramental administrations—become the ones who gain peace in this life and eternal life in the world to come.[102]

Talmage adds, "The sacrament has not been established as a specific means of securing remission of sins; nor for any other special blessing, aside from that of a fresh endowment of the Holy Spirit, which, however, comprises all needful blessings."[103] Likewise, Andrew C. Skinner, former dean of religious education at Brigham Young University, writes:

> Then, as now, those who partake of the sacrament in worthiness enter into a covenant with God the Father. According to prayers offered by priesthood holders when blessing the sacrament, followers promise to always remember the broken body and spilled blood of God's Only Begotten Son, to take upon themselves the name of God's Son, and to keep his commandments. God, in turn, promises that worthy disciples of his Son will always have his Spirit to be with them. During his mortal ministry Jesus said that those who consumed the emblems of his

[100] Church of Jesus Christ of Latter-day Saints, *Gospel Principles*, 136.
[101] Church of Jesus Christ of Latter-day Saints, 136.
[102] McConkie, *Mormon Doctrine*, 661.
[103] Talmage, *The Articles of Faith*, 179.

body and blood worthily would be given eternal life and their bodies would be raised up.[104]

Thus, we can say the remission of sins is not given to Latter-day Saints when the sacrament is observed, but covenants are renewed, and those who keep the observance of the sacrament are promised eternal life. Although the sacrament is not viewed as a dispensation of grace whereby the remission of sins is offered, it is nonetheless a requirement for Latter-day Saints. Then member of the Quorum of Twelve Apostles Joseph Fielding Smith said, "To meet together often for [the partaking of the sacrament] is a requirement made of members of the Church, which is just as binding upon them in its observance as the requirement in relation to any other principle or ordinance of the gospel. No member of the Church who refuses to observe this sacred ordinance can retain the inspiration and guidance of the Holy Ghost."[105] Thus, though remission of sins is not offered via the sacrament, the continual presence of the Holy Ghost seems dependent on one's observance of this ordinance.

The Sabbath Day

For Latter-day Saints, the Sabbath day is indeed a holy day and is reserved for sacrament meetings, family events, and rest. *Gospel Principles* explains, "The Sabbath day is every seventh day. It is a holy day ordained by God for us to rest from our daily labors and worship Him."[106] The manual explains further, "Jesus taught that the Sabbath day was made for our benefit. The purpose of the Sabbath is to give us a certain day of the week on which to direct our thoughts and actions toward God. It is not a day merely to rest from work. It is a sacred day to be spent in worship and reverence."[107] The command to keep the Sabbath continues for current Latter-day Saints. Apostle Joseph Fielding Smith noted, "The commandment to keep holy the Sabbath day is just as binding upon the people of the earth today as it ever was. While it is true that man was not made for the Sabbath, but the Sabbath for man, we should not misinterpret this saying and ignore the great commandment, for that would incur the displeasure of the Lord."[108]

---

[104] Andrew C. Skinner, "Sacrament of the Lord's Supper" in Millet et al., *LDS Beliefs*, 549.
[105] Joseph Fielding Smith, *Doctrines of Salvation*, 2:338.
[106] Church of Jesus Christ of Latter-day Saints, *Gospel Principles*, 139.
[107] Church of Jesus Christ of Latter-day Saints, 139.
[108] Joseph Fielding Smith, *Church History and Modern Revelation*, 1:218.

What, then, does it mean for Latter-day Saints to "keep the Sabbath holy"? *Gospel Principles* clarifies:

> The Lord asks us, first, to sanctify the Sabbath day. . . . Second, He asks us to rest from daily work. This means we should perform no labor that would keep us from giving our full attention to spiritual matters. . . . We should consider righteous things we can do on the Sabbath. For example, we can keep the Sabbath day holy by attending Church meetings; reading the scriptures and the words of our Church leaders; visiting the sick, the aged, and our loved ones; listening to uplifting music and singing hymns; praying to our Heavenly Father with praise and thanksgiving; performing Church service; preparing family history records and personal histories; telling faith-promoting stories and bearing our testimony to family members and sharing spiritual experiences with them; writing letters to missionaries and loved ones; fasting with a purpose; and sharing time with children and others in the home.[109]

Brigham Young University's Brent L. Top explains further: "Sabbath observance is not merely a matter of doing or not doing certain things. It involves our attitudes and innermost desires and feelings—our love, devotion, and appreciation for the Lord and his infinite sacrifice. It reminds us that there is no rest, no peace, and no salvation in the world or in following after its many false gods. The Sabbath is a constant reminder of our unique relationship to God."[110]

Though there are some very positive aspects of the Sabbath for Latter-day Saints, there are also some negative "don'ts." Then member of the Quorum of Twelve Apostles Spencer W. Kimball declared, "To many, Sabbath breaking is a matter of little moment, but to our Heavenly Father it is one of the principal commandments."[111] In 1940, the First Presidency of the LDS Church, then composed of Heber J. Grant, Anthony W. Ivins, and Charles W. Nibley, issued a statement about keeping the Sabbath. They said, "Let all unnecessary labor be suspended and let no encouragement be given by the attendance of members of the Church at places of amusement and recreation on the Sabbath day. If Sunday is spent in our meetings and in our homes great blessings will come

---

[109] Church of Jesus Christ of Latter-day Saints, *Gospel Principles*, 141–42.
[110] Brent L. Top, "Sabbath" in Millet et al., *LDS Beliefs*, 546.
[111] Edward L. Kimball, *The Teachings of Spencer W. Kimball;* 217 (see chap. 3, n. 137).

to our families and communities."[112] Similarly, in 1992 the First Presidency of the LDS Church, then consisting of Ezra Taft Benson, Gordon B. Hinckley, and Thomas S. Monson, issued a statement concerning the Sabbath. They declared:

> We sense that many Latter-day Saints have become lax in their observance of the Sabbath day. We should refrain from shopping on the Sabbath and participating in other commercial and sporting activities that now commonly desecrate the Sabbath. We urge all Latter-day Saints to set this holy day apart from activities of the world and consecrate themselves by entering into a spirit of worship, thanksgiving, service, and family-centered activities appropriate to the Sabbath. As Church members endeavor to make their Sabbath activities compatible with the intent and Spirit of the Lord, their lives will be filled with joy and peace.[113]

In 1974, President Spencer W. Kimball discussed the Sabbath during his conference address. He said, "We call attention also to the habit in which many buy their commodities on the Sabbath. Many employed people would be released for rest and worship on the Sabbath if we did not shop on that day. Numerous excuses and rationalizations are presented to justify the Sabbath buying. We call upon all of you to keep the Sabbath holy and make no Sunday purchases."[114] Later, in 1978, President Kimball addressed the issue again. He said, "Sabbath-breakers too are those who buy commodities or entertainment on the Sabbath, thus encouraging pleasure palaces and business establishments to remain open—which they otherwise would not do. If we buy, sell, trade, or support such on the Lord's day we are as rebellious as the children of Israel, the dire consequences of whose transgressions against this and other commandments should be a permanent warning to us all."[115]

In a final word about the Sabbath, when considering whether or not the Sabbath is important, we look once more to *Gospel Principles*. The manual states, "If we honor the Sabbath day, we may receive great spiritual and

[112] Heber J. Grant, Anthony W. Ivins, and Charles W. Nibley, "First Presidency Message," *Liahona* magazine, October 1940, 195–96.
[113] Ezra Taft Benson, Gordon B. Hinckley, and Thomas S. Monson, "First Presidency Statement on the Sabbath," *Ensign*, January 1993, 2.
[114] Spencer W. Kimball, "Conference Address" in *Conference Report* (Salt Lake City: Church of Jesus Christ of Latter-day Saints, October 1974), 6.
[115] Spencer W. Kimball, "The Sabbath—a Delight," *Ensign*, January 1978, 5.

temporal blessings. The Lord has said if we keep the Sabbath day with thanks-giving and cheerful hearts, we will be full of joy."[116]

Fasting

The next theme found in *Gospel Principles* is that of fasting. The manual clear-ly states prayer and fasting should always be coupled together and that fasting should be done with a specific purpose in mind, namely, to overcome weak-nesses, to seek guidance, to know truth, to help others embrace truth, or for comfort.[117] With these purposes in mind, Latter-day Saints are encouraged to fast often and regularly. *Gospel Principles* states, "One Sunday each month Latter-day Saints observe a fast day. On this day we neither eat nor drink for two consecutive meals. If we were to eat our evening meal on Saturday, then we would not eat or drink until the evening meal on Sunday."[118] The authors continue, "All members who are physically able should fast. We should en-courage our children to fast after they have been baptized, but we should never force them. The fast day is a special day for us to humble ourselves before the Lord in fasting and prayer. It is a day to pray for forgiveness from our sins and for the power to overcome our faults and to forgive others."[119] The manual also notes fasting produces "peace, improved health, and spiritual guidance."[120] It also declares, "When we fast wisely and prayerfully, we develop our faith. With that faith we will have greater spiritual power."[121]

McConkie explains further:

Fasting, with prayer as its companion, is designed to increase spiritu-ality; to foster a spirit of devotion and love of God; to increase faith in the hearts of men, thus assuring divine favor; to encourage humility and contrition of soul; to aid in the acquirement of righteousness; to teach men his nothingness and dependence upon God; and to hasten those who properly comply with the law of fasting along the path to salvation.[122]

---

[116] Church of Jesus Christ of Latter-day Saints, *Gospel Principles*, 142.
[117] Church of Jesus Christ of Latter-day Saints, 145–46.
[118] Church of Jesus Christ of Latter-day Saints, 146.
[119] Church of Jesus Christ of Latter-day Saints, 146.
[120] Church of Jesus Christ of Latter-day Saints, 147.
[121] Church of Jesus Christ of Latter-day Saints, 148.
[122] McConkie, *Mormon Doctrine*, 276.

President Joseph F. Smith concurs with both McConkie and *Gospel Principles*. He writes:

> It would be a simple matter for people to comply with this requirement to abstain from food and drink one day each month, and to dedicate what would be consumed during that day to the poor, and as much more as they pleased. The Lord has instituted this law; it is simple and perfect, based on reason and intelligence, and would not only prove a solution to the question of providing for the poor, but it would result in good to those who observe the law. It would call attention to the sin of over-eating, place the body in subjugation to the spirit, and so promote communion with the Holy Ghost, and insure a spiritual strength and power which the people of the nation so greatly need.[123]

As Smith mentioned, Latter-day Saints give the money that would have been spent on the two meals during the fast weekend to the "fast offering" of the LDS Church. This offering is used to further the work of an entity known as Bishop's Storehouses, free grocery stores that function as food distribution hubs for needy Latter-day Saints, and other community members. This is one way Latter-day Saints see themselves as positive, helpful members of their community and communities beyond their own.

Sacrifice, Work and Personal Responsibility, Service

Sacrifice is the next topic addressed in *Gospel Principles*. Along with sacrifice are the natural complements of work, personal responsibility, and service. *Gospel Principles* states, "Sacrifice means giving to the Lord whatever He requires of our time, our earthly possessions, and our energies to further His work."[124] Indeed, this issue is of such importance that it is found within Latter-day Saint temple rituals. The Endowment Ceremony, as of 1990, includes the following words:

> The posterity of Adam down to Moses, and from Moses to Jesus Christ offered up the first fruits of the field, and the firstlings of the flock, which continued until the death of Jesus Christ, which ended sacrifice by the shedding of blood. And as Jesus Christ has laid down his life for the redemption of mankind, so we should covenant to sacrifice

[123] Joseph F. Smith, *Gospel Doctrine* (Salt Lake City: Deseret, 1919), 237–38.
[124] The Church of Jesus Christ of Latter-day Saints, *Gospel Principles*, 149.

all that we possess, even our own lives if necessary, in sustaining and defending the Kingdom of God.[125]

Gospel Principles explains further, "If we are to be a living sacrifice, we must be willing to give everything we have for The Church of Jesus Christ of Latter-day Saints—to build the kingdom of God on the earth and labor to bring forth Zion."[126] McConkie concurs with this sentiment. He writes, "*Sacrifice* is the crowning test of the gospel. Men are tried and tested in this mortal probation to see if they will put first in their lives the things of the kingdom of God. To gain eternal life, they must be willing, if called upon, to sacrifice all things for the gospel."[127] *Gospel Principles* concludes, "Only through sacrifice can we become worthy to live in the presence of God. Only through sacrifice can we enjoy eternal life. Many who have lived before us have sacrificed all they had. We must be willing to do the same if we would earn the rich reward they enjoy."[128]

When sacrificing all one has for the sake of the work of the LDS Church, one's work and personal responsibility come immediately to the forefront. Work is, as *Gospel Principles* notes, an "eternal principle."[129] The manual explains:

> Our Heavenly Father and Jesus Christ have shown us by Their examples and teachings that work is important in heaven and on earth. God worked to create the heavens and the earth. He caused the seas to gather in one place and the dry land to appear. He caused the grass, herbs, and trees to grow on the land. He created the sun, the moon, and the stars. He created every living thing in the sea or on the land. Then He placed Adam and Eve on the earth to take care of it and to have dominion over all living things.[130]

McConkie adds:

---

[125] "The Mormon Temple Endowment Ceremony," Mormons in Transition, posted August 18, 2011, http://mit.irr.org/mormon-temple-endowment-ceremony.
[126] Church of Jesus Christ of Latter-day Saints, *Gospel Principles*, 151.
[127] McConkie, *Mormon Doctrine*, 663.
[128] Church of Jesus Christ of Latter-day Saints, *Gospel Principles*, 153.
[129] Church of Jesus Christ of Latter-day Saints, 155.
[130] Church of Jesus Christ of Latter-day Saints, 155.

Work is the great basic principle which makes all things possible both in time and in eternity. Men, spirits, angels, and Gods use their physical and mental powers in work. . . . Without work there would be neither existence, creation, redemption, salvation, or temporal necessities for mortal man. Deity worked for six days in the creation of this earth and then rested on the seventh. The Father's work and glory is to bring to pass the immortality and eternal life of man. Our Lord's mission was to work out the infinite and eternal atonement. Man is commanded to work both temporally and spiritually—to work out his salvation with fear and trembling before God, and to earn his living by the sweat of his face until he returns to the ground. *Work is a blessing that brings salvation, idleness a curse that assures damnation.*[131]

Similarly, work is an important aspect of life inside the family unit. Latter-day Saint parents are fully expected and taught to provide for the welfare, both physical and spiritual, of their children and anyone else in their home. Even children are expected and taught to work within the confines of the family unit, at least as far as their abilities allow them to do so. This promotes the understanding that work is important for all Latter-day Saints in all places. Idleness, as McConkie mentioned, is understood to have a significantly negative impact on the person. "From the earliest days of the Church, the prophets have taught Latter-day Saints to be independent and self-sustaining and to avoid idleness. True Latter-day Saints will not voluntarily shift from themselves the burden of their own support. So long as they are able, they will supply themselves and their families with the necessities of life."[132]

The final partner of sacrifice mentioned in *Gospel Principles* is service. As with many other organizations, the LDS Church defines service as "helping others who need assistance."[133] This service is to be given to all who need help and should be provided by all persons: young and old, rich and poor, male and female. The reason for service, according to Latter-day Saints, is simple: "Through the service of men and women and boys and girls, God's work is done."[134] However, service is more than serving God and others, as there is an aspect of serving oneself when serving others. *Gospel Principles* states,

---

[131] McConkie, *Mormon Doctrine*, 847.
[132] Church of Jesus Christ of Latter-day Saints, *Gospel Principles*, 158.
[133] Church of Jesus Christ of Latter-day Saints, 161.
[134] Church of Jesus Christ of Latter-day Saints, 163.

"When we serve others we gain important blessings. Through service we increase our ability to love. We become less selfish. As we think of the problems of others, our own problems seem less serious. We must serve others to gain eternal life. God has said that those who live with Him must love and serve His children."[135]

The Lord's Law of Health

Probably one of the best-known but least understood aspects of Latter-day Saint life is the Lord's Law of Health, or the Word of Wisdom. Doctrine and Covenants 89 spells out this commandment for Latter-day Saints. This section forbids Latter-day Saints to consume "wine or strong drink," tobacco, or "hot drinks." It also avers that Latter-day Saints should refrain from consuming copious amounts of meat but should use meat "sparingly." Positively, section 89 encourages Latter-day Saints to use "wholesome herbs," fruits, and grain regularly for food. *Gospel Principles* offers reasons for this section and its teachings:

> One of the great blessings we received when we came to earth was a physical body. We need a physical body to become like our Heavenly Father. Our bodies are so important that the Lord calls them temples of God. Our bodies are holy. Because our bodies are important, our Father in Heaven wants us to take good care of them. He knows that we can be happier, better people if we are healthy. . . . For this reason He has told us which things are good for our health and which things are bad. Much of the information God has given us concerning good health is found in Doctrine and Covenants 89. This revelation is called the Word of Wisdom.[136]

There are more than just temporal, earthly reasons to follow the Word of Wisdom: "We must obey the Word of Wisdom to be worthy to enter the temple. If we do not obey the Word of Wisdom, the Lord's Spirit withdraws from us."[137] McConkie is helpful here for another summary understanding. He argues, "As a revealed law of health, dealing particularly with dietary matters, [section 89] contains both positive and negative instructions. Its affirmative provision gives directions for the use of meat and grain by both man and

---

[135] Church of Jesus Christ of Latter-day Saints, 164.
[136] Church of Jesus Christ of Latter-day Saints, 167.
[137] Church of Jesus Christ of Latter-day Saints, 167.

animals; its prohibitions direct man to refrain from the use of certain specific harmful things."[138]

The Word of Wisdom mentions three particular substances (interpreted as four specific items) that are not to be consumed by Latter-day Saints: strong drinks, tobacco, and hot drinks. McConkie explains: "By strong drinks is meant alcoholic beverages; hot drinks, according to the Prophet's own statement, mean tea and coffee. Accordingly the negative side of the Word of Wisdom is a command to abstain from *tea, coffee, tobacco*, and *liquor*."[139] Speaking about alcohol and tobacco, President Joseph F. Smith said, "Young men or middle-aged men who have had experience in the Church should not be ordained to the Priesthood nor recommended to the privileges of the House of the Lord, unless they will abstain from the use of tobacco and intoxicating drinks. This is the rule of the Church, and should be observed by all its members."[140] Likewise, then member of the Quorum of Twelve Apostles George Albert Smith, speaking of tobacco, noted:

I want to say to you, in my judgment, that the use of tobacco, a little thing as it seems to some men, has been the means of destroying their spiritual life, has been the means of driving from them the companionship of the Spirit of our Father, has alienated them from the society of good men and women, and has brought upon them the disregard and reproach of the children that have been born to them, and yet the devil will say to a man, Oh, it's only a little thing![141]

Concerning hot drinks, Joseph Smith said, "I understand that some of the people are excusing themselves in using tea and coffee, because the Lord only said 'hot drinks' in the revelation of the Word of Wisdom. Tea and coffee are what the Lord meant when he said 'hot drinks.'"[142]

Recently, much discussion has been had concerning the meaning of "hot drinks" and whether or not caffeine is forbidden or if coffee and tea are the specifically forbidden items. Interestingly, in the everyday outworking

[138] McConkie, *Mormon Doctrine*, 845.
[139] McConkie, 845.
[140] Church of Jesus Christ of Latter-day Saints, *Teachings of the Latter-day Prophets*, 740 (see chap. 2, n. 104).
[141] George Albert Smith, "Conference Talk" in *Conference Report*, ed. Church of Jesus Christ of Latter-day Saints (Salt Lake City: Church of Jesus Christ of Latter-day Saints, April 1918), 40.
[142] Church of Jesus Christ of Latter-day Saints, *Teachings of the Latter-day Prophets*, 740.

of Latter-day Saint life, caffeine is usually regarded as the issue, and many Latter-day Saints decry the use of it altogether, not just in coffee and tea. This is not just an issue within the Latter-day Saint community. Indeed, people who are not members of the LDS Church ask about the consumption of caffeine regularly and usually assume Latter-day Saints do not consume caffeine at all. The question among Latter-day Saints became so common that the April 2008 edition of *New Era* magazine published a frequently asked question concerning caffeine, as well as an official response. The question reads, "Is there anything wrong with drinking sodas with caffeine in them? Is caffeine bad? The Word of Wisdom doesn't mention it." The answer offered by the authors reads, simply, "Doctrine and Covenants 89:9 says we shouldn't drink 'hot drinks.' The only official interpretation of this term is the statement made by early Church leaders that it means tea and coffee. Caffeine is not specifically mentioned as the reason not to drink these drinks."[143] Similarly, in response to an NBC News broadcast in 2012, the LDS Church issued a statement on its website concerning issues with the broadcast in an effort to clarify misconceptions. The Mormon Newsroom blog states, "Finally, another small correction: Despite what was reported, the Church revelation spelling out health practices does not mention the use of caffeine. The Church's health guidelines prohibit alcoholic drinks, smoking or chewing of tobacco, and 'hot drinks'—taught by Church leaders to refer specifically to tea and coffee."[144] Therefore, it should be understood that caffeine is not specifically forbidden, but coffee and tea are. Further, the temperature of the coffee and tea is of no importance, even though the Word of Wisdom specifically designates "hot drinks" as forbidden. Hot or iced coffee, along with hot or iced tea, are forbidden for use by Latter-day Saints.

In summary, the Word of Wisdom is intended for Latter-day Saints not as an exhaustive list, but as an overall philosophy of health. *Gospel Principles* states:

> We should avoid anything that we know is harmful to our bodies. We
> should not use any substance that is habit forming. We should also

---

[143] Church of Jesus Christ of Latter-day Saints, "Is there anything wrong with drinking sodas with caffeine in them? Is caffeine bad? The Word of Wisdom doesn't mention it" in *New Era*, April 2008, 41.

[144] Church of Jesus Christ of Latter-day Saints, "Mormonism in the News: Getting It Right, August 29," *The Newsroom Blog*, posted August 29, 2012, http://www.mormonnewsroom.org/article/mormonism-news--getting-it-right-august-29.

avoid overeating. The Word of Wisdom does not tell us everything to avoid or consume, but it does give us guidelines. It is a valuable temporal law. It is also a great spiritual law. By living the Word of Wisdom, we become stronger spiritually. We purify our bodies so the Spirit of the Lord can dwell with us.[145]

Charity, Honesty, and Tithes and Offerings

The next three items that impact the daily life of the Latter-day Saint all relate, to some degree, to finances. Charity is defined simply as "that pure love which our Savior Jesus Christ has. He has commanded us to love one another as He loves us. The scriptures tell us that charity comes from a pure heart. We have pure love when, from the heart, we show genuine concern and compassion for all our brothers and sisters."[146] Similarly, charity is described as the most desirable of all virtues attainable by Latter-day Saints. "Above all the attributes of godliness and perfection, *charity* is the one most devoutly to be desired. Charity is more than love, far more; it is everlasting love, perfect love, the pure love of Christ which endureth forever. It is love so centered in righteousness that the possessor has no aim or desire except for the eternal welfare of his own soul and for the souls of those around him."[147]

Charity is not an implanted human behavior. Indeed, it must be given from above. Millet writes:

We must pray for charity. We must plead for it. We must ask with all the energy of heart to be so endowed. As we do so, there will come moments of surpassing import, sublime moments in which our whole souls seem to reach out to others with a kind of fellowship and affection that we would not otherwise know. Such love is beyond anything earthly, above and beyond anything that mortals can explain or produce. It provides moral courage to those who face difficult challenges. It unites husbands, wives, and children and grants them a foretaste of eternal life. It welds classes and congregations and wards and stakes in a union that is the foundation for Zion. And it comes from the Lord, who is the source of all that is godlike.[148]

---

[145] Church of Jesus Christ of Latter-day Saints, *Gospel Principles*, 169.
[146] Church of Jesus Christ of Latter-day Saints, 173.
[147] McConkie, *Mormon Doctrine*, 121.
[148] Robert L. Millet, "Charity," in Millet et al., *LDS Beliefs*, 102.

Not only must charity be practiced as it is given from above; it is one of the principles in the life of the Latter-day Saint that leads to exaltation. *Gospel Principles* notes, "Jesus taught that we should give food to the hungry, shelter to those who have none, and clothes to the poor. When we visit the sick and those who are in prison, it is as if we were doing these things for Him instead. He promises that as we do these things, we will inherit His kingdom."[149] In a similar vein, McConkie declares, "Charity is a gift of the Spirit which must be gained if one is to have salvation."[150]

Similar to charity, honesty is a necessary aspect of Latter-day Saint life. Article of Faith 13 states, "We believe in being honest." Bruce McConkie explains further:

> Perfect *honesty* is one of the invarying characteristics exhibited by all who are worthy to be numbered with the saints of God. Honest persons are fair and truthful in speech, straightforward in their dealings, free from deceit, and above cheating, stealing, misrepresentation, or any other fraudulent action. Honesty is the companion of truth, dishonesty of falsehood; honesty is of God, dishonesty of the devil, for he was a liar from the beginning.[151]

Within a Latter-day Saint framework, honesty goes further than simply telling the truth and refusing to cheat or commit some sort of fraud. There is a significant spiritual consequence that comes with honesty. Indeed, *Gospel Principles* declares candidly, "Complete honesty is necessary for our salvation."[152] This idea of complete honesty means being extremely vigilant about one's actions and words. "To become completely honest, we must look carefully at our lives. If there are ways in which we are being even the least bit dishonest, we should repent of them immediately. When we are completely honest, we cannot be corrupted. We are true to every trust, duty, agreement, or covenant, even if it costs us money, friends, or our lives."[153] Former member of the Quorum of Twelve Apostles Mark E. Petersen, during the October 1971 General Conference, said:

---

[149] Church of Jesus Christ of Latter-day Saints, *Gospel Principles*, 175.
[150] McConkie, *Mormon Doctrine*, 121.
[151] McConkie, 364.
[152] Church of Jesus Christ of Latter-day Saints, *Gospel Principles*, 182.
[153] Church of Jesus Christ of Latter-day Saints, 182.

But we do not believe in honesty merely as a matter of policy. It is far more important than that. Honesty is a principle of salvation in the kingdom of God. Without it there can be no salvation. Just as no man or woman can be saved without baptism, so no one can be saved without honesty. As we cannot advance in the kingdom of heaven without a resurrection, so we cannot move into celestial realms without honesty.[154]

The final cog in the gears of this particular line of thinking deals with tithes and offerings. Doctrine and Covenants 119:4 reads, "And after that, those who have thus been tithed shall pay one-tenth of all their interest annually; and this shall be a standing law unto them forever, for my holy priesthood, saith the Lord." President Howard W. Hunter offered a simple explanation of this text. He said, "The law is simply stated as 'one-tenth of all their interest.' Interest means profit, compensation, increase. It is the wage of one employed, the profit from the operation of a business, the increase of one who grows or produces, or the income to a person from any other source."[155] McConkie explains further:

One tenth of the *interest* or *increase* of each member of the Church is payable as *tithing* into the *tithing funds* of the Church *each year*. Salaries, wages, bequests, inheritances, the increase of flocks, herds, and crops, and all income of whatever nature are subject to the law of tithing. Payment of the requisite tenth does not comply with the law unless the property and money so donated go into the tithing funds of the Church; it is not left with the individual to choose where his tithing contributions shall be made.[156]

The LDS Church uses the tithes of Latter-day Saints for several projects. *Gospel Principles* notes that tithes are used to (1) "build, maintain, and operate temples, meetinghouses, and other buildings"; (2) "provide operating funds for stakes, wards, and other units of the Church"; (3) "help the missionary program"; (4) "educate young people in Church schools, seminaries, and

---

[154] Mark E. Petersen, "Conference talk" in *Conference Report*, ed. The Church of Jesus Christ of Latter-day Saints (Salt Lake City: The Church of Jesus Christ of Latter-day Saints, October, 1971), 63.

[155] Howard W. Hunter, "Conference Talk" in *Conference Report*, ed. Church of Jesus Christ of Latter-day Saints (Salt Lake City: Church of Jesus Christ of Latter-day Saints, April 1964), 35.

[156] McConkie, *Mormon Doctrine*, 796.

institutes"; (5) "print and distribute lesson materials"; and (6) "help in family history and temple work."[157]

And though the tithes of faithful Latter-day Saints are for the building up of the LDS Church and its work on the earth, tithes are also required for entrance into the celestial kingdom of heaven. McConkie explains: *"Payment of an honest tithing is essential to the attainment of those great blessings which the Lord has in store for his saints.* Indeed, the law of consecration itself is the celestial law of property and money, and to gain the celestial world man must be able to abide this higher law, to say nothing of the lesser law of tithing."[158]

Once per year, all Latter-day Saints are required to consult with their bishop in something called a *tithing settlement*, that is, an accounting of one's tithing to make sure a full and complete tithe has been paid. McConkie explains:

> As the end of each year certain convenient days are set apart for *tithing settlement.* On these days church members are privileged to go over their personal tithing records with their bishop, and to receive counsel from him, so that the tithing status of each member is clearly known both to him and his ecclesiastical judge. As a matter of wisdom, tithing should be paid when income is received, though it is possible to comply with the law by a lump sum contribution at the time of tithing settlement.[159]

Missionary Work

Like most faith groups around the world, the Church of Jesus Christ of Latter-day Saints is a missionary organization. All faithful Latter-day Saints are expected to serve as missionaries in order to spread the message of the LDS church around the world. As of 2017, there were 104,641 full-time and Church-service missionaries serving for the LDS Church.[160] *Gospel Principles* declares, "The Lord's Church has always been a missionary church. When the Savior lived on the earth, He ordained Apostles and Seventies and gave them the authority and responsibility to preach the gospel."[161] Further:

---

[157] Church of Jesus Christ of Latter-day Saints, *Gospel Principles*, 186–87.
[158] McConkie, *Mormon Doctrine*, 797.
[159] McConkie, 799.
[160] Church of Jesus Christ of Latter-day Saints, "2016 Statistical Report for 2017 April Conference," Newsroom, April 1, 2017, http://www.mormonnewsroom.org/article/2016-statistical-report-2017-april-conference.
[161] Church of Jesus Christ of Latter-day Saints, *Gospel Principles*, 189.

Since that time, over one million missionaries have been called and sent forth to preach the gospel. The message they take to the world is that Jesus Christ is the Son of God and our Savior. They testify that the gospel has been restored to the earth through a prophet of God. The missionaries are given the responsibility to preach the gospel to all people, to baptize them, and to teach them to do all the things that the Lord has commanded. Latter-day Saint missionaries go at their own expense to all parts of the world to preach the gospel message.[162]

The purpose of the missionary, as stated by the LDS missionary manual *Preach My Gospel*, is as follows:

You are called to represent Jesus Christ in helping people become clean from their sins. You do this by inviting them to come unto Jesus Christ and become converted to His restored gospel. To come to the Savior they must have faith in Him unto repentance—making the necessary changes to bring their life into agreement with His teachings. You can help people develop such faith by teaching them the restored gospel by the Spirit and inviting them to commit to live according to its teachings. Keeping this commitment prepares them for the covenants of baptism and confirmation and the precious gift of the Holy Ghost.[163]

As an LDS missionary, you can declare success when you've accomplished the following:

[You] feel the Spirit testify to people through you; love people and desire their salvation; obey with exactness; live so that you can receive and know how to follow the Spirit, who will show you where to go, what to do, and what to say; develop Christlike attributes; work effectively every day, do your very best to bring souls to Christ, and seek earnestly to learn and improve; help build up the Church wherever you are assigned to work; warn people of the consequences of sin; invite [people] to make and keep commitments; teach and serve other missionaries; [and] go about doing good and serving people at every opportunity, whether or not they accept your message.[164]

---

[162] Church of Jesus Christ of Latter-day Saints, 191.
[163] Church of Jesus Christ of Latter-day Saints, *Preach My Gospel,* 2 (see chap. 3, n. 27).
[164] Church of Jesus Christ of Latter-day Saints, 10–11.

Put concisely, "your purpose [as a missionary] is to invite others to come unto Christ by helping them receive the restored gospel through faith in Jesus Christ and His Atonement, repentance, baptism, receiving the Holy Ghost, and enduring to the end."[165]

Again, like previous issues addressed in this chapter, missionary work is about more than those with whom the missionary is sharing. Personal spiritual benefits may also be reaped from performing missionary work. "The Lord told the Prophet Joseph Smith that missionaries would receive great blessings."[166] Those blessings may very well entail entrance into the celestial kingdom. *Gospel Principles* states, "[Jesus Christ] has also said that those who work for the salvation of others will have their sins forgiven and will bring salvation to their own souls."[167]

Developing Our Talents, Obedience

For Latter-day Saints, talents and abilities are special gifts received in the premortal existence and retained when gaining a human body on the earth. They are received directly from God, and He expects them to be used for the betterment of oneself, others, and society as a whole.

> We all have special gifts, talents, and abilities given to us by our Heavenly Father. When we were born, we brought these gifts, talents, and abilities with us. . . . We have a responsibility to develop the talents we have been given. Sometimes we think we do not have many talents or that other people have been blessed with more abilities than we possess. Sometimes we do not use our talents because we are afraid that we might fail or be criticized by others. We should not hide our talents. We should use them. Then others can see our good works and glorify our Heavenly Father.[168]

And like other items previously discussed, talents and abilities are used not only for the building up of others, but for oneself as well and for one's eternal status. *Gospel Principles* states:

---

[165] Church of Jesus Christ of Latter-day Saints, 11.
[166] Church of Jesus Christ of Latter-day Saints, *Gospel Principles*, 194.
[167] Church of Jesus Christ of Latter-day Saints, 194.
[168] Church of Jesus Christ of Latter-day Saints, 197.

A talent is one kind of stewardship. The parable of the talents tells us that when we serve well in our stewardship, we will be given greater responsibilities. If we do not serve well, our stewardship will eventually be taken from us. We are also told in the scriptures that we will be judged according to our works. By developing and using our talents for other people, we perform good works. The Lord is pleased when we use our talents wisely. He will bless us if we use our talents to benefit other people and to build up His kingdom here on earth. Some of the blessings we gain are joy and love from serving our brothers and sisters here on earth. We also learn self-control. All these things are necessary if we are going to be worthy to live with our Heavenly Father again.[169]

Thus, it can be said that though talents are not directly linked to entrance into the celestial kingdom, the development of one's talents and the use of them for the sake of others will then develop further personal attributes necessary for entrance into the celestial kingdom. In this way, talents are an indirect door through which the celestial kingdom is found.

Obedience is the opposite side of the same coin and the way by which Latter-day Saints can show their love for Heavenly Father and Jesus Christ. Brent L. Top writes, "Obedience—willfully submitting to the commandments of God and seeking to conform one's life to his mind and will—is foundational and fundamental to one's Christian discipleship."[170] Similarly, in 1921, President Heber J. Grant offered his understanding of the need for obedience:

Of what good is our faith, our repentance, our baptism, and all the sacred ordinances of the gospel by which we have been made ready to receive the blessings of the Lord, if we fail, on our part, to keep the commandments? All that we expect, or all that we are promised, is predicated on our own actions, and if we fail to act, or to do the work which God has required of us, we are little better than those who have not received the principles and ordinances of the gospel. We have only started, and when we rest there, we are not following our faith by our works, and are under condemnation, our salvation is not attained.[171]

---

[169] Church of Jesus Christ of Latter-day Saints, 199.
[170] Brent L. Top, "Obedience" in Millet et al., *LDS Beliefs*, 455.
[171] Church of Jesus Christ of Latter-day Saints, *Teachings of the Latter-day Prophets*, 436.

McConkie, likewise, adds, "*Obedience* is the first law of heaven, the corner-stone upon which all righteousness and progression rest. It consists in compliance with divine law, in conformity to the mind and will of Deity, in complete subjugation to God and his commands. To obey gospel law is to yield obedience to the Lord, to execute the commands of and be ruled by him whose we are."[172]

Obedience, though, is more than showing one's faithfulness to Heavenly Father and Jesus Christ. There is a sacramental element as well. McConkie notes, "All men are commanded to believe the gospel, repent of their sins, enter in at the gate of baptism, get on the strait and narrow path, and endure to the end in righteousness by obedience to all the laws and ordinances of the gospel. They thereby attain a hope of eternal life in the kingdom of God."[173] *Gospel Principles* teaches:

> Each of us should ask ourselves why we obey God's commandments. Is it because we fear punishment? Is it because we desire the rewards for living a good life? Is it because we love God and Jesus Christ and want to serve Them? It is better to obey the commandments because we fear punishment than not to obey them at all. But we will be much happier if we obey God because we love Him and want to obey Him. When we obey Him freely, He can bless us freely. . . . Obedience also helps us progress and become more like our Heavenly Father. But those who do nothing until they are commanded and then keep the commandments unwillingly lose their reward. . . . By keeping God's commandments, we prepare for eternal life and exaltation.[174]

Former member of the Quorum of Twelve Apostles Mark E. Peterson said:

> One of the great things about the gospel is that the Lord determined that in order for us to become like him we must be held strictly in a certain line of living. We must make it clear to ourselves as we study the gospel that there is a definite way that we must travel and that we must not vary from it. The gospel is very specific. We cannot vary from the way the Lord gives us because we must consider the commandments as a formula whereby we may build into ourselves the

---

[172] McConkie, *Mormon Doctrine*, 539.
[173] McConkie, 540.
[174] Church of Jesus Christ of Latter-day Saints, *Gospel Principles*, 201–2.

Christlike traits of character that were required, and in doing so then we become Christlike.[175]

Similarly, President Spencer W. Kimball noted, "All blessings, then, are conditional upon faithfulness. One is ordained to the priesthood with a conditional promise; one is married and sealed in the temple on condition of his faithfulness. And so far as I know there is nothing—no blessing in the world— that anyone can receive except through faithfulness."[176] Former member of the Quorum of Twelve Apostles Delbert L. Stapley, during the October 1977 General Conference, said:

> One goal that most of us share in this life is the desire to achieve true joy and lasting happiness. There is only one way to do this, and that is by being obedient to all the commandments of God. As members of The Church of Jesus Christ of Latter-day Saints, we have voluntarily entered into holy covenants, promising to obey the Lord's commandments. Willing, righteous obedience leads to celestial life: indeed, there is no eternal progress without it.[177]

Indeed, *True to the Faith*, an officially published manual like *Gospel Principles*, states, "God gives commandments for your benefit. They are loving instructions for your happiness and your physical and spiritual well-being. The Prophet Joseph Smith taught that obedience to the commandments leads to blessings from God."[178]

The idea of obedience also extends to following the current members of the First Presidency and the Quorum of Twelve Apostles, all regarded as prophets, seers, and revelators. In 2015, then president Thomas S. Monson wrote, "If you want to see the light of heaven, if you want to feel the inspiration of Almighty God, if you want to have that feeling within your bosom that your Heavenly Father is guiding you, then follow the prophets of God. When

---

[175] Mark E. Peterson, "Conference Talk" in *Area Conference Report*, ed. Church of Jesus Christ of Latter-day Saints (Manchester, UK: Church of Jesus Christ of Latter-day Saints, 1976), 11.

[176] Church of Jesus Christ of Latter-day Saints, ed., *Teachings of the Latter-day Prophets*, 436.

[177] Delbert L. Stapley, "Conference Address" in *Conference Report*, ed. Church of Jesus Christ of Latter-day Saints (Salt Lake City: Church of Jesus Christ of Latter-day Saints, October 1977), 26.

[178] Church of Jesus Christ of Latter-day Saints, *True to the Faith* (Salt Lake City: Church of Jesus Christ of Latter-day Saints, 2004), 108–9.

you follow the prophets, you will be in safe territory."[179] Likewise, William R. Walker, former member of the First Quorum of Seventy, during a Church Educational System devotional, said, "I count it a blessing to live in the day when Thomas S. Monson is the Lord's prophet. As we follow him and try to be more like him, we will inevitably succeed in being more faithful disciples of the Lord Jesus Christ."[180] In June 1981, then member of the Quorum of Twelve Apostles Ezra Taft Benson gave a talk entitled "Fourteen Fundamentals in Following the Prophet." Some of those fundamentals include "the living prophet is more vital to us than the Standard Works," "the living prophet is more important to us than a dead prophet," and "the prophet and the presidency—the living prophet and the First Presidency—follow them and be blessed—reject them and suffer."[181]

The Family

Within the idea of the family, *Gospel Principles* lists four specific subcategories: the eternal nature of the family, family responsibilities, eternal marriage, and the law of chastity. The family unit within Latter-day Saint life is, without question, the most important unit in the LDS Church. Indeed, in 1995, the members of the First Presidency and the Quorum of Twelve Apostles issued a statement entitled "The Family: A Proclamation to the World."[182] This statement, because it was issued by the two highest governing bodies, is the LDS Church's official stance on the family and its official statement on matters of the family. It begins, "We, the First Presidency and the Council of the Twelve Apostles of The Church of Jesus Christ of Latter-day Saints, solemnly proclaim that marriage between a man and a woman is ordained of God and that the family is central to the Creator's plan for the eternal destiny of His children." The document continues, "The family is ordained of God. Marriage between man and woman is essential to His eternal plan." In closing, the LDS leaders warn, "We warn that individuals who violate covenants of chastity, who abuse spouse or offspring, or who fail to fulfill family responsibilities will

---

[179] Thomas S. Monson, "Follow the Prophets," *Ensign,* January 2015, 5.
[180] William R. Walker, "Follow the Prophet," *Ensign,* April 2014, 41.
[181] Ezra Taft Benson, "Fourteen Fundamentals in Following the Prophet," address given February 26, 1980, Brigham Young University, *Liahona,* June 1981, https://www.lds.org/liahona/1981/06/fourteen-fundamentals-in-following-the-prophet?lang=eng.
[182] The quotations in this paragraph are from the First Presidency and Council of the Twelve Apostles of the Church of Jesus Christ of Latter-day Saints, "The Family: A Proclamation to the World," September 23, 1995, https://www.lds.org/topics/family-proclamation?lang=eng&old=true.

one day stand accountable before God. Further, we warn that the disintegration of the family will bring upon individuals, communities, and nations the calamities foretold by ancient and modern prophets."

Gospel Principles offers a brief explanation for the foundation of this strong belief in the family unit. It reads:

> After Heavenly Father brought Adam and Eve together in marriage, He commanded them to have children. He has revealed that one of the purposes of marriage is to provide mortal bodies for His spirit children. Parents are partners with our Heavenly Father. He wants each of His spirit children to receive a physical body and to experience earth life. When a man and a woman bring children into this world, they help our Heavenly Father carry out His plan.[183]

Brent L. Top explains:

> Latter-day Saints have a unique understanding of how "the family is ordained of God" because of our belief that we lived in a family setting as spirits before we came to earth, that the family is the basic unit of society on earth, that at death the righteous will also be organized by families in the post-earth spirit world, and that family relationships will continue for those resurrected and exalted in God's celestial kingdom. Before we were born on earth, we lived in the family of God, where we were taught, reared, and nurtured by Heavenly Parents. We observed and were part of a celestial family—seeing how perfect parents love and nurture their beloved children. We understood that the plan of salvation provided the means whereby we could be united as families throughout all eternity in a state of perfect happiness and joy.[184]

Not only were families together and of utmost importance in the premortal spirit world and at present; they can also be together in the afterlife in the postmortal spirit world. *Gospel Principles* explains:

> Families can be together forever. To enjoy this blessing we must be married in the temple. When people are married outside the temple,

---

[183] Church of Jesus Christ of Latter-day Saints, *Gospel Principles*, 207.
[184] Brent L. Top, "Family" in Millet et al., *LDS Beliefs*, 211.

the marriage ends when one of the partners dies. When we are married in the temple by the authority of the Melchizedek Priesthood, we are married for time and eternity. If we keep our covenants with the Lord, our families will be united eternally as husband, wife, and children. Death cannot separate us.[185]

Brent Top adds, "The eternal family comes full circle—premortal spirit sons and daughters organized in a heavenly family, born and reared in earthly homes, reunited with and organized by families in the postmortal spirit world, and, if true to their covenants, resurrected to celestial glory, sealed to their earthly family, and endowed with power to create an eternal family unit."[186] McConkie notes, "*Eternal families* have their beginning in celestial marriage here in mortality. Faithful members of them continue in the family unit in eternity, in the highest heaven of the celestial world, where they have eternal increase."[187]

In summary, *Gospel Principles* offers the following: "The family is the most important unit in The Church of Jesus Christ of Latter-day Saints. The Church exists to help families gain eternal blessings and exaltation. The organizations and programs within the Church are designed to strengthen us individually and help us live as families forever."[188] Indeed, marriage and family are so important for Latter-day Saints that *Gospel Principles* declares:

> Our exaltation depends on marriage, along with other principles and ordinances, such as faith, repentance, baptism, and receiving the gift of the Holy Ghost. We believe that marriage is the most sacred relationship that can exist between a man and a woman. This sacred relationship affects our happiness now and in the eternities. . . . Some of the blessings we can enjoy for eternity are as follows: 1. We can live in the highest degree of the celestial kingdom of God. 2. We can be exalted as God is and receive a fulness of joy.[189]

---

[185] Church of Jesus Christ of Latter-day Saints, *Gospel Principles*, 209.
[186] Top, "Family," 212–13.
[187] McConkie, *Mormon Doctrine*, 273.
[188] Church of Jesus Christ of Latter-day Saints, *Gospel Principles*, 211.
[189] Church of Jesus Christ of Latter-day Saints, 219–21.

Millet also summarizes the Latter-day Saint understanding of the family well. He writes, "And surely heaven could never be heaven without our family."[190]

Temple Work and Family History

The final tooth in the cog for entrance into the exalted level of the celestial kingdom is temple and family history work. These complementary works are of utmost importance to Latter-day Saints and are a regular thought in their daily life. Temples are of such importance that, as of this writing, there are 159 operating temples with 11 more under construction and 12 announced for construction. In fact, the importance of temples cannot be overstated. *True to the Faith* states, "The principal purpose of temples is to provide the ordinances necessary for our exaltation in the celestial kingdom. Temple ordinances lead to the greatest blessings available through the Atonement of Jesus Christ. All we do in Church—our meetings and activities, our missionary efforts, the lessons we teach and the hymns we sing—should point us to the Savior and the work we do in holy temples. . . . Only the home can compare with temples in sacredness."[191] Andrew C. Skinner wrote, "Temples are places of eternal linking: families are linked together forever; the living are linked to their kindred dead; heaven and earth are linked as one; worshippers are linked to the Savior."[192] McConkie writes:

> Holy sanctuaries wherein sacred ordinances, rites, and ceremonies are performed which pertain to salvation and exaltation in the kingdom of God are called *temples*. They are the most sacred places of worship on earth; each one is literally a *House of the Lord*, a house of the great Creator, a house where he and his Spirit may dwell, to which he may come, or send his messengers, to confer priesthood and keys and to give revelation to his people.[193]

Similarly, *Gospel Principles* declare:

> Temples of The Church of Jesus Christ of Latter-day Saints are special buildings dedicated to the Lord. Worthy Church members may

---

[190] Robert L. Millet, *Precept upon Precept* (Salt Lake City: Deseret, 2016), 344.
[191] Church of Jesus Christ of Latter-day Saints, *True to the Faith*, 170.
[192] Andrew C. Skinner, "Temples" in Millet et al., *LDS Beliefs*, 616.
[193] McConkie, *Mormon Doctrine*, 780.

go there to receive sacred ordinances and make covenants with God. Like baptism, these ordinances and covenants are necessary for our salvation. They must be performed in the temples of the Lord. We also go to the temple to learn more about Heavenly Father and His Son, Jesus Christ. We gain a better understanding of our purpose in life and our relationship with Heavenly Father and Jesus Christ. We are taught about our premortal existence, the meaning of earth life, and life after death.[194]

Probably one of the most-asked-about subjects finding its center in the temple is the topic of Latter-day Saint temple garments. *True to the Faith* explains:

Once you are endowed, you have the blessing of wearing the temple garment throughout your life. You are obligated to wear it according to the instructions given in the endowment. Remember that the blessings that are related to this sacred privilege depend on your worthiness and your faithfulness in keeping temple covenants. The garment provides a constant reminder of the covenants you have made in the temple. You should treat it with respect at all times. You should not expose it to the view of those who do not understand its significance, and you should not adjust it to accommodate different styles of clothing. When you wear it properly, it provides protection against temptation and evil. Wearing the garment is an outward expression of an inward commitment to follow the Savior.[195]

Similarly, the Mormon Newsroom, the official media outlet for the LDS Church, posted an article in 2014 about the temple garments. The article states:

Temple garments are worn by adult members of the Church who have made sacred promises of fidelity to God's commandments and the gospel of Jesus Christ in temples of The Church of Jesus Christ of Latter-day Saints. To Church members, the modest temple garment, worn under normal clothing, along with the symbolic vestments worn during temple worship, represent the sacred and personal aspect of

---

[194] Church of Jesus Christ of Latter-day Saints, *Gospel Principles*, 235.
[195] Church of Jesus Christ of Latter-day Saints, *True to the Faith*, 173.

their relationship with God and their commitment to live good, honorable lives.[196]

Temples are more, though, than specialized buildings for teaching the living. They also function as intermediary points of connection for the salvation for the dead. Within temples, endowments, baptisms, and sealings (weddings) are performed for the living and also for, and on behalf of, the dead. *Gospel Principles* states, "Many of our ancestors are among those who died without hearing about the gospel while on the earth. They now live in the spirit world. There they are taught the gospel of Jesus Christ. Those who have accepted the gospel are waiting for the temple ordinances to be performed for them. As we perform these ordinances in the temple for our ancestors, we can share their joy."[197] Similarly, *True to the Faith* teaches, "People who have died without essential gospel ordinances may receive those ordinances through the work done in temples. You may do this work in behalf of your ancestors and others who have died. Acting for them, you can be baptized and confirmed, receive the endowment, and participate in the sealings of husband to wife and children to parents."[198] The authors also assert, "As you receive priesthood ordinances in behalf of those who have died, you become a savior on Mount Zion for them. Your effort approaches the spirit of the Savior's atoning sacrifice—you perform a saving work for others that they cannot do."[199]

As mentioned, one of the important issues within temple work is performing temple rituals for, and on behalf of, those who have died. To find those individuals, "Latter-day Saints are encouraged to participate in family history activities. Through these activities we learn about our ancestors so that we can perform ordinances for them. Family history involves three basic steps: 1. Identify our ancestors. 2. Find out which ancestors need temple ordinances performed. 3. Make certain that the ordinances are performed for them."[200] To identify these ancestors, significant genealogical and family history work must be performed. McConkie affirms:

---

[196] Church of Jesus Christ of Latter-day Saints, "Temple Garments," Mormon Newsroom, accessed January 31, 2018, http://www.mormonnewsroom.org/article/temple-garments.
[197] Church of Jesus Christ of Latter-day Saints, *Gospel Principles*, 236.
[198] Church of Jesus Christ of Latter-day Saints, *True to the Faith*, 171–72.
[199] Church of Jesus Christ of Latter-day Saints, 63.
[200] Church of Jesus Christ of Latter-day Saints, *Gospel Principles*, 236.

Before vicarious ordinances of salvation and exaltation may be performed for those who have died without a knowledge of the gospel, but who presumably would have received it had the opportunity come to them, they must be accurately and properly identified. Hence, *genealogical research* is required. To aid its members in intelligent and effective research, the Church maintains in Salt Lake City one of the world's greatest *genealogical societies*. Much of the genealogical source material of various nations of the earth has been or is being microfilmed by this society; millions of dollars is being spent; and a reservoir of millions of names and other data about people who lived in past generations is available for study.[201]

Conclusion

As can be seen, Latter-day Saint soteriology is both simple and complex. It is simple because the fourth Article of Faith states that Latter-day Saints believe salvation rests in faith, repentance, baptism, and the reception of the Holy Ghost. However, it is complex because the third Article of Faith states all humans may have salvation "by obedience to the laws and ordinances of the Gospel." It is simple because faith, repentance, baptism, and the reception of the Holy Ghost are not multifaceted. It is complex because of the multitiered system of the afterlife and the various sets of laws (telestial, terrestrial, and celestial) one must keep in order to enter the various kingdoms of the postmortal existence. It is simple because faith, repentance, baptism, and the gift of the Holy Ghost are identifiable markers. It is complex because no authoritative list exists to delineate for Latter-day Saints the exact nature of telestial, terrestrial, or celestial law. One can deduce a potential set of laws to be followed, but without an authoritative set, the average Latter-day Saint can never be sure if he is doing all the things required for exaltation. One only needs to look to Spencer W. Kimball's infamous *The Miracle of Forgiveness* to see how difficult average life can be for a Latter-day Saint.[202]

---

[201] McConkie, *Mormon Doctrine*, 308–9.

[202] Spencer W. Kimball's *The Miracle of Forgiveness*, first published in 1969, was, as *Salt Lake Tribune* writer Peggy Fletcher Stack wrote, a "much-circulated 1969 treatise on guilt, wrongdoing, and repentance by then-apostle Kimball." See Peggy Fletcher Stack, "LDS Classic 'Miracle of Forgiveness' Fading Away, and Some Mormons Say It's Time," *Salt Lake Tribune*, July 24, 2015, http://archive.sltrib.com/article.php?id=2762815&itype=CMSID.

For all intents and purposes, the Latter-day Saint must rely on 2 Nephi 25:23 and whatever interpretation of that verse he finds helpful: "For we labor diligently to write, to persuade our children, and also our brethren, to believe in Christ, and to be reconciled to God; for we know that it is by grace that we are saved, after all we can do." Though some Latter-day Saint authors, at least to some degree, dismiss this verse, the catalog found in *Gospel Principles* seems to create a significant list of those things humans can do. Likewise, Latter-day Saints can rely on encouragement from their leaders. Elder Neil L. Anderson of the Quorum of Twelve Apostles said:

> Your spiritual destiny will have obstacles, delays, and equipment mal-functions. There will be mistakes. You may wonder if you are going to make it. Don't be discouraged! You will also have moments of hope and faith as doors open and obstacles are overcome. Continue, persist, above all, believe in Christ and learn to follow Him and His prophets; endure, as Nephi said, with a "brightness of hope" (2 Nephi 31:20). As you do, I promise you, one day you will hear your name. You will make it.[203]

[203] Neil L. Anderson, "Don't Be Discouraged" in *We're with You: Counsel and Encouragement from Your Brethren*, comp. Deseret Book (Salt Lake City: Deseret, 2016), 280.

Chapter 5

History and Organization

A s we have seen over the preceding chapters, the Church of Jesus Christ of Latter-day Saints is indeed a large organization with complex systems and beliefs. It also has a complex and fascinating history, a look at which will help inform our current study. One major aspect of their history is their reason for existence in the first place, specifically, something Latter-day Saints call the Great Apostasy and the Restoration. Also intimately connected to their history and the apostasy is their understanding of church polity. All of these issues will be addressed in this chapter.

History

The Church of Jesus Christ of Latter-day Saints was started in the midst of ongoing religious fervor and revivalism during the mid-nineteenth century. The history of the LDS Church begins with its founder, Joseph Smith Jr. Born December 23, 1805, in Sharon, Vermont, to Joseph and Lucy Mack Smith, Joseph Jr. would soon have an impact on the religious landscape of the world that none could have imagined.

Raised in the context of a Christian home, Joseph was interested in religion from an early age. He frequently visited the local Methodist, Baptist, and Presbyterian churches to ask questions of the ministers from the varied denominations. He posed the same questions to each minister but received differing answers. Joseph was greatly bothered by the seeming lack of unity between the three Christian denominations represented around his home.

During a personal Bible study one evening in his parents' home, young Smith came to Jas 1:5: "If any of you lack wisdom, let him ask of God, that

giveth to all men liberally, and upbraideth not; and it shall be given him"
(KJV). This passage sparked Joseph's interest, leading him to walk out into
a grove of woods nearby to seek after God's will. According to the officially
accepted account of the events in the grove, Joseph began praying upon arrival
and, soon after he started praying, his First Vision purportedly took place.[1]
Smith recounted being visited by God the Father and Christ the Son during
this vision. The two personages supposedly told him not to join any currently
existing church because God was repulsed by their creeds. Joseph hurried back
home and began telling family members and friends about his vision.

The next major event in Smith's life came on the evening of September
21, 1823, when he allegedly received another heavenly visitor. This vision,
however, was different. In the 1820 vision, Joseph was given only general
information about not joining any existing church. In 1823, the heavenly messenger, the angel Moroni, informed Joseph of the existence of a book of golden
plates. Moroni told Smith that he would unearth the buried plates and would
eventually translate them. Smith was also given the exact location of the plates
and was told he would receive specific instructions as to when he could uncover the plates and begin the work of translation. After attempting to gain access
to the plates earlier than instructed (Smith tried to uncover the plates the next
day, September 22, 1823), Moroni visited Smith again and told him he would
not be able to unearth the plates until September 22, 1827.

The expected day arrived and Smith returned to the Hill Cumorah, the
location of the plates, and removed the plates from the hill. Along with the
plates, Smith also received a breastplate and a pair of "seer stones" set into
something resembling primitive spectacles, which he called the Urim and
Thummim. Smith began the translation process. David Whitmer, a leader in
the early church, described this process:

> Smith would put the seer stone into a hat, and put his face in the hat,
> drawing it closely around his face to exclude the light; and in the dark-
> ness the spiritual light would shine. A piece of something resembling
> parchment would appear, and on that appeared the writing. Under it
> was the interpretation in English. Brother Joseph would read off the
> English to Oliver Cowdry, who was his principal scribe, and when
> it was written down and repeated to Brother Joseph to see if it was

---

[1] For an excellent discussion of the other accounts of Smith's First Vision, see Abanes, *One
Nation under Gods,* 14–22 (see chap. 3, n. 145).

correct, then it would disappear, and another character with the interpretation would appear. Thus the Book of Mormon was translated by the gift and power of God, and not by any power of man.[2]

With the production and publication of the Book of Mormon, Smith was able to begin spreading his message to a wider audience and soon found that people were listening to the message. On April 6, 1830, approximately thirty believers met in Fayette, New York, in the home of David Whitmer, and organized the Church of Christ. Six people were listed as founders of this new church, and Joseph Smith and Oliver Cowdry were unanimously received and elected as the teachers of the Church. At first the Church was called the Church of Christ, but as early as 1831 members began referring to themselves as "saints." On May 3, 1834, while in Kirtland, Ohio, a revelation was purportedly received by Smith, renaming the church the Church of the Latter-day Saints. Finally, on April 26, 1838, a revelation was reportedly received in which the name was officially changed to the Church of Jesus Christ of Latter-day Saints. After the Latter-day Saints moved to Kirtland, Ohio, to escape persecution, the church grew very rapidly and a temple was constructed in Kirtland. Nonmembers had a strong dislike for the Latter-day Saints because of the political power the group wielded in the small town of Kirtland and because their beliefs varied from orthodox Christianity. In fact, in 1832, Joseph was tarred and feathered by a mob in Kirtland because of reports that he had made sexual advances toward a seventeen-year-old girl in the community. After persecution became unbearable, Joseph received a revelation instructing the Latter-day Saints to leave Kirtland and move to Missouri. Eventually settling in Independence, Missouri, the Latter-day Saints enjoyed relative peace, but, as had happened in the past, persecution quickly replaced the peace and stability of the new location. Smith received another revelation relocating the Latter-day Saints to Far West, Missouri, where the Saints helped establish a new settlement. After a skirmish with the Missouri State Militia, the Saints relocated to Illinois and settled in Nauvoo. Unlike at the previous movements, the Saints were welcomed into Illinois by the major political parties (Whig and Democrat), as each of the parties hoped the Saints would join their ranks in order to gain political power over the opposing party (nearly 15,000 Latter-day Saints moved from Missouri to Illinois in 1839). Joseph was quickly elected mayor of Nauvoo, commissioned as a lieutenant general in the Illinois State Militia, and

---

[2] Whitmer, *An Address to All Believers in Christ*, 12 (see chap. 3, n. 36).

placed in command of the Nauvoo legion. In 1844, a rift formed in the ranks of the Church because Joseph began publicly proposing plural marriage. Those who left the Church purchased a printing press and began publishing information derogatory of Smith and the Church. Eventually, Smith's followers destroyed the press, and Joseph was arrested for violating the First Amendment to the US Constitution. Joseph and his brother Hyrum were placed in the jail in Carthage, Illinois. On the second day of his imprisonment, a mob approached the jail, and Joseph and Hyrum were killed on June 27, 1844.

After Joseph's death, the Church was thrust into a leadership crisis. Bringhurst and Hamer note that at least seven men had legitimate claims to succeed Smith as the second president.[3] The two main groups formed during this transition period were a group led by Brigham Young and the smaller Reorganized Church of Jesus Christ of Latter-day Saints (now the Community of Christ), led by Joseph Smith III and Emma Smith. The larger group moved west due to a revelation received by Young. The westward trek was racked with difficulties, but the group eventually arrived on the Wasatch Front and settled in the Great Salt Lake Valley. Once in the Salt Lake area, the Saints began working on establishing their new community, which they referred to as Zion.[4]

One of the most significant problems faced by the early Salt Lake Latter-day Saints was opposition to their practice of plural marriage. As early as April 5, 1841, Joseph Smith began entering into plural marriages, and on July 12, 1843, he issued a revelation making plural marriage an official practice of the early Latter-day Saints. This practice followed the Saints from Illinois to Utah. As the Utah territory grew and statehood was sought, the practice of plural marriage would come to the forefront. Because plural marriage was against United States common law, the United States Congress would not entertain any notion of granting statehood to the Utah territory as long as the leadership of the territory maintained the practice. The continual calls from the Latter-day Saints for religious freedom and the continued insistence on the part of the federal government that the practice be stopped eventually resulted in a number of laws being passed through the United States Congress: the Morrill Anti-Bigamy Act of 1862, the Edmunds Act of 1882, and the Edmunds–Tucker Act of 1887. Together, these three laws disincorporated the LDS Church, disenfranchised polygamists of their right to vote, banned polygamists from holding public office

---

[3] Bringhurst and Hamer, *Scattering of the Saints*, 5 (see chap. 1, n. 1).
[4] For an excellent discussion of the concept of Zion in Latter-day Saint thought, see Millet, "The Development of the Concept of Zion in Mormon Theology" (see chap. 1, n. 54).

and from jury duty, imposed a $50,000 fine on the LDS Church, and declared all elected seats in the territory of Utah open. The United States government also seized all financial and land assets of the LDS Church, making it impossible for the Church to pay the fine levied on it for the practice of plural marriage. After living through such difficult times and realizing the United States government would not be persuaded, President Wilford Woodruff, after prayer and consultation with his counselors, issued a revelation (called the Manifesto) on September 24, 1890, banning plural marriage. Six years later, on January 4, 1896, the Utah territory was granted statehood. A similar situation occurred with reference to African Americans gaining the right to hold the priesthood.[5]

From Joseph Smith to current president Russell M. Nelson, seventeen men have served as president of the LDS Church. Especially noteworthy administrations include Joseph Smith's, Brigham Young's, Wilford Woodruff's, Spencer W. Kimball's, and Gordon B. Hinckley's. Significant growth and/or development took place under each of these administrations. Introduced as the seventeenth president of the Church on January 16, 2018, Russell M. Nelson was a member of the Quorum of the Twelve Apostles from 1984 to 2018, serving as its president from 2015 until becoming president of the Church.

The Great Apostasy and Restoration

The history of the Church of Jesus Christ of Latter-day Saints is a long, complicated, and fascinating study in the history of the American religious landscape. The LDS Church, as a restorationist movement, would, basically, have no reason for existence if there were no falling away from authentic, historic, primitive Christianity. Though multiple movements claim to have restored authentic Christianity, the LDS Church ranks as one of the largest, most powerful, and most easily identified restorationist movements. This restoration was needed, Latter-day Saints believe, because of an event that took place after the death of the last New Testament apostle. This event, known to Latter-day Saints as the Great Apostasy, was the foundation for the existence of the LDS Church. If this great falling away took place, then Christianity needed to be restored. If this great falling away did not take place, then Christianity did not need to be restored. It has often been said that the Church of Jesus Christ of Latter-day Saints stands or falls on the story of Joseph Smith. However, it seems more proper to say the existence of the LDS Church stands of falls with

---

[5] For an excellent discussion, see Abanes, *One Nation under Gods*, 355–74.

their belief in the Great Apostasy. Thus, the Great Apostasy is a central theme within the storyline of the LDS Church.

Latter-day Saint missionaries around the world have, for years, shared the basic message of Mormonism with anyone who would listen. The topic of the Great Apostasy is found very early in the missionary discussions. *Preach My Gospel*, the current missionary manual for Latter-day Saints, contains information about this apostasy within the first discussion. The manual states:

> After the death of Jesus Christ, wicked people persecuted the Apostles and Church members and killed many of them. With the death of the Apostles, priesthood keys and the presiding priesthood authority were taken from the earth. The Apostles had kept doctrines of the gospel pure and maintained the order and standard of worthiness for Church members. Without the Apostles, over time the doctrines were corrupted, and unauthorized changes were made in Church organization and priesthood ordinances, such as baptism and conferring the gift of the Holy Ghost.[6]

Gospel Principles also contains information concerning the apostasy. The authors assert:

> Throughout history, evil people have tried to destroy the work of God. This happened while the Apostles were still alive and supervising the young, growing Church. Some members taught ideas from their old pagan or Jewish beliefs instead of the simple truths taught by Jesus. Some rebelled openly. In addition, there was persecution from outside the Church. Church members were tortured and killed for their beliefs. One by one, the Apostles were killed or otherwise taken from the earth. Because of the wickedness and apostasy, the apostolic authority and priesthood keys were also taken from the earth. The organization that Jesus Christ had established no longer existed, and confusion resulted. More and more error crept into Church doctrine, and soon the dissolution of the Church was complete. The period of time when the true Church no longer existed on earth is called the Great Apostasy.[7]

---

[6] Church of Jesus Christ of Latter-day Saints, *Preach My Gospel*, 35 (see chap. 3, n. 27).
[7] Church of Jesus Christ of Latter-day Saints, *Gospel Principles*, 91–92 (see chap. 1, n. 69).

Similarly, James Talmage offers his understanding, unsurprisingly, not at all inconsistent with *Preach My Gospel* or *Gospel Principles*. The only difference between the two manuals and Talmage is, as will be seen, the ink spilled over the subject. Talmage wrote:

> The question may fairly arise in the mind of the earnest investigator, have these authorities and powers, together with their associated gifts of the Spirit, remained with men from the apostolic age to the present; in short, has there been a Church of Christ upon the earth during this long interval? In answer, let these facts be considered: Since the period immediately following the ministrations of the apostles of old, and until the present century, no organization has maintained a claim to direct revelation from God; in fact, the teachings of the professed ministers of the gospel for centuries have been to the effect that such gifts of God have ceased, that the days of miracles have gone, and that the present depends for its guiding code wholly upon the past. A self-suggesting interpretation of history indicates that there has been a great departure from the way of salvation as laid down by the Savior, a universal apostasy from the Church of Christ. Scarcely had the Church been organized by the Savior, whose name it bears, before the powers of darkness arrayed themselves for conflict with the organized body. . . .
>
> In the first quarter of the fourth century, however, a change in the attitude of paganism toward Christianity was marked by the conversion of Constantine the Great, under whose patronage the Christian profession grew in favor, and became in fact the religion of the state. But what a profession, what a religion was it by this time! Its simplicity had departed; earnest devotion and self-sacrificing sincerity were no longer characteristic of the Church's ministers; these professed followers of the humble Prophet of Nazareth, these self-styled associates of the meek and lowly Jesus, these loudly-proclaimed lovers of the Man of Sorrow, lived amid conditions strangely inconsistent with the life of their great Exemplar. Church offices were sought after for the distinction of honor and wealth accompanying them; ministers of the gospel affected the state of worldly authority; bishops sought the pomp of princes, archbishops lived as kings, and popes like emperors. With these unauthorized changes and unscriptural innovations, came many changes in the ordinances of the so-called church; the rites of

baptism were perverted; the sacrament was altered; public worship
became an exhibition of art; men were canonized; martyrs were made
subjects of adoration; blasphemy grew apace, in that men without authority essayed to exercise the prerogatives of God in calling others
to what still bore the name of spiritual office. Ages of darkness came
upon the earth; the power of Satan seemed almost supreme.[8]

True to the Faith, another officially published manual, offers a short explanation of the time of apostasy. The authors note, "During the Great Apostasy,
people were without divine direction from living prophets. Many churches
were established, but they did not have priesthood power to lead people to the
true knowledge of God the Father and Jesus Christ. Parts of the holy scriptures
were corrupted or lost, and no one had authority to confer the gift of the Holy
Ghost or perform other priesthood ordinances."[9]

Tad R. Callister, currently serving as Sunday school general president for
the LDS Church, has written a book-length work about this time of apostasy,
entitled *The Inevitable Apostasy*. Indeed, in speaking with Callister, one learns
very quickly of his research and reading interests in the Great Apostasy. In the
work, Callister writes:

While acknowledging the rapid growth in Christ's Church following
his ascension, The Church of Jesus Christ of Latter-day Saints nonetheless makes a bold and startling statement. It declares there was a
turning point that occurred shortly after the death of the apostles—
an apostasy or falling away that eventually resulted in a total loss of
Christ's Church from the earth. While an apostasy *of* the Church is
not the same as an apostasy of individuals *from* the Church, the former cannot occur without the latter. Individual members of Christ's
Church may reject its teachings and ordinances without affecting the
authority and integrity of the Church. When, however, a sufficient
number of persuasive individuals apostatize, and in the process the
official Church doctrines and ordinances become perverted, then,
inevitably, the priesthood or divine power that sustains and sets the
Church apart from all other worldly organizations is lost. That constitutes an apostasy *of* the Church. From that point forward the ongoing

---

[8] Talmage, *The Articles of Faith*, 203–4 (see chap. 2, n. 10).
[9] Church of Jesus Christ of Latter-day Saints, *True to the Faith*, 13 (see chap. 4, n. 178).

institution may propagate some truths; it may be a fraternity of sorts; it may render service and satisfy certain social needs. All this is good. But it will lack the prime reason for its existence—the power to save and exalt man.[10]

The Latter-day Saint belief in and understanding of the Great Apostasy is rooted in the First Vision of Joseph Smith. In the officially published version of Smith's First Vision, he recounts reading Jas 1:5 and wanting to inquire of God for knowledge and wisdom concerning which church he should join. He recalls going out into the woods to pray, where he was visited by what he perceived to be Heavenly Father and Jesus Christ. In his published history, included within the standard works, Smith recollected:

> My object in going to inquire of the Lord was to know which of all the sects was right, that I might know which to join. No sooner, therefore, did I get possession of myself, so as to be able to speak, than I asked the Personages who stood above me in the light, which of all the sects was right (for at this time it had never entered into my heart that all were wrong)—and which I should join. I was answered that I must join none of them, for they were all wrong; and the Personage who addressed me said that all their creeds were an abomination in his sight; that those professors were all corrupt; that: "they draw near to me with their lips, but their hearts are far from me, they teach for doctrines the commandments of men, having a form of godliness, but they deny the power thereof." He again forbade me to join with any of them.

This is recorded in Joseph Smith, History 1:18–20, and is found within the pages of the Pearl of Great Price. Although he published a number of varying versions of this First Vision, the one quoted above is the officially accepted and published version and, as can be seen, offers no real hope for any churches in existence at the time of Smith's question-and-answer time with the heavenly visitors.

As can be seen from all of the previously quoted material, the apostasy, according to Latter-day Saints, caused the true teachings of Christianity to be lost. This is the reason for Smith purportedly being told not to join any sects. One of the main doctrines lost during this time was authority: authority for

---

[10] Tad R. Callister, *The Inevitable Apostasy* (Salt Lake City: Deseret, 2006), 12–13.

teachings, baptism, and conferring the gift of the Holy Ghost. Enter here the idea of the Latter-day Saint priesthood and priesthood authority. *Gospel Principles* declares:

> The priesthood is the eternal power and authority of God. Through the priesthood He created and governs the heavens and the earth. By this power the universe is kept in perfect order. . . . Our Heavenly Father delegates His priesthood power to worthy male members of the Church. The priesthood enables them to act in God's name for the salvation of the human family. Through it they can be authorized to preach the gospel, administer the ordinances of salvation, and govern God's kingdom on earth.[11]

Tad R. Callister agrees:

> The priesthood is the power to act for God and perform his work as though he himself were present. . . . The priesthood is like a spiritual power of attorney given by God to mortals. With this power a man can teach with authority, heal the sick, perform miracles, administer the saving ordinances, and regulate the affairs of the Church, just as the Savior would do if he were present. Thus, the priesthood becomes a form of divine investiture of authority by which the acts and words of the priesthood bearer become the acts and words of the Savior. In a sense, the priesthood is the power to think God's thoughts, to speak his words, and to be his hands. . . . Each time a worthy priesthood bearer gives a blessing or performs an ordinance, he is entitled to think God's thoughts, to speak his words, and to be his hands.[12]

McConkie explains further, "As pertaining to eternity, priesthood is the eternal power and authority of Deity by which all things exist; by which they are created, governed, and controlled; by which the universe and worlds without number have come rolling into existence; by which the great plan of creation, redemption, and exaltation operates throughout immensity. It is the power of God."[13] McConkie continues:

---

[11] Church of Jesus Christ of Latter-day Saints, *Gospel Principles*, 67.
[12] Callister, *The Inevitable Apostasy*, 293–94.
[13] McConkie, *Mormon Doctrine*, 594 (see chap. 2, n. 11).

As pertaining to man's existence on this earth, priesthood is the power and authority of God delegated to man on earth to act in all things for the salvation of men. It is the power by which the gospel is preached; by which the ordinances of salvation are performed so that they will be binding on earth and in heaven; by which men are sealed up unto eternal life, being assured of the fulness of the Father's kingdom hereafter; and by which in due course the Lord will govern the nations of the earth and all that pertains to them.[14]

According to Latter-day Saint thought, because this priesthood authority was lost during the Great Apostasy, it needed to be restored to the earth. This restoration began in 1820 when Joseph Smith had his first vision. The restoration of the priesthood was needed, as *Gospel Principles* states, because humans "must have priesthood authority to act in the name of God when performing the sacred ordinances of the gospel, such as baptism, confirmation, administration of the sacrament, and temple marriage. If a man does not have the priesthood, even though he may be sincere, the Lord will not recognize ordinances he performs."[15] The priesthood, with all of the ordinances and authority attached to it, creates the structure through which the LDS Church is organized. We will now turn our attention to how that organization is worked out practically.

LDS Church Organization

The organization of the Church of Jesus Christ of Latter-day Saints is equally as complex as their history and beliefs. The easiest way to understand LDS Church organization is to consider it in terms of concentric circles of influence. Indeed, many LDS writers make it a point for their readers to understand that these circles of influence, or spheres of responsibility, are critical. Tad R. Callister writes:

The Lord will never give us a responsibility in life without the right to receive revelation to help us fulfill it. What does that mean? It means that every person has the right to receive revelation to help in his or her individual quest for exaltation because every one of us has been commanded to seek eternal life. It means that every student has the right to

[14] McConkie, 594.
[15] Church of Jesus Christ of Latter-day Saints, *Gospel Principles*, 67.

receive revelation in his or her studies because God has commanded us to "seek learning, even by study and also by faith" (D&C 88:118). It means that every individual has the right to receive revelation to find and become a better companion because God has commanded us to marry. It means that every parent has the right to receive revelation in order to give good and wise counsel to his or her children because God has commanded us to multiply and replenish the earth. And it means that every member with a Church calling has the right to receive revelation to help him or her magnify that calling, because it was God who inspired the call in the first place. Inherent in every God-given responsibility in life is the right to receive God-given direction by way of revelation.[16]

Concerning one's concentric circle, or sphere of responsibility, being his or her own, Callister writes:

> God is a God of order; therefore, revelation is given in an orderly way. If one or more persons were to receive revelation for another person's sphere of responsibility, then confusion would result. . . . If someone claims revelation for the bishop or stake president or prophet, you may know with certainty those revelations are not of the Lord. Certainly people are welcome to give suggestions and provide advice in council settings, but the final decision is to be made by those who have the right to receive the revelation associated with their calling. God does not operate through multiple channels for a single responsibility because He is a God of order.[17]

Similarly, McConkie writes, "Where the Church is concerned revelation comes only through the appointed channels. No one but the President of the Church, who holds and exercises the fulness of the keys, can announce revelation to the Church."[18]

At the center of the smallest circle is the individual person who is a Latter-day Saint. He or she is expected to receive revelation for himself or herself as the need dictates. McConkie writes, "With reference to their own personal affairs, the saints are expected to gain personal revelation and guidance

---

[16] Callister, *The Inevitable Apostasy*, 347.
[17] Callister, 348.
[18] McConkie, *Mormon Doctrine*, 646.

rather than to run to the First Presidency or some other church leaders to be told what to do."[19] The idea of personal revelation is indispensable to all Latter-day Saints and is a part of daily life. McConkie continues, "Our Lord's true Church is established and founded upon revelation. Its identity as the true Church continues as long as revelation is received to direct its affairs, for the gates of hell can never prevail against that power of faith and righteousness which pulls down revelations from heaven."[20]

In the following circle is the father in any Latter-day Saint family. As the father, and holder of the priesthood in and for his family, he is authorized to act on behalf of God for his family and receive revelation for his family only. He is the representative for God to his family. To take Callister's words in the context of a family, it would not be in order for a wife to receive revelation for the family if that revelation is contrary to her husband's. Likewise, it would not be in order for a child to receive revelation for the entire family. Rather, the parents would receive revelation for the family as a whole. Although the father's authority is specifically for himself and his family, as the concentric circles begin moving outward, his authority may be superseded by one holding more authority because the responsibility given is of a greater sphere of influence.

In the next circle of influence is the bishop of the local ward. The local ward is an organized group of Latter-day Saints, arranged geographically, and usually numbering approximately 500 individual members. McConkie explains, "The basic ecclesiastical district or church unit in and through which the programs of the Church are administered is the ward. Several wards form a stake of Zion. A bishop is the presiding ward officer; all Aaronic Priesthood quorums are ward quorums; and substantially all of the actual operation of all the programs of the Church takes place in the ward rather than in some larger or higher unit."[21] Similarly, *True to the Faith* explains:

> Each ward or branch (a smaller congregation) comprises a specific geographic area. Different organizations in the ward or branch contribute

---

[19] McConkie, 645.

[20] McConkie, 646.

[21] McConkie, 827. The priesthood is split into two groups: Aaronic and Melchizedek. The Aaronic priesthood is the lower office, and the Melchizedek priesthood is the higher office. Skinner writes, "The Aaronic Priesthood deals with the temporal matters and outward ordinances of the law and gospel. The Melchizedek Priesthood holds the 'keys of all the spiritual blessings of the church—to have the privilege of receiving the mysteries of the kingdom,' 'even the key of the knowledge of God' (D&C 107:18–19; 84:19)." See Andrew C. Skinner, "Aaronic Priesthood" in Millet et al., *LDS Beliefs*, 5 (see chap. 4, n. 26).

to the Lord's work: high priests groups; elders quorums; the Relief Society, for women ages 18 years and older; Aaronic Priesthood quorums, for young men ages 12 through 17; the Young Women program, for young women ages 12 through 17; Primary, for children ages 18 months to 11 years; and the Sunday School, for all Church members ages 12 and older. Each of these organizations fulfills important roles in teaching the gospel, giving service, and supporting parents in their sacred duty to help their children become converted to the gospel of Jesus Christ. These organizations also work together to help members share the gospel with others.[22]

Concerning the bishop, Andrew C. Skinner writes:

The title bishop designates the ecclesiastical leader, holding the keys of presidency, over a ward. Each ward bishop serves simultaneously as president of the Aaronic Priesthood in the ward and as the president of the priests quorum. As the presiding high priest in the ward, he is responsible for all its members and is a judge in Israel, who judges, counsels, and delegates among his congregation just as Moses judged, led, and delegated. . . . A bishop is given the gift to discern all the gifts of the Spirit in order that every member of his ward may be benefited thereby.[23]

Most often, this gift for the bishop is exercised in choosing speakers for any given sacrament service, in choosing callings for a particular member's service, in counseling individuals or couples, and in other temporal and spiritual matters. Members of the ward bishopric, or the bishop and his two counselors, usually make these decisions as a group. McConkie explains, "A ward bishopric, a quorum of three high priests, consists of a bishop and two counselors. They are set apart to preside over and direct the affairs of the kingdom in a particular ward."[24]

In the next circle is the stake president, including his two counselors, making up the stake presidency. In Latter-day Saint life, the stake president is the ruling authority for a slightly larger geographical area than that of a ward.

[22] Church of Jesus Christ of Latter-day Saints, *True to the Faith*, 36.
[23] Andrew C. Skinner, "Bishop" in Millet et al., *LDS Beliefs*, 71.
[24] McConkie, *Mormon Doctrine*, 89.

Most geographic areas where the Church is organized are divided into stakes. The term *stake* comes from the prophet Isaiah, who prophesied that the Latter-day Church would be like a tent, held secure by stakes (see Isa 33:20; 54:2). There are usually 5 to 12 wards and branches in a stake. Each stake is presided over by a stake president, assisted by two counselors. Stake presidents report to and receive direction from the Presidency of the Seventy or the Area Presidency.[25]

Talmage explains further:

Where the Saints are permanently located, Stakes of Zion are organized, each Stake comprising a number of wards or branches. Over each Stake is placed a Stake Presidency, consisting of a president and two counselors, who are High Priests properly chosen and set apart to this office. The Stake Presidency is assisted in judicial function by a Standing High Council, composed of twelve High Priests chosen and ordained to the office. This Council is presided over by the Stake Presidency, and forms the highest judicial tribunal of the Stake.[26]

The Stake President, along with his two counselors and the High Council, are charged with receiving revelation for those within the stake. Practically, this usually involves the recommendation for the calling of new bishops in a ward, resolving any issues which may arise within the stake, organizing the regular meeting of the stake conference, and other spiritual and temporal matters.

In the next sphere of influence is the area presidency. Stakes are, around the world, organized into areas of the LDS Church. The area presidency consists of a president and two counselors and the members of these groups are usually made up of General Authorities of the Church.[27] Area presidencies are made up of a president, most often a member of the First or Second Quorum of Seventy, and two counselors chosen either from the general authorities or from any of the Quorums of Seventies. Area presidencies are charged with overseeing all stakes, specifically stake presidencies, within their geographic

[25] Church of Jesus Christ of Latter-day Saints, *True to the Faith*, 36.
[26] Talmage, *The Articles of Faith*, 215.
[27] A general authority is any member of Latter-day Saint leadership in the following groups: the First Presidency, the Quorum of Twelve Apostles, the Presidency of the Seventy, the First Quorum of Seventy, the Second Quorum of Seventy, and the Presiding Bishopric.

realm of oversight. This includes the receiving of revelation for those stakes, practically meaning the calling of stake presidents, the resolution of issues, the organization of area conferences, and other spiritual and temporal matters. *True to the Faith* explains, "An area is the largest geographic division of the Church. . . . An Area Presidency consists of a president, who is usually assigned from the First or Second Quorum of the Seventy, and two counselors, who may be assigned from any Quorum of the Seventy. Area Presidencies serve under the direction of the First Presidency, the Quorum of the Twelve, and the Presidency of the Seventy."[28]

The next and larger circle of influence are the Quorums of Seventies. There are, at present, eight Quorums of Seventy, from the First Quorum of Seventy to the Eighth Quorum of Seventy. These groups oversee the work of the LDS Church across the world and function primarily as area presidencies. The First and Second Quorum of Seventy are general authorities and function in a slightly different capacity, mainly as area presidents. A group of seven presidents of these quorums is known as the Presidency of the Seventy, and, as in all other groupings of leadership, one man is designated as the senior president of the Presidency of the Seventy.

The next and still larger concentric circle of influence and revelatory authority is that of the Quorum of Twelve Apostles. Skinner notes:

> Apostles are special witnesses of the name of Christ—his divinity and reality—in all the world. . . . [T]he Church of Jesus Christ in this last dispensation is guided by the Quorum of Twelve Apostles, which regulates the affairs of God's kingdom on earth under the direction of three presiding high priests who form the First Presidency. As they did in Jesus' day, the apostles in the Quorum of the Twelve (and in the First Presidency) hold the keys of the priesthood, the controlling authority of the Church delegated to men on earth by God.[29]

Likewise, McConkie proclaims, "Every apostle who is set apart as a member of the Council or Quorum of the Twelve is given the keys of the kingdom. Since keys are the right of presidency and the kingdom of God on earth is the Church, it follows that each apostle so set apart receives the inherent power

---

[28] Church of Jesus Christ of Latter-day Saints, *True to the Faith*, 35.
[29] Andrew C. Skinner, "Apostle" in Millet et al., *LDS Beliefs*, 50.

and authority to preside over the Church and direct all of its affairs."[30] *Gospel Principles* explains further:

> An Apostle is a special witness of the name of Jesus Christ in all the world. The Apostles administer the affairs of the Church throughout the world. Those who are ordained to the office of Apostles in the Melchizedek Priesthood are usually set apart as members of the Quorum of the Twelve Apostles. Each one is given all the keys of the kingdom of God on earth, but only the senior apostle, who is the President of the Church, actively exercises all of the keys. The others act under his direction.[31]

Along with members of the First Presidency and the Patriarch of the Church, each of the members of the Quorum of Twelve Apostles is viewed as a prophet, seer, and revelator. McConkie notes, "Members of the First Presidency, Council of the Twelve, and the Patriarch to the Church—because they are appointed and sustained as prophets, seers, and revelators to the Church—are known as living oracles."[32] Thus, the members of the Quorum of Twelve Apostles, because they are "appointed and sustained as prophets, seers, and revelators to the Church" may receive revelation for the entire Church. However, it is not received to each of them individually and revealed individually. The Quorum of the Twelve Apostles, together as a group, holds the same power as the First Presidency as a group, but the only apostle who can reveal new revelation to the entire Church, alone, is the senior apostle, also called the President of the Church. As with lower groups, the Quorum of the Twelve Apostles also has one leader set apart as president; he is given the title President of the Quorum of the Twelve Apostles. The President of the Quorum of the Twelve is also the next President of the Church "in waiting."

The final group within Latter-day Saint leadership is the First Presidency, a group consisting of three members: the president of the Church, the first counselor, and the second counselor. While all three men are given the title "president," only the actual president of the Church, the longest serving, most senior of the apostles, serves as the sole person within Latter-day Saint life exercising all of the keys of the kingdom of God on the earth.

---

[30] McConkie, *Mormon Doctrine*, 49.
[31] Church of Jesus Christ of Latter-day Saints, *Gospel Principles*, 77.
[32] McConkie, *Mormon Doctrine*, 547.

The fulness of these keys can be exercised only in the event an apostle becomes the senior apostle of God on earth, for unless he does there will always be someone above him to direct his labors. The senior apostle is always chosen and set apart as the President of the Church, and through this system of apostolic succession, the Lord has made provision for the continuation and preservation of his kingdom on earth.[33]

Similarly, Skinner writes:

The senior apostle of God on the earth is the president of the Church, the only individual authorized to exercise all priesthood keys in their fulness. He and two counselors form the First Presidency, the supreme governing body or presiding quorum over the whole Church, separate and apart from the Quorum of the Twelve Apostles, though the latter is designated as a body, or "quorum, equal in authority and power" to the First Presidency (D&C 107:24). This means that when the First Presidency is dissolved upon the death of the president of the Church, the Twelve are authorized to exercise all of the power, authority, and prerogatives previously vested in the First Presidency.[34]

When the president of the Church dies, the two remaining members of the First Presidency move back into the Quorum of Twelve Apostles, technically making them the Quorum of Fourteen Apostles. Of the fourteen men, the longest serving, most senior apostle is appointed as the next president of the Church. With this, the number of apostles in the quorum is reduced to thirteen. The new president of the Church then chooses his two counselors, most often from the remaining apostles. While any man holding the Aaronic and Melchizedek Priesthoods may be chosen to serve as counselors to the president, history shows that the two counselors are chosen from the members of the Quorum of Twelve Apostles. After the two counselors are chosen, the number of apostles within the Quorum is reduced to eleven. With this, the members of the First Presidency, in consultation with the remaining members of the Quorum of Twelve Apostles, begin the process of selecting a new member of the Quorum of Twelve Apostles. Once the process is complete and the new apostle is ordained and sustained by the membership of the Church at the next

[33] McConkie, 49.
[34] Skinner, "Apostle," 51.

General Conference, the full First Presidency and Quorum of Twelve Apostles is complete, and work continues until the process is needed upon the death of the president of the Church.

Because of the significantly large organizational structure of the LDS Church, a brief summary will be offered for the sake of clarity and conclusion. *Gospel Principles* offers the most succinct organizational summary:

> A prophet, acting under the direction of the Lord, leads the Church. This prophet is also the President of the Church. He holds all the authority necessary to direct the Lord's work on earth (see D&C 107:65, 91). Two counselors assist the President. Twelve Apostles, who are special witnesses of the name of Jesus Christ, teach the gospel and regulate the affairs of the Church in all parts of the world. Other general officers of the Church with special assignments, including the Presiding Bishopric and the Quorums of the Seventy, serve under the direction of the First President and the Twelve. . . . The Church has grown much larger than it was in the days of Jesus. As it has grown, the Lord has revealed additional units of organization within the Church. When the Church is fully organized in an area, it has local divisions called stakes. A stake president and his two counselors preside over each stake. The stake has 12 high councilors who help do the Lord's work in the stake. Melchizedek Priesthood quorums are organized in the stake under the direction of the stake president. Each stake is divided into smaller areas called wards. A bishop and his two counselors preside over each ward. In areas of the world where the Church is developing, there are districts, which are like stakes. Districts are divided into smaller units called branches, which are like wards.[35]

Conclusion

One could say with ease that the history of the Church of Jesus Christ of Latter-day Saints is complex, fascinating, and filled with intrigue. To say LDS Church organization is complex may be an understatement. There are multiple aspects of Church leadership and varying roles within Church hierarchy that could, as the old adage says, make one's head spin. However complex the

---

[35] Church of Jesus Christ of Latter-day Saints, *Gospel Principles*, 98.

history and organization of the Church of Jesus Christ of Latter-day Saints may be, there is one overarching concept that ties each of the pieces together, namely, the Latter-day Saint belief in the loss and restoration of priesthood authority. Priesthood authority, the right to conduct the business of the Kingdom of God on the earth, really is the lynchpin of LDS history and organization. The priesthood keys, the authority to act on behalf of Heavenly Father, are the center of Latter-day Saint thought and life. Talmage offers the most complete reasoning for this belief:

> [I]t is evident that the Church was literally driven from the earth; in the first ten centuries immediately following the ministry of Christ, the authority of the priesthood was lost from among men, and no worldly power could restore it. But the Lord in His mercy provided for the re-establishment of His Church in the last days, and for the last time; and prophets of olden time fore-saw this era of renewed enlightenment, and sang in joyous tones of its coming. It has already been shown that this restoration was effected by the Lord through the Prophet Joseph Smith, who, together with Oliver Cowdry, in 1829 received the Aaronic Priesthood under the hands of John the Baptist; and later the Melchizedek Priesthood under the hands of the former-day apostles, Peter, James, and John. By the authority thus bestowed, the Church has been again organized, with all its former completeness, and mankind once more rejoices in the priceless privileges of the counsels of God. The Latter-day Saints declare their high claim to the true Church organization, similar in all essentials to the organization effected by Christ among the Jews; this people of the last days profess to have the Priesthood of the Almighty, the power to act in the name of God, which power commands respect both on earth and in heaven.[36]

Indeed, the LDS Church believes it has the Old Testament priesthoods of Aaron and Melchizedek, making it God's uniquely chosen organization for the expansion of the kingdom through the spreading of Heavenly Father's message on the earth, and according to Latter-day Saint thought, none other can make the same claim.

---

[36] Talmage, *The Articles of Faith*, 206–7.

Chapter 6

Are Mormons Christians?

O ne question should consistently enter the mind of the follower of Jesus. That question centers around the eternal state of every person with
whom the Christian comes into contact. We should, on a constant basis, be asking ourselves this question: do I know the eternal status of the persons around
me? Of all the topics we consistently find ourselves discussing, such as sports,
family matters, hobbies, work-related issues, and other interests, the topic of
Jesus should be the most important. In Matthew 16, Jesus has discussions with
the Pharisees and Sadducees about signs of the coming kingdom, and after
leaving the religious leaders, Jesus has a more private discussion with his disciples. Jesus's first recorded words in this dialogue with his disciples upon
reaching Caesarea Philippi is a question, namely, "Who do people say that the
Son of Man is?" As the talk unfolds and the disciples offer the answers of others, Jesus directs the question specifically to his disciples, asking, "But who do
you say that I am?" (vv. 13–15). Jesus could have spoken with the disciples on
any range of topics, but he chose to ask about their understanding of his status.
It is plain from the text that Jesus was not asking because he lacked a messianic
self-identity or had issues with his personal merit. He was asking his followers
what others were saying and what they themselves say because he was specifically interested in how individuals thought of him in light of the kingdom
of God. Indeed, Luke 19 records one of Jesus's boldest statements on this
topic. In this passage, Jesus is in conversation with Zacchaeus concerning his
spiritual status. Interestingly, Jesus tells this social outcast, otherwise known
as a tax collector, that he plans to stay at his home for the evening. Many in
the crowd did not appreciate Jesus staying in the home of a tax collector and

began deriding his decision, saying, "He's gone to stay with a sinful man" (v. 7). When Zacchaeus responded positively to Jesus's message, Jesus made an amazing proclamation to Zacchaeus specifically and, by extension, to his audience at large. Jesus said, "Today salvation has come to this house, because he too is a son of Abraham. For the Son of Man has come to seek and to save the lost" (vv. 9–10). A similar account is found in Luke 5 between Jesus and Levi, soon to be renamed Matthew. After Levi leaves all of his tax-collecting goods at the tax booth and follows Jesus, Levi hosts Jesus in his home for a meal. Not only were Jesus and Levi in attendance, but the text indicates that "there was a large crowd of tax collectors and others who were guests with them" (v. 29). And just as in the Zacchaeus account, some in the crowd were unhappy with this party of sinners close to Jesus. Those unhappy religious leaders asked Jesus's disciples why he would eat with such untouchables. Jesus responded similarly to his Luke 19 statement, saying, "It is not those who are healthy who need a doctor, but those who are sick. I have not come to call the righteous, but sinners to repentance" (vv. 31–32).

One thing should be obvious from these passages. Jesus's main mission was to seek out sinners and call them to repentance. This was not just an issue for Jesus. This was *the issue* for Jesus. As we read in Luke 15, his most pressing concern was looking for lost sheep, finding them, and bringing them into the fold of the kingdom. The most effective way Jesus found to accomplish this mission was simply to make sure his mission was expressed verbally to all those around him.

As followers of Jesus, Christ's ambassadors on the earth, we are to follow his example. We are to, as he expressed, pick up our crosses and follow him (Matt 16:24). So we must constantly ask ourselves about others around us. We must be willing to move outside of our comfort zones and express concern for our family, friends, neighbors, coworkers, and any others around us. We must consistently ask ourselves the following questions. Are my family members followers of Jesus? Are my friends followers of Jesus? Are my coworkers followers of Jesus? What about people with whom we may not have interpersonal relationships: bank tellers, gas station attendants, grocery store workers, coffee shop baristas? Do we carry the same burden for those with whom we may not have a personal relationship as those with whom we do? What about those who may come to our front doors to sell magazines, offer cable television subscriptions, or present a religious message? Do we become irritated with them, or are we, as Peter instructs in 1 Pet 3:15–16, always ready to make a defense for the hope that is in us, with gentleness and respect? How ready, willing, and able are we to share the message of Jesus with those around us?

Many have likely had missionaries from other faith traditions come to the front door and ask to share a message about their faith. From personal conversations with representatives of other faith traditions, we learn quickly the most common response to an attempt to share a religious message is either no answer at the door or a door closed very quickly. When a religious spokesperson rings the front door bell, the missionary is likely either a Jehovah's Witness or a Latter-day Saint. And of those two groups, more have probably had Latter-day Saints than Jehovah's Witnesses at the front door. Young men, dressed very conservatively and looking like professional salesmen, approach hundreds of thousands of doors every year to share the message of Mormonism. With more than 74,000 active missionaries around the world, the Church of Jesus Christ of Latter-day Saints has missionaries in most nations.[1] Similarly, there are fifteen active missionary training centers around the world in places such as Utah, Brazil, England, Ghana, South Africa, and Spain.[2] LDS missionaries are nearly everywhere on the earth, and there are hundreds of thousands, maybe millions, of missionaries-in-waiting in LDS families.

Most often, when LDS missionaries come to the door, the topic of Christianity is likely to come up very quickly. Indeed, LDS missionaries are instructed to say within the first few moments of the initial discussion, "Central to our Father's plan is Jesus Christ's Atonement."[3] That is a very Christian-sounding statement and would immediately raise thoughts of Christianity in most hearers. Likewise, the LDS missionary manual, *Preach My Gospel*, when defining the purpose of the missionary, states, "The gospel of Jesus Christ defines both your message and your purpose; that is, it provides both the 'what' and the 'why' of missionary work."[4] Two things should be obvious from this: the name of Jesus and the message of Jesus are of paramount importance for LDS missionaries.

LDS missionary handbooks, though, are not the only source of pressing Mormonism as Christian in the minds of members and nonmembers. Former LDS Church president Gordon B. Hinckley, speaking in 1998, asked, "Am I a

---

[1] Church of Jesus Christ of Latter-day Saints, "Missionary Program," news release, April 2, 2016, http://www.mormonnewsroom.org/.article/2015-statistical-report-april-2016-general-conference.
[2] Church of Jesus Christ of Latter-day Saints, "Missionary Program."
[3] Church of Jesus Christ of Latter-day Saints, *Preach My Gospel*, 31–32 (see chap. 3, n. 27).
[4] Church of Jesus Christ of Latter-day Saints, 5.

Christian?" He answered, "Of course I am. I believe in Christ. I talk of Christ. I pray through Christ. I'm trying to follow Him and live His gospel in my life."[5] Hinckley is not alone. Other LDS authors, speakers, and sources have offered the same answer. The official website for the LDS Church, www.lds. org, makes the same claim. Their article "Are Mormons Christians?" reads:

> Members of The Church of Jesus Christ of Latter-day Saints un-equivocally affirm themselves to be Christians. They worship God the Eternal Father in the name of Jesus Christ. When asked what the Latter-day Saints believe, Joseph Smith put Christ at the center: "The fundamental principles of our religion is the testimony of the apostles and prophets concerning Jesus Christ, 'that he died, was buried, and rose again the third day, and ascended up to heaven;' and all other things are only appendages to these, which pertain to our religion." The modern-day Quorum of the Twelve Apostles reaffirmed that testi-mony when they proclaimed, "Jesus is the Living Christ, the immortal son of God. . . . His way is the path that leads to happiness in this life and eternal life in the world to come."[6]

In a similar vein, Robert L. Millet argues, "Latter-day Saints are Chris-tians. We love Christ, we admire Christ, we worship Christ, we look to Christ, we treasure the words of Christ spoken by him and his anointed servants, and we have given our lives to Christ. We rejoice in his mercy and exult in his grace. His atoning sacrifice is the fundamental principle of Mormonism. He is the center of our faith."[7] In another work, Millet writes:

> In recent years the criticism of Latter-day Saints and a movement to exclude them from the category of *Christian* have intensified. There are those who feel uncomfortable with them because of their belief in modern prophets and additional scripture. Others reject the LDS claim to Christianity because the Church does not subscribe to the creeds of Christendom or is not in the historical Christian tradition. On what basis, then, do the Latter-day saints themselves claim to be Christian?

---

[5] Church of Jesus Christ of Latter-day Saints, "Crown of Gospel Is upon Our Heads," news release, June 20, 1998, http://www.ldschurchnewsarchive.com/articles/31188/Crown-of-gos-pel-is-upon-our-heads.html.
[6] Church of Jesus Christ of Latter-day Saints, "Are Mormons Christian?," LDS.org, November 2013, https://www.lds.org/topics/christians?lang=eng.
[7] Millet, "Christian" in Millet et al., *LDS Beliefs*, 110 (see chap. 4, n. 26).

They believe in Jesus Christ; that he is the Son of the Eternal Father, the Only Begotten in the flesh; that Christ is God, that he is Lord and Savior, the Redeemer of the world; that we are saved by obedience to his commandments and by virtue of his atoning blood; that only through reliance upon his merits, mercy, and grace can people find happiness here and eternal reward hereafter; and that his was the only perfect and sinless life, a life to be emulated and followed. Jesus Christ is the central figure in the doctrine and practice of The Church of Jesus Christ of Latter-day Saints. That so many misunderstand, prejudge, and exclude is sad and strangely ironic.[8]

Without question, Millet, a former dean of religious education at Brigham Young University, believes wholeheartedly that Mormons are indeed Christians. His argument is based on the Latter-day Saint belief in and acceptance of Jesus Christ, along with the central role Jesus plays within Latter-day Saint theology and practice.

Bruce McConkie offers a helpful understanding as well:

Christianity is the true religion of the Christians. Hence, true and acceptable Christianity is found among the saints who have the fulness of the gospel, and a perverted Christianity holds sway among the so-called Christians of apostate Christendom. In these circles it is believed and taught that Christianity had its beginning with the mortal ministry of our Lord. Actually, of course, Adam was the first Christian, for both he and the saints of all ages have rejoiced in the very doctrines of salvation restored to earth by our Lord in his ministry.[9]

He continues, "As the day of the great apostasy set in, the term Christian continued to be applied to the supposed followers of Christ, even though in reality they had departed from the true doctrines. Today those who purport to believe in Christ though they may not actually accept him as the Son of God, are called Christians."[10]

In 1991, Stephen Robinson, then a professor at the School of Religious Education at Brigham Young University, published a work entitled *Are Mormons Christians?* This was a groundbreaking work in the field of comparative

---

[8] Millet, *The Mormon Faith*, 164 (see chap. 2, n. 47).
[9] McConkie, *Mormon Doctrine*, 132 (see chap. 2, n. 11).
[10] McConkie, 132.

religion, as it was one of the first major, book-length works written by a Latter-day Saint maintaining that Mormons are indeed Christians. Robinson takes on some of the major arguments from non-Mormon writers and thinkers concerning the question proposed by the title of the work. His major contentions focus around what he calls "exclusions," of which he lists six: definition, misrepresentation, name-calling, historical, biblical, and doctrinal.[11] In the conclusion, he writes:

> When the charge is made that "Mormons aren't Christians," the very first impression created in the mind of the average individual is that Latter-day Saints don't believe in Jesus Christ. Most often those who make this charge *intend* that their uninformed hearers or readers will get this impression. Yet in the arguments offered to support the assertion the only issue that really matters is never even raised: Do the Latter-day Saints believe in Jesus Christ? Do they accept him as Lord? Do they believe that he is the way, the truth, and the life, and that no man cometh unto the Father but by him? These crucial questions are never asked. And why aren't they? Because these critics of the Latter-day Saints know that to open the box is to lose the argument, for no one who is even remotely familiar with the beliefs of the Latter-day Saints—not even their most hostile critics—can deny the Latter-day Saints' belief in Jesus Christ as the Son of God, as the Savior of the world, and as the only source of salvation available to human beings.[12]

He contends:

> That is, if Augustine or Luther or John Paul II can express opinions or insist on beliefs that differ from the Christian mainstream and yet still be considered Christians, then Joseph Smith and Brigham Young cannot be disqualified from bearing that title when they express the same or similar opinions. If theological or ecclesiastical diversity can be tolerated among mainstream Christian churches without charges of their being "non-Christian," then diversity of a similar kind, or to a similar degree, ought to be tolerated in the Latter-day Saints. This is simply an issue of playing on a level field.[13]

---

[11] Stephen E. Robinson, *Are Mormons Christians?* (Salt Lake City: Bookcraft, 1991).
[12] Robinson, 112.
[13] Robinson, viii.

Similarly, an article posted on the official website of the Church of Jesus Christ of Latter-day Saints attempts to answer the question, "Are Mormons Christian?"[14] The article begins, "Members of The Church of Jesus Christ of Latter-day Saints unequivocally affirm themselves to be Christians. They worship God the Eternal Father in the name of Jesus Christ." The article continues and outlines three basic objections for believing Mormons are not Christians, specifically: (1) Mormons do not accept post New Testament creeds, confessions, and councils; (2) Mormons are not within the lineage of traditional Christianity; and (3) Mormons believe in an open canon. The article concludes:

> Converts across the world continue to join The Church of Jesus Christ of Latter-day Saints in part because of its doctrinal and spiritual distinctiveness. That distinctiveness flows from the knowledge restored to this earth, together with the power of the Holy Ghost present in the Church because of restored priesthood authority, keys, ordinances, and the fulness of the gospel of Jesus Christ. The fruits of the restored gospel are evident in the lives of its faithful members. While members of The Church of Jesus Christ of Latter-day Saints have no desire to compromise the distinctiveness of the restored Church of Jesus Christ, they wish to work together with other Christians—and people of all faiths—to recognize and remedy many of the moral and family issues faced by society. The Christian conversation is richer for what the Latter-day Saints bring to the table. There is no good reason for Christian faiths to ostracize each other when there has never been more urgent need for unity in proclaiming the divinity and teachings of Jesus Christ.

Former director of the public affairs department of the LDS Church, Michael Otterson, in an article written for the *Washington Post*'s On Faith column, also posed the question "Are Mormons Christian?"[15] He wrote, "The question, 'Are Mormons Christian?' is a good starting point for this discussion. When some conservative Protestants say Mormons aren't Christian, it is deeply offensive to Latter-day Saints. Yet when Latter-day Saints assert their

---

[14] Church of Jesus Christ of Latter-day Saints, "Are Mormons Christian?" accessed 23 April 2017, available at https://www.lds.org/topics/christians?lang=eng&old=true.

[15] The quotations from this article are from Michael Otterson, "Are Mormons Christians?" On Faith, accessed January 31, 2018, https://www.onfaith.co/onfaith/2007/12/10/are-mormons-christians/7620.

Christianity, some of those same Christians bitterly resent it. Why? Because both sides are using the same terms to describe different things." He continued:

> When someone says Mormons aren't Christian . . . he or she usually means that Mormons don't embrace the traditional interpretation of the Bible that includes the Trinity. "Our Jesus" is somehow different from "their Jesus." Further, they mean that some Mormon teachings are so far outside Christian orthodoxy of past centuries that they constitute almost a new religion. The irony is that most Latter-day Saints wouldn't argue with those statements. When a Mormon says he or she is Christian, they are not trying to minimize differences or fudge the issues. Mormons are well aware of the many deep doctrinal differences with other Christians. For instance, Mormons reject the Trinity as non-biblical, and believe the concept to be a product of the creeds that emerged from the 4th and 5th centuries. Further, while embracing the Bible, they don't interpret it the same way as some Protestants—for instance, that the earth was literally created in six days of 24 hours. Neither do they believe that the scriptural canon was closed with a period and an exclamation mark after the death of the apostles, but that God is perfectly able to talk to prophets today as He did in ancient times. But for Mormons, these belief differences have nothing to do with whether or not they are Christian in the true meaning of the word. . . . For Latter-day Saints who try to live their lives as they believe Jesus taught, assertions that they aren't Christian are as bewildering as they are wounding.

He went on to assert, "Mormons have no argument with assertions that they are not 'creedal Christians,' or not 'orthodox' Christians or 'Trinitarian Christians.' Frankly, the whole point of Mormonism is that it is different. Just how different is best explained not by pastors of other faiths, or by secular journalists or by those whose self-interest lies in marginalizing a growing religion, but by Mormons themselves."

Likewise, during the April 2002 General Conference, then LDS Church president Gordon B. Hinckley offered his words concerning the status of Mormonism within the larger Christian context:

> As a Church we have critics, many of them. They say we do not believe in the traditional Christ of Christianity. There is some substance

to what they say. Our faith, our knowledge is not based on ancient tradition, the creeds which came of a finite understanding and out of the almost infinite discussions of men trying to arrive at a definition of the risen Christ. Our faith, our knowledge comes of the witness of a prophet in this dispensation who saw before him the great God of the universe and His Beloved Son, the resurrected Lord Jesus Christ. They spoke to him. He spoke with Them. He testified openly, unequivocally, and unabashedly of that great vision. It was a vision of the Almighty and of the Redeemer of the world, glorious beyond our understanding but certain and unequivocating in the knowledge which it brought. . . . I know that Jesus Christ is His Only Begotten Son, the Redeemer of the world, who gave His life that we might have eternal life and who rules and reigns with His Father. I know that They are individual beings, separate and distinct one from another and yet alike in form and substance and purpose.[16]

Furthermore, in an address during the April 1998 General Conference, President Hinckley offered similar words:[17]

There are some of other faiths who do not regard us as Christians. That is not important. How we regard ourselves is what is important. We acknowledge without hesitation that there are differences between us. Were this not so there would have been no need for a restoration of the gospel. . . .

We must not become disagreeable as we talk of doctrinal differences. There is no place for acrimony. But we can never surrender or compromise that knowledge which has come to us through revelation and the direct bestowal of keys and authority under the hands of those who held them anciently.

He also remarked that Latter-day Saints must be respectful when discussing matters of faith with members of other religious groups, adding, "But in all of

---

[16] Gordon B. Hinckley, "We Look to Christ," Church of Jesus Christ of Latter-day Saints General Conference website, April 2002, https://www.lds.org/general-conference/2002/04/we-look-to-christ?lang=eng.

[17] Quotations from this address are taken from Gordon B. Hinckley, "We Bear Witness of Him," Church of Jesus Christ of Latter-day Saints General Conference website, April 1998, https://www.lds.org/general-conference/1998/04/we-bear-witness-of-him?lang=eng.

this there is no doctrinal compromise. There need not be and must not be on our part."

Just a few months later, in June 1998, President Hinckley spoke to Latter-day Saints in Switzerland, mentioning members of other faiths who do not regard Latter-day Saints as Christians. LDS *Church News* records:

> In bearing testimony of Jesus Christ, President Hinckley spoke of those outside the Church who say Latter-day Saints "do not believe in the traditional Christ. No, I don't. The traditional Christ of whom they speak is not the Christ of whom I speak. For the Christ of whom I speak has been revealed in this the Dispensation of the Fulness of Times. He, together with His Father, appeared to the boy Joseph Smith in the year 1820, and when Joseph left the grove that day, he knew more of the nature of God than all the learned ministers of the gospel of the ages."[18]

With all these statements from Latter-day Saint scholars and Church leaders in mind, along with the information from previous chapters, we now turn to the question asked by the chapter title: are Mormons Christians? This is assuredly a deeply personal and volatile question to ask and attempt to answer. As quoted earlier, there are many biblical texts exhorting followers of Jesus to show intimate concern for the eternal state of others. This concern for their eternal state is not out of animosity, hatred, or anger, but out of love and fear for the souls of men and women. Joe Carter, an evangelical writer, expressed this well: "We can't love our neighbor and turn a blind eye to their eternal fate. We should therefore pray diligently that our friends and family who put their trust in [something other than Christianity] might come to know and accept the true Gospel of Jesus Christ."[19] In Luke 10:27, Jesus instructed his followers to love God with everything and to love their neighbors as themselves. As Carter stated, we cannot love our neighbors and simply refuse to tell them about the Jesus of the New Testament. This holds true for all of our neighbors, whether those neighbors are members of the same church we attend, are members of our same faith, or are members of another faith. We must show concern for the

---

[18] Church of Jesus Christ of Latter-day Saints, "Crown of Gospel Is upon Our Heads," *Church News* (June 20, 1998), 7.
[19] Joe Carter, "The FAQs: Are Mormons Christian?," *The Gospel Coalition,* April 24, 2012, https://www.thegospelcoalition.org/article/the-faqs-are-mormons-christian.

eternal state of all individuals. That includes our neighbors, friends, and family members who are Latter-day Saints.

Latter-day Saint leaders such as Gordon B. Hinckley offer little middle ground in their statements. Hinckley believed there are differences between orthodox Christianity and Mormonism, but Mormons worship and serve Jesus, so they must be Christian. Otterson proclaimed that Latter-day Saints have no issue with being termed non-Christian if, by "Christian" the person means "orthodox Christian" or "Trinitarian Christian" or "creedal Christians." He said most Latter-day Saints would not argue with the statement that Mormons are different from Christians if, again, by "Christian" one means the specifics he stated. The LDS article cited earlier indicates that Latter-day Saints do not want to give up doctrinal distinctives, and Hinckley argued that he and his fellow Latter-day Saints should never do so. Indeed, Hinckley said there is no need for doctrinal compromise. In a similar vein, Tad R. Callister, currently a general authority, said during the October 2011 Semiannual General Conference:

> That is the genius of the Book of Mormon—there is no middle ground. It is either the word of God as professed, or it is a total fraud. This book does not merely claim to be a moral treatise or theological commentary or collection of insightful writings. It claims to be the word of God—every sentence, every verse, every page. Joseph Smith declared that an angel of God directed him to gold plates, which contained the writings of the prophets in ancient America, and that he translated those plates by divine powers. If that story is true, then the Book of Mormon is holy scripture, just as it professes to be; if not, it is a sophisticated but, nonetheless, diabolical hoax.[20]

After alluding to the "liar, lunatic, or Lord" analogy of C. S. Lewis, Callister argued, "Likewise, we must make a simple choice with the Book of Mormon: it is either of God or the devil. There is no other option."[21]

Taking this into consideration, we must now make a decision concerning the state of the Church of Jesus Christ of Latter-day Saints. Callister could not be more correct: the Book of Mormon is either from God or from the devil.

---

[20] Tad R. Callister, "The Book of Mormon—a Book from God," Church of Jesus Christ of Latter-day Saints General Conference website, October 2011, https://www.lds.org/general-conference/2011/10/the-book-of-mormon-a-book-from-god?lang=eng.
[21] Callister.

And extending that analogy one step further, we may say the Church of Jesus
Christ of Latter-day Saints is either from God or from the devil. There is no
middle ground. One evangelical missions organization, the North American
Mission Board, concludes:

> When taken as doctrine, there is no other way to describe the teachings
> of The Church of Jesus Christ of Latter-day Saints than as cultic. Mor-
> mon teaching is not orthodox nor biblical in that it does not hold to
> the inerrancy of Scripture, nor to the full, eternal divinity of Christ. On
> those two points alone, Mormon teaching does not qualify as orthodox
> Christianity. Obviously, the question "Are Mormons Christians?" is
> not controversial because of a mere disagreement over classification.
> The real issue is whether the LDS Church is a valid, authentic, faithful
> expression of the Christian faith. On this question, we must simply
> accept the fact that evangelicals and LDS will disagree.[22]

A recognized leader among evangelicals, R. Albert Mohler Jr., current
president of The Southern Baptist Theological Seminary in Louisville, Kentucky, in an online debate with a Latter-day Saint author, wrote:

> Without doubt, Mormonism borrows Christian themes, personalities,
> and narratives. Nevertheless, it rejects what orthodox Christianity af-
> firms and it affirms what orthodox Christianity rejects. It is not Christi-
> anity in a new form or another branch of the Christian tradition. By its
> own teachings and claims, it rejects that very tradition. Richard John
> Neuhaus, a leading Roman Catholic theologian, helpfully reminds us
> that "Christian" is a word that "is not honorific but descriptive." Chris-
> tians do respect the Mormon affirmation of the family and the zeal of
> Mormon youth in their own missionary work. Christians must affirm
> religious liberty and the right of Mormons to practice and share their
> faith. Nevertheless, Mormonism is not Christianity by definition or
> description.[23]

---

[22] The North American Mission Board, "Are Mormons Christians?" Apologetics, NAMB.net,
accessed January 31, 2018, https://www.namb.net/apologetics/faq-are-mormons-christians.
[23] R. Albert Mohler, "Are Mormons Christians?—a Beliefnet.com Debate," Albert Mohler
website, June 29, 2007, http://www.albertmohler.com/2007/06/29/are-mormons-christians-
a-beliefnetcom-debate/.

Similarly, Brett Kunkle, a leader for the evangelical ministry Stand to Reason, in answering the question "Are Mormons Christians?" wrote:

> What's the point of this discussion? Are we just trying to beat up on the Mormons? Of course not. In John 17:3, Jesus says, "Now this is eternal life: that they know you, the only true God, and Jesus Christ, whom you have sent." According to Jesus, what does eternal life consist of? Knowing God. Any God? No, the *only true* God. Of course, if there is only one true God, any god who is not *that* God is a false god. And a false god cannot give you eternal life. Mormons and Christians worship different gods.[24]

There is indeed more to this than, as Robinson suggested, playing on a level field. The question at hand is more than merely considering Joseph Smith and Brigham Young as offering views equally as divergent as Martin Luther and Augustine. Neither Luther nor Augustine argued for a physical deity who is connected, in some way, to another planet with, as some Latter-day Saints will conjecture, its own deity. Similarly, neither Luther nor Augustine argued for a time in the past during which Jesus did not exist and then came into existence through the creative power of Heavenly Father and Heavenly Mother as the first spirit child of that relationship.[25] Augustine and Luther, and other Christian leaders in the early and later church, in fact, bluntly branded beliefs like this heretical and unbiblical. There is more to this than just degrees of difference. Hinckley argued that Mormons do not believe in the same Jesus as orthodox Christians when he said, speaking to the Latter-day Saints in Switzerland and France, "[I] do not believe in the traditional Christ. No, I don't. The traditional Christ of whom they speak is not the Christ of whom I speak."[26]

In all of this, the First Vision of Joseph Smith must be brought in as well. During his initial vision in 1820, Smith purported to have seen Heavenly Father and Jesus Christ and received a message from them. He was told not to join any existing churches, recounting it in Joseph Smith History 1:1–20, because they "were all wrong; and [Jesus Christ] said that all their creeds were

---

[24] Brett Kunkle, "Are Mormons Christians?," *Stand to Reason*, August 2011, https://www.str.org/articles/are-mormons-christians#.WQFxJ1LMxmA.

[25] For a discussion on the idea of Heavenly Mother, see Church of Jesus Christ of Latter-day Saints, "Mother in Heaven," LDS.org, https://www.lds.org/topics/mother-in-heaven?lang=eng&old=true.

[26] Church of Jesus Christ of Latter-day Saints, "Crown of Gospel Is upon Our Heads."

an abomination in his sight; that those professors were all corrupt; that: 'they draw near to me with their lips, but their hearts are far from me, they teach for doctrines the commandments of men, having a form of godliness, but they deny the power thereof.'" The content of this vision is plain: existing churches at the time of Joseph Smith, and their leaders, because of their beliefs, were an abomination and the leaders were corrupt. Millet explains:

> The empire of Alexander the Great, as a political entity, did not survive his death in 323 B.C., but the cultural empire he founded lasted for nearly one thousand years, until the rise of Islam and the Arab conquests in the seventh century after Christ. Greek, or Hellenistic, influence was profound—upon the Roman Empire, upon the world of Judaism, and, unfortunately, upon the early Christian Church. . . . But it was only a matter of time before the teachings of the prophets and ideas of the philosophers would come in conflict; those with eyes to see were aware that attempts to merge the doctrines of the temple of God with the doctrines of Plato would be abortive to the Christian faith. Early ecumenism would lead to shared impotence. And so it did.[27]

He continued, "The pressing problem was idolatry. . . . The problem was that man had fashioned unto himself a god, an unknown god, the unreachable and the unknowable Essence, the Wholly Other. Whether Catholic or Protestant, Jew or Muslim, the religious leaders of the nineteenth century, with their congregants—even the most sincere among them, and surely there were many—had lost their way."[28] Indeed, the very idea of idolatry, as Millet mentions, is foundational to the existence of Mormonism. According to Latter-day Saint logic, had the Great Apostasy not taken place, there would be no need for any restoration; hence, there would have been no need for Joseph Smith. It was this supposed Great Apostasy, bringing with it the loss of priesthood authority and the prophetic voice, that necessitated a restoration of first-century Christianity and, eventually, that Joseph Smith be the agent of the restoration during the early nineteenth century.

It should not be shocking, then, for a Latter-day Saint to hear a Christian describe LDS beliefs as corrupt or an abomination, to use words from the First

---

[27] Millet, *Restored and Restoring*, 4 (see chap. 3, n. 23).
[28] Millet, 6.

Vision. It was in the spring of 1820 that this battle began between Christianity and Mormonism, and it was Joseph Smith who threw the first stone. Yet today, when Christians, hopefully lovingly, share their faith with Latter-day Saints, they are often called anti-Mormon, bigots, or outright hate-filled. It is often wondered why Latter-day Saints can use words like "corrupt," "abomination," "impotent," or "idolatrous" to describe orthodox Christianity without the same vitriolic reaction from orthodox Christians as would be found from Latter-day Saints. Or, more forcefully, phrases like these from Bruce McConkie make the point further. He wrote:

> The titles church of the devil and great and abominable church are used to identify all churches or organizations of whatever name or nature—whether political, philosophical, educational, economic, social, fraternal, civic, or religious—which are designed to take men on a course that leads away from God and his laws and thus from salvation in the kingdom of God. Salvation is in Christ, is revealed by him from age to age, and is available only to those who keep his commandments and obey his ordinances. These commandments are taught in, and these ordinances are administered by, his Church. There is no salvation outside this one true Church, the Church of Jesus Christ. There is one Christ, one Church, one gospel, one plan of salvation, one set of saving ordinances, one group of legal administrators.[29]

He concluded, "Any church or organization of any kind whatever which satisfies the innate religious longings of man and keeps him from coming to the saving truths of Christ and his gospel is therefore not of God."[30] We know from previous materials that only through the Church of Jesus Christ of Latter-day Saints can "saving truths of Christ and his gospel" be found. Similarly, Talmage writes:

> I submit that to deny the materiality of God's person is to deny God; for a thing without parts has no whole, and an immaterial body cannot exist. The Church of Jesus Christ of Latter-day Saints proclaims against the incomprehensible God, devoid of "body, parts, and passions," as a

[29] McConkie, *Mormon Doctrine*, 138.
[30] McConkie, 138.

thing impossible of existence, and asserts its belief in and allegiance to the true and living God of scripture and revelation.[31]

McConkie asks further, "Does anyone really suppose that the sects of modern Christendom—with their silks and robes and rituals; with their notions of a salvation without works and by grace alone; with neither signs, nor miracles, nor apostles, nor prophets, nor revelation—does anyone really believe such a Christianity is the same as that of Jesus and Peter and Paul?"[32] Again, why can Latter-day Saints use such language concerning historic, orthodox Christianity and not be called bigoted or hateful or anti-Christian when the same type of language cannot be used by Christians concerning Latter-day Saint beliefs without being denounced with the same modifiers?

Latter-day Saints would likely answer this question simply: their worship of and central focus on Jesus Christ makes them Christians. Indeed, they would probably go as far as to say the restoration to Joseph Smith in 1820 makes Latter-day Saints the true orthodox, historic Christian church. Here is where we find ourselves using the same terms but defining those terms with different dictionaries. When an orthodox, historic Christian, or what is sometimes called a traditional Christian, makes the claim that a group is or is not Christian, the claim is made for theological reasons. The claims are not made in hateful, arrogant, or unloving ways, or if they are, they should not be. Indeed, 1 Pet 3:15–16 enjoins Christians to be ready to offer Christ to all who ask, yet with gentleness and respect. Though Latter-day Saints call themselves Christians because they worship, adore, and are focused on their conception of Christ, historically orthodox Christians simply do not accept Latter-day Saint Christology as Christian. Nor do Christians accept Latter-day Saint Theology Proper as Christian. These differences are not raised out of hate or anger, but out of concern for the souls of men and women. Evangelicals are usually the ones making these claims in a clarion fashion, and, to be fair, they are difficult claims to make because human emotion is involved and the hurt that can come from such claims cuts very deeply for those impacted by them. However, the claims coming from Latter-day Saints are equally hurtful to anyone involved in a Christian church: we are said to be unorthodox, ignorant, and corrupt. Orthodox, historic Christians stand firmly with Gordon B. Hinckley's statement,

[31] Talmage, *The Articles of Faith*, 48.
[32] Bruce R. McConkie, *The Mortal Messiah* (Salt Lake City: Deseret, 1980), 3:436–37.

"We acknowledge without hesitation that there are differences between us."[33] We also stand firm with the thought, "We must not become disagreeable as we talk of doctrinal differences. There is no place for acrimony."[34] In the end, we also agree with Hinckley's call to stand fast in one's beliefs. He said, "But in all of this there is no doctrinal compromise. There need not be and must not be on our part."[35] Therefore, when Christians say Latter-day Saints are not Christians, it is not out of anger, hatred, or bigotry; it is out of a desire not to compromise our deeply held doctrinal beliefs. Indeed, the North American Mission Board puts it best:

> Our conclusion that Mormonism is not "Christian" in this narrower, theological sense does not imply any animosity or hostility toward Latter-day Saints. Devout Mormons tend to be good citizens, to espouse high, conservative moral values, and to make common cause with conservative Christians on such important social issues as abortion. Nor do evangelicals single out Mormonism on this issue, since we reach similar conclusions about a variety of "Christian" religious groups whose teachings differ radically from biblical, historic Christian orthodoxy. Our intent is to draw attention to the serious differences between Mormonism and biblical Christianity in order that believers may be prepared to share the truth with their LDS friends and loved ones.[36]

With this as a foundation, Christians continue to do the work we believe Jesus Christ set out for us in the New Testament, specifically, to continue to spread the message of the gospel to the ends of the earth and to all peoples, regardless of any religious affiliation those peoples may or may not have. We do this, in agreement with McConkie, because we believe very strongly, that "worship of the true and living God leads to salvation; the worship of false and dead deities does not. Perfect worship is manifest by living in such a manner as to be like the Venerated One. Thus, the extent of man's knowledge of God determines the excellence of his worship and the progress he makes toward salvation."[37] Likewise, we agree with Millet—though obviously on the orthodox

---

[33] Hinckley, "We Bear Witness of Him."
[34] Hinckley.
[35] Hinckley.
[36] North American Mission Board, "Are Mormons Christians?"
[37] McConkie, *A New Witness for the Articles of Faith*, 55 (see chap. 3, n. 9).

Christian side of the analogy—who wrote, "Those who are content with what they have are perfectly free to express the same to LDS missionaries. Those who are curious, unsatisfied with their present faith or way of life, or those who may be seeking for answers to some of life's puzzling questions, may find an encounter with the Latter-day Saints worth their time and attention."[38] Surely Christians should not try to force any person to listen to the message of Christ or convert unbelievers by conscription. Do Christians wholeheartedly believe their doctrines and believe all who die without accepting the message of Christ are lost, separated from God's mercy, grace, and forgiveness in an eternal hell? Absolutely, and there is no doctrinal compromise on those issues (and many others). However, Christians should not be unruly or combative while sharing the message of Christ. Paul told Christians in Eph 6:12, "For our struggle is not against flesh and blood, but against the rulers, against the authorities, against the cosmic powers of this darkness, against evil, spiritual forces in the heavens."

Therefore, in the end, Christians are forced to say one thing: the Church of Jesus Christ of Latter-day Saints is not Christian in that it has its own distinctive and divergent beliefs, separate from historic, orthodox Christianity, many of which have been bluntly declared heretical and unbiblical for thousands of years. Likewise, the founder of the movement decried all of historic, orthodox Christianity as spurious, an abomination, and its leaders as corrupt as he followed what he purportedly heard in a vision. Similarly, modern Latter-day Saint leaders continue to say their beliefs are different from historic, orthodox Christianity. Also, Latter-day Saints have their own books of revelatory authority, along with continuing revelatory authority invested in the currently recognized prophets, seers, and revelators.

Conclusion

What, then, should Christians do when they encounter Latter-day Saints? What are the next steps? Are there fruitful ways to share the message of the New Testament Jesus with members of the Church of Jesus Christ of Latter-day Saints? Many Christians involved in ministry to Latter-day Saints disagree, methodologically, over the most effective ways to reach members of the LDS Church. This disagreement is not a source of discord among Christians; it is simply a methodological issue and assuredly should not raise any question on the

---

[38] Millet, *The Mormon Faith*, 181.

issue of Christian fellowship. Some believe the Christian evangelist must get a person to what he might call "full, unadulterated Mormonism" before sharing the New Testament gospel. Put differently, this means the Christian evangelist should work to make sure the Latter-day Saint knows and believes "all of Mormonism" before working to see him convert to Christianity. This methodology sees the most fruit in showing the stark contrasts between Christian and Latter-day Saint theology. Others believe it is vital to tear down Latter-day Saint belief and history, and once the Latter-day Saint member feels broken and downtrodden because his entire system of thinking has been seemingly destroyed, then the message of the New Testament Jesus can be inserted and the person's faith in religion can be rebuilt. While none of these are necessarily wrong or unbiblical, a lack of gentleness and respect often manifests during these types of presentations. A more biblically centered approach may produce more fruit because of the promises found in the text itself. In Rom 1:16, Paul declares, "For I am not ashamed of the gospel, because it is the power of God for salvation to everyone who believes, first to the Jew, and also to the Greek." Put simply, the message of Jesus is the power of God for salvation, not tearing down another belief system or building someone up in another belief system. The message of Jesus, the gospel, is the answer. It alone is the power of God for salvation. Thus, when Christians encounter members of the Church of Jesus Christ of Latter-day Saints, or any other faith tradition, the unique role of the Christian is to share the message of Jesus with that person.

Interestingly, all other faith traditions other than historic, orthodox Christianity have one common denominator, specifically, faith and works having a bearing on salvation together. There is no salvation by grace alone, through faith alone, in Christ alone in any other religious tradition. With this in mind, the Christian should always emphasize three specific points when sharing the message of Jesus with members of other faith traditions: grace, mercy, and forgiveness. These three points should be stressed because they are the hallmarks of the salvation Christians receive from God. In Eph 2:4–9, Paul said:

> But God, who is rich in mercy, because of his great love that he had for us, made us alive with Christ even though we were dead in trespasses. You are saved by grace! He also raised us up with him and seated us with him in the heavens in Christ Jesus, so that in the coming ages he might display the immeasurable riches of his grace through his kindness to us in Christ Jesus. For you are saved by grace through faith,

and this is not from yourselves; it is God's gift—not from works, so that no one can boast.

Similarly, Paul wrote in Eph 1:7, "In him we have redemption through his blood, the forgiveness of our trespasses, according to the riches of his grace." When considering the message of Jesus, the non-Christian may hear of grace, mercy, and forgiveness and not think much of them. However, when considering the message of grace, mercy, and forgiveness in light of other religious traditions, it is indeed like the proverbial cool drink of water in a hot desert. Sharing the message of Jesus with a non-Christian, especially considering that Jesus has paid the full price for the sins of humans, can be the most refreshing, satisfying message a member of another faith tradition could ever hear. This is especially so when that message of salvation is coupled heavily with grace, mercy, and forgiveness, and it is with these three aspects of the gospel that Christians should treat members of the LDS Church, and, further, all members of any other religious group. Likewise, the three legs (grace, mercy, and forgiveness) of the gospel stool should be communicated as clearly and strongly with Latter-day Saints as possible. Members of other faith traditions live daily under the guilt heaped on them by the necessity of works. Wondering if one has ever done enough would be a tiring way of life. The message of the incarnation, atonement, and resurrection of Jesus is truly the best thing for the ears of a non-Christian. The gospel is truly God's power for salvation, and all people around the world are in desperate need of hearing that message.

To those readers who are believers in the Jesus of the New Testament: let us be the bearers of the greatest news in the history of creation to all who will hear. Let us not be the ones who fail to share Christ with our family, friends, coworkers, neighbors, and others around us within our circle of influence. Let us share with passion, with consistency, and with compassion. To those readers who are not believers in the Jesus of the New Testament: know that the God of Abraham, Isaac, and Jacob, the Holy One of Israel, the Creator of the universe, loves you. However, your actions, attitudes, and makeup as a human separate you from God.

In Rom 3:23, Paul declares, "For all have sinned and fall short of the glory of God." In similar fashion, Paul declares in Rom 6:23a that we face the penalty of death for that sin: "For the wages of sin is death." However, the greatest news ever told in the universe is the second half of Rom 6:23: ". . . but the gift of God is eternal life in Christ Jesus our Lord." Likewise, know that Jesus died for you so that you need only to trust that Jesus did enough to pay the penalty due to you for your sins. Indeed, Jesus died in your place! Placing your trust in his death will give you access to God as never before. Paul declared in Rom 10:9–10, "If you confess with your mouth, 'Jesus is Lord,' and believe in your heart that God raised him from the dead, you will be saved. One believes with the heart, resulting in righteousness, and one confesses with the mouth, resulting in salvation."

Furthermore, Paul contends in Eph 2:8–9, "For you are saved by grace through faith, and this is not from yourselves; it is God's gift—not from works, so that no one can boast." Basically, we were made to be in relationship with God, but we ruined that relationship. Nevertheless, God offers a heavenly fix through his son Jesus Christ. Placing one's trust in Christ restores the relationship, and that relationship is based on the grace of God, not on our works. Salvation is all of God and not of us. Trust Christ today! There is no better news to be found anywhere.

Select Bibliography

Books

Abanes, Richard. *Becoming Gods*. Eugene, OR: Harvest House, 2004.

―――. *One Nation under Gods*. New York: Four Walls Eight Windows, 2002.

Allen, James B., and Glen M. Leonard. *The Story of the Latter-day Saints*. Salt Lake City: Deseret, 1976.

Allison, Gregg R. *Historical Theology*. Grand Rapids: Zondervan, 2011.

Allred, Gordon, comp. *God the Father*. Salt Lake City: Deseret, 1979.

Allred, Janice, ed. *God the Mother*. Salt Lake City: Signature, 1997.

Andrus, Hyrum L. *Doctrinal Commentary on the Pearl of Great Price*. Salt Lake City: Deseret, 1972.

―――. *The Glory of God and Man's Relation to Deity*. Provo, UT: Extension Publications of Brigham Young University, 1964.

Ankerberg, John, and John Weldon. *Behind the Mask of Mormonism*. Eugene, OR: Harvest House, 1996.

Aquinas, Thomas. *Summa Theologiae*. Edited by Timothy McDermott. Allen, TX: Christian Classics, 1991.

Arbaugh, George B. *Revelation in Mormonism: Its Character and Changing Forms*. Chicago: University of Chicago Press, 1932.

Arrington, Leonard J., and Davis Bitton. *The Mormon Experience: A History of the Latter-day Saints*. New York: Alfred A. Knopf, 1979.

Audi, Robert, ed. *Cambridge Dictionary of Philosophy*. 2nd ed. New York: Cambridge University Press, 1999.

Augustine. *On the Trinity*. Vol. 3 of *Nicene and Post-Nicene Fathers*. Edited by Philip Schaff. Peabody, MA: Hendrickson, 1999.

Ballard, M. Russell. *Our Search for Happiness*. Salt Lake City: Deseret, 1993.

Beck, Martha. *Leaving the Saints*. New York: Crown, 2005.

Beckwith, Francis J., William Lane Craig, and J. P. Moreland. *To Everyone an Answer*. Downers Grove, IL: InterVarsity, 2004.

Beckwith, Francis J., Norman Geisler, Ron Rhodes, Phil Roberts, Jerald Tanner, and Sandra Tanner. *The Counterfeit Gospel of Mormonism*. Eugene, OR: Harvest House, 1998.

Beckwith, Francis J., and Gregory Koukl. *Relativism: Feet Firmly Planted in Mid-Air.* Grand Rapids: Baker, 1998.

Beckwith, Francis J., and Stephen E. Parrish. *The Mormon Concept of God: A Philosophical Analysis.* Lewiston, NY: Edwin Mellon, 1991.

———. *See the Gods Fall.* Joplin, MO: College Press, 2000.

Beckwith, Francis J., Carl Mosser, and Paul Owen, eds. *The New Mormon Challenge.* Grand Rapids: Zondervan, 2002.

Beilby, James K. *For Faith and Clarity.* Grand Rapids: Baker Academic, 2006.

Bennett, Isaiah. *Inside Mormonism: What Mormons Really Believe.* San Diego: Catholic Answers, 1999.

Bennion, Lowell L. *The Religion of the Latter-day Saints.* Salt Lake City: Church of Jesus Christ of Latter-day Saints, 1940.

Benson, Ezra Taft. *Come unto Christ.* Salt Lake City: Deseret, 1983.

———. *The Teachings of Ezra Taft Benson.* Salt Lake City: Bookcraft, 1989.

Bergera, Gary James, ed. *Line upon Line: Essays on Mormon Doctrine.* Salt Lake City: Signature, 1989.

Berrett, William E. *Teachings of the Doctrine and Covenants.* Salt Lake City: Deseret, 1956.

Blackman, Milton, Jr. *Joseph Smith's First Vision.* 2nd ed. Salt Lake City: Bookcraft, 1980.

Blomberg, Craig, and Stephen Robinson. *How Wide the Divide?* Downers Grove, IL: InterVarsity, 1997.

Bradley, Francis H. *Essays on Truth and Reality.* Oxford: Clarendon, 1914.

Braswell, George, Jr. *Understanding Sectarian Groups in America.* Nashville: Broadman, 1986.

Bringhurst, Newell G., and John C. Hamer, eds. *Scattering of the Saints: Schism within Mormonism.* Independence, MO: John Whitmer, 2007.

Brodie, Fawn M. *No Man Knows My History.* New York: Vintage, 1995.

Brown, Colin. *Philosophy & the Christian Faith.* Downers Grove, IL: InterVarsity, 1968.

Burton, Rulon T. *We Believe: Doctrines and Principles of the Church of Jesus Christ of Latter-day Saints.* Salt Lake City: Tabernacle, 1994.

Bushman, Claudia Lauper, and Richard Lyman Bushman. *Building the Kingdom: A History of Mormons in America.* New York: Oxford University Press, 2001.

Bushman, Richard Lyman. *Joseph Smith: Rough Stone Rolling.* New York: Alfred A. Knopf, 2005.

———. *Joseph Smith and the Beginnings of Mormonism.* Urbana: University of Illinois Press, 1984.

Callister, Tad R. *The Inevitable Apostasy.* Salt Lake City: Deseret, 2006.

Campbell, Eugene E., ed. *The Essential Brigham Young.* Salt Lake City: Signature, 1992.

Cannon, Donald Q., and Larry E. Dahl, eds. *The Prophet Joseph Smith's King Follett Discourse: A Six Column Comparison of Original Notes and Amalgamations, with Introduction and Commentary.* Provo, UT: Religious Studies Center, Brigham Young University, 1983.

Cannon, George Q. *Gospel Truth.* Compiled by Jerreld L. Newquist. Salt Lake City: Deseret, 1957, 1987.

Carson, D. A. *The Gagging of God.* Grand Rapids: Zondervan, 1996.

Carson, D. A., and John D. Woodbridge, eds. *Scripture and Truth.* Grand Rapids: Baker, 1992.

Cheesman, Paul R., ed. *The Book of Mormon: The Keystone Scripture.* Provo, UT: Brigham Young University Religious Studies Center, 1988.

Church of Jesus Christ of Latter-day Saints. *Area Conference Report.* Manchester, UK: Church of Jesus Christ of Latter-day Saints, 1976.

———. *Conference Report.* Salt Lake City: Church of Jesus Christ of Latter-day Saints, April 1907.

———. April 1916.

———. April 1918.

———. April 1921.

———. April 1964.

———. October 1931.

———. October 1955.

———. October 1958.

———. October 1967.

———. October 1971.

———. October 1977.

Church of Jesus Christ of Latter-day Saints. *Doctrine and Covenants Student Manual.* Salt Lake City: Church of Jesus Christ of Latter-day Saints, 1981.

———. *Doctrines of the Gospel Student Manual.* Salt Lake City: Church of Jesus Christ of Latter-day Saints, 1986.

———. *Eternal Progression.* Salt Lake City: Church of Jesus Christ of Latter-day Saints, 1986.

———. *Explanatory Introduction.* In Doctrine and Covenants. Salt Lake City: Church of Jesus Christ of Latter-day Saints, 1992.

———. *The Family.* Salt Lake City: Church of Jesus Christ of Latter-day Saints, 1995.

———. *Gospel Fundamentals.* Salt Lake City: Church of Jesus Christ of Latter-day Saints, 2002.

———. *The Gospel of Jesus Christ.* Salt Lake City: Church of Jesus Christ of Latter-day Saints, 1986.

———. *Gospel Principles.* Salt Lake City: Church of Jesus Christ of Latter-day Saints, 1997.

————. *Hymns of The Church of Jesus Christ of Latter-day Saints*. Salt Lake City: Church of Jesus Christ of Latter-day Saints, 1998.

————. *Instructions for the Discussions*. Salt Lake City: Church of Jesus Christ of Latter-day Saints, 1986.

————. *Introduction to the Book of Mormon*. Salt Lake City: Church of Jesus Christ of Latter-day Saints, 2013.

————. *Introductory Note*. In Pearl of Great Price. Salt Lake City: Church of Jesus Christ of Latter-day Saints, 1992.

————. *Living a Christlike Life*. Salt Lake City: Church of Jesus Christ of Latter-day Saints, 1986.

————. *The Living Christ*. Salt Lake City: Church of Jesus Christ of Latter-day Saints, 2000.

————. *Melchizedek Priesthood Personal Study Guide*. Salt Lake City: Church of Jesus Christ of Latter-day Saints, 1972.

————. *Membership in the Kingdom*. Salt Lake City: Church of Jesus Christ of Latter-day Saints, 1986.

————. *The Plan of Our Heavenly Father*. Salt Lake City: Intellectual Reserve, 1986.

————. *Preach My Gospel*. Salt Lake City: Church of Jesus Christ of Latter-day Saints, 2004.

————. *The Restoration*. Salt Lake City: Church of Jesus Christ of Latter-day Saints, 1986.

————. *Revelations in Context*. Salt Lake City: Church of Jesus Christ of Latter-day Saints, 2016.

————. *Teachings of the Latter-day Prophets*. Salt Lake City: Church of Jesus Christ of Latter-day Saints, 1986.

————. *Teachings of the Living Prophets*. Salt Lake City: Church of Jesus Christ of Latter-day Saints, 2010.

————. *Topical Guide*. Salt Lake City: Church of Jesus Christ of Latter-day Saints, 2006.

————. *True to the Faith*. Salt Lake City: Church of Jesus Christ of Latter-day Saints, 2004.

————. *We're with You*. Salt Lake City: Deseret, 2016.

Clark, James R., comp. *Messages of the First Presidency of the Church of Jesus Christ of Latter-day Saints (1833–1951)*. 6 vols. Salt Lake City: Bookcraft, 1971.

Condie, Spencer J. *In Perfect Balance*. Salt Lake City: Bookcraft, 1993.

Copleston, Frederick. *A History of Philosophy*. 9 vols. New York: Doubleday, 1993–1994.

Craig, William Lane, ed. *Philosophy of Religion: A Reader and Guide*. New Brunswick, NJ: Rutgers University Press, 2002.

————. *Reasonable Faith*. 3rd ed. Wheaton, IL: Crossway, 2008.

Crawley, Peter L., ed. *The Essential Parley Pratt*. Salt Lake City: Signature, 1990.

Culver, Robert Duncan. *Systematic Theology*. Ross-shire, UK: Christian Focus, 2005.

Curriculum Department of the Church of Jesus Christ of Latter-day Saints, ed. *Teachings of Presidents of the Church: Brigham Young*. Salt Lake City: Church of Jesus Christ of Latter-day Saints, 1997.

———. *Teachings of Presidents of the Church: Spencer Kimball*. Salt Lake City: Church of Jesus Christ of Latter-day Saints, 2006.

Dahl, Larry E., and Charles D. Tate, eds. *The Lectures on Faith in Historical Perspective*. Provo, UT: Religious Studies Center, Brigham Young University, 1990.

Dana, Bruce E. *The Eternal Father and His Son*. Springville, UT: Cedar Fort, 2004.

———. *Mysteries of the Kingdom*. Springville, UT: Bonneville, 2001.

Davies, Douglas, ed. *Mormon Identities in Transition*. London: Cassells, 1996.

Dawson, Lorne L. *Comprehending Cults: The Sociology of New Religious Movements*. New York: Oxford University Press, 1998.

———, ed. *Cults and New Religious Movements: A Reader*. Malden, MA: Blackwell, 2003.

Devine, Philip E. *Relativism, Nihilism, and God*. Notre Dame, IN: University of Notre Dame Press, 1989.

Durham, G. Homer, ed. *The Discourses of Wilford Woodruff*. Salt Lake City: Bookcraft, 1946.

———. *The Gospel Kingdom: Selections from the Writings and Discourses of John Taylor*. Salt Lake City: Improvement Era, 1941.

Erickson, Millard J. *Christian Theology*. Grand Rapids: Baker, 1999.

———. *Truth or Consequences*. Downers Grove, IL: InterVarsity, 2001.

———. *What Does God Know and When Does He Know It?* Grand Rapids: Zondervan, 2003.

Faulconer, James E. *Tools for Scripture Study*. Provo, UT: Foundation for Ancient Research and Mormon Study, 1999.

———, ed. *Transcendence in Religion and Philosophy*. Indianapolis: Indiana University Press, 2003.

Feinburg, John S. *No One Like Him*. Wheaton, IL: Crossway, 2001.

Frame, John S. *The Doctrine of God*. Phillipsburg, NJ: P&R, 2002.

———. *The Doctrine of the Knowledge of God*. Phillipsburg, NJ: P&R, 1987.

Garrett, James Leo, Jr. *Systematic Theology*. 2 vols. North Richland Hills, TX: BIBAL, 2000–2001.

Gates, Susa Young. *The Life Story of Brigham Young*. New York: Macmillan, 1930.

Geer, Thelma. *Mormonism, Mama & Me*. Chicago: Moody, 1986.

THE SAINTS OF ZION

Geisler, Norman L. *Creating God in the Image of Man?* Minneapolis: Bethany House, 1997.

———. *Systematic Theology.* 4 vols. Minneapolis: Bethany House, 2002–2005.

———, ed. *Inerrancy.* Grand Rapids: Zondervan, 1980.

Geisler, Norman L., and Paul D. Feinberg. *Introduction to Philosophy.* Grand Rapids: Baker, 2003.

Geisler, Norman L., and H. Wayne House. *The Battle for God: Responding to the Challenge of Neotheism.* Grand Rapids: Kregel, 2001.

Geisler, Norman L., and Ron Rhodes. *When Cultists Ask: A Popular Handbook on Cultic Misrepresentations.* Grand Rapids: Baker, 1999.

Giles, Kevin. *The Eternal Generation of the Son.* Downers Grove, IL: InterVarsity, 2012.

Givens, Terryl L. *By the Hand of Mormon: The American Scripture That Launched a New World Religion.* New York: Oxford University Press, 2002.

Givens, Terryl L., and Philip L. Barlow, eds. *Oxford Handbook of Mormonism.* New York: Oxford University Press, 2015.

Goldman, Alan H. *Moral Knowledge.* New York: Routledge, 1988.

Gonzalez, Justo L. *The Story of Christianity: The Early Church to the Present Day.* Peabody, MA: Hendrickson, 2001.

Gottlieb, Robert, and Peter Wiley. *America's Saints: The Rise of Mormon Power.* New York: Harcourt Brace Jovanovich, 1986.

Grant, Heber J., and G. Homer Durham. *Gospel Standards.* Salt Lake City: Deseret, 1941.

Grenz, Stanley J. *A Primer of Postmodernism.* Grand Rapids: Eerdmans, 1996.

Groothius, Douglas. *Truth Decay: Defending Christianity against the Challenges of Postmodernism.* Downers Grove, IL: InterVarsity, 2000.

Grudem, Wayne. *Systematic Theology: An Introduction to Biblical Doctrine.* Grand Rapids: Zondervan, 1994.

Guinness, Os. *Time for Truth.* Grand Rapids: Baker, 2000.

Gundry, Stanley, ed. *Five Views on Law and Gospel.* Grand Rapids: Zondervan, 1999.

Hansen, Klaus J. *Quest for Empire: The Political Kingdom of God and the Council of Fifty in Mormon History.* Lincoln: University of Nebraska Press, 1967.

Harris, James P., ed. *The Essential James Talmage.* Salt Lake City: Signature, 1997.

Hatch, Nathan O. *The Democratization of American Christianity.* New Haven, CT: Yale University Press, 1989.

Henry, Carl F. H. *God, Revelation, and Authority.* 6 vols. Wheaton, IL: Crossway, 1999.

Herrick, James A. *The Making of the New Spirituality.* Downers Grove, IL: InterVarsity, 2003.

Hicks, Peter. *The Journey So Far.* Grand Rapids: Zondervan, 2003.

Hill, Donna. *Joseph Smith: The First Mormon*. New York: Doubleday, 1984.

Hill, Marvin S., ed. *The Essential Joseph Smith*. Salt Lake City: Signature, 1995.

Hinckley, Gordon B. *Discourses of President Gordon B. Hinckley: Volume 1: 1995–1999*. Salt Lake City: Deseret, 2005.

———. *Discourses of President Gordon B. Hinckley: Volume 2: 2000–2004*. Salt Lake City: Deseret, 2005.

———. *Faith: The Essence of True Religion*. Salt Lake City: Deseret, 1989.

Hoekema, Anthony. *The Four Major Cults: Christian Science, Jehovah's Witnesses, Mormonism, Seventh-day Adventism*. Grand Rapids: Eerdmans, 1963.

———. *Mormonism*. Grand Rapids: Eerdmans, 1963.

Huffman, Douglas S., and Eric L. Johnson. *God under Fire*. Grand Rapids: Zondervan, 2002.

Hunter, Milton R. *Pearl of Great Price Commentary: A Selection from the Revelations, Translations, and Narrations of Joseph Smith*. Salt Lake City: Bookcraft, 1951.

Hutchinson, Janis. *The Mormon Missionaries*. Grand Rapids: Kregel, 1995.

Illinois State Bar Association. *Revised Laws of Illinois*. Vandalia, IL: Greiner and Sherman, 1833.

Jenkins, Philip. *Mystics and Messiahs*. New York: Oxford University Press, 2000.

Jenson, Andrew. *LDS Biographical Encyclopedia*. 4 vols. Salt Lake City: Andrew Jenson History, 1901–1936.

Jessee, Dean C., ed. *The Personal Writings of Joseph Smith*. Salt Lake City: Deseret, 1984.

Johanson, W. F. Waler. *What Is Mormonism All About? Answers to the 150 Most Commonly Asked Questions about the Church of Jesus Christ of Latter-day Saints*. New York: St. Martin's Griffin, 2002.

Kant, Immanuel. *Critique of Pure Reason*. Edited by Paul Guyer and Allen W. Wood. New York: Cambridge University Press, 1998.

Kimball, Edward L., ed. *The Teachings of Spencer W. Kimball*. Salt Lake City: Bookcraft, 1982.

Kimball, Spencer W. *President Kimball Speaks Out*. Salt Lake City: Deseret, 1981.

Krakauer, Jon. *Under the Banner of Heaven: A Story of Violent Faith*. New York: Doubleday, 2003.

Kyle, Richard. *The Religious Fringe*. Downers Grove, IL: InterVarsity, 1993.

Ludlow, Daniel H. *A Companion to Your Study of the Book of Mormon*. Salt Lake City: Deseret, 1976.

———. *Principles and Practices of the Restored Gospel*. Salt Lake City: Deseret, 1992.

———, ed. *Encyclopedia of Mormonism*. New York: Macmillan, 1992.

————. *Latter-day Prophets Speak: Selections from the Sermons and Writings of Church Presidents.* Salt Lake City: Bookcraft, 1993.

Lundquist, John M., and Stephen D. Ricks, eds. *By Study and Also by Faith: Essays in Honor of Hugh W. Nibley on the Occasion of His Eightieth Birthday, 27 March 1990.* 2 vols. Salt Lake City: Deseret, Foundation for Ancient Research and Mormon Studies, 1990.

Lundwall, N. B., comp. *Masterful Discourses and Writings of Orson Pratt.* Salt Lake City: Bookcraft, 1962.

Madsen, Brigham D., ed. *The Essential B. H. Roberts.* Salt Lake City: Signature, 1999.

Marquardt, H. Michael, and Wesley P. Walters. *Inventing Mormonism: Tradition and the Historical Record.* Salt Lake City: Smith Research Associates, 1994.

Matthews, Robert J. *A Bible! A Bible!* Salt Lake City: Bookcraft, 1990.

Maxwell, Neal A. *All These Things Shall Give Thee Experience.* Salt Lake City: Deseret, 1979.

————. *Wonderful Flood of Light.* Salt Lake City: Bookcraft, 1990.

McConkie, Bruce. *The Foolishness of Teaching.* Salt Lake City: Church of Jesus Christ of Latter-day Saints, 1981.

————. *Millennial Messiah.* Salt Lake City: Deseret, 1982.

————. *Mormon Doctrine.* Salt Lake City: Deseret, 1966.

————. *Mormon Doctrine.* 2nd ed. Salt Lake City: Deseret, 1979.

————. *The Mortal Messiah.* Salt Lake City: Deseret, 1980.

————. *A New Witness for the Articles of Faith.* Salt Lake City: Deseret, 1985.

McConkie, Joseph Fielding. *The Spirit of Revelation.* Salt Lake City: Deseret, 1984.

McConkie, Joseph Fielding, and Robert L. Millet. *Sustaining and Defending the Faith.* Salt Lake City: Bookcraft, 1985.

McConkie, Joseph Fielding, Robert L. Millet, and Brent L. Top. *Doctrinal Commentary on the Book of Mormon.* 4 vols. Salt Lake City: Bookcraft, 1987–1992.

McConkie, Mark L., ed. *Sermons and Writings of Bruce R. McConkie.* Salt Lake City: Bookcraft, 1998.

McGuckin, John Anthony, ed. *We Believe in One Lord Jesus Christ.* Downers Grove, IL: InterVarsity, 2009.

McKay, David O. *Gospel Ideals.* 7 vols. Salt Lake City: Improvement Era, 1953.

McKeever, Bill. *Answering Mormons' Questions.* Minneapolis: Bethany House, 1991.

McKeever, Bill, and Eric Johnson. *Mormonism 101.* Grand Rapids: Baker, 2000.

McLachlan, James M., and Lloyd Ericson, eds. *Discourses in Mormon Theology.* Salt Lake City: Greg Kofford Books, 2007.

McMurrin, Sterling. *Philosophical Foundations of Mormon Theology.* Salt Lake City: Signature, 2000.

————. *The Theological Foundations of the Mormon Religion*. Salt Lake City: Signature, 2000.

Mead, Frank S., Samuel S. Hill, and Craig D. Atwood. *Handbook of Denominations in the United States*, 12th ed. Nashville: Abingdon, 2005.

Millet, Robert L. *Alive in Christ*. Salt Lake City: Deseret, 1997.

————. *By Grace Are We Saved*. Salt Lake City: Bookcraft, 1989.

————. *Christ-Centered Living*. Salt Lake City: Bookcraft, 1994.

————. *A Different Jesus?* Grand Rapids: Eerdmans, 2005.

————. *An Eye Single to the Glory of God*. Salt Lake City: Deseret, 1991.

————. *Getting at the Truth*. Salt Lake City: Deseret, 2004.

————. *Grace Works*. Salt Lake City: Deseret, 2003.

————. *I Will Fear No Evil*. Salt Lake City: Bookcraft, 2002.

————. *Life in Christ*. Salt Lake City: Bookcraft, 1990.

————. *Lost and Found*. Salt Lake City: Deseret, 2001.

————. *Magnifying Priesthood Power*. Bountiful, UT: Horizon, 1974.

————. *The Mormon Faith*. Salt Lake City: Shadow Mountain, 1998.

————. *Precept upon Precept*. Salt Lake City: Deseret, 2016.

————. *Restored and Restoring*. Salt Lake City: Eborn, 2014.

————. *What Happened to the Cross? Distinctive LDS Teachings*. Salt Lake City: Deseret, 2007.

————. *When a Child Wanders*. Salt Lake City: Deseret, 1996.

————. *Within Reach*. Salt Lake City: Deseret, 1995.

————, ed. *No Weapon Shall Prosper*. Salt Lake City: Deseret, 2011.

————. *Joseph Smith: Selected Sermons and Writings*. New York: Paulist, 1989.

————. *"To Be Learned Is Good If . . ."* Salt Lake City: Bookcraft, 1987.

Millet, Robert L., and Robert J. Matthews, eds. *Plain and Precious Truths Restored: The Doctrinal and Historical Significance of the Joseph Smith Translation*. Salt Lake City: Bookcraft, 1995.

Millet, Robert L., and Gerald R. McDermott. *Claiming Christ: A Mormon-Evangelical Debate*. Grand Rapids: Brazos, 2007.

Millet, Robert L., and Noel B. Reynolds, eds. *Latter-day Christianity: 10 Basic Issues*. Provo, UT: Foundation for Ancient Research and Mormon Studies, 1998.

Millet, Robert L., Camille Fronk Olson, Andrew C. Skinner, and Brent L. Top, eds. *LDS Beliefs*. Salt Lake City: Deseret, 2011.

Moore, Raymond D. *Mormonism against Itself*. Bloomington, IN: 1st Books, 2001.

Moreland, J. P. *Scaling the Secular City*. Grand Rapids: Baker, 1998.

Moreland, J. P., and William Lane Craig. *Philosophical Foundations for a Christian Worldview*. Downers Grove, IL: InterVarsity, 2003.

Morris, Thomas V. *Our Idea of God: An Introduction to Philosophical Theology*. Vancouver, BC: Regent College Publishing, 1991.

Mullen, Robert. *The Latter-day Saints: The Mormons Yesterday and Today*. Garden City, NY: Doubleday, 1966.

Musser, Joseph W., ed. *Michael, Our Father and Our God*. Salt Lake City: Truth, 1945.

Netland, Harold. *Encountering Religious Pluralism*. Downers Grove, IL: InterVarsity, 2001.

Newell, Coke. *Latter Days: An Insider's Guide to Mormonism*. New York: St. Martin's Griffin, 2000.

Nibley, Hugh W. *Teachings of the Book of Mormon: Semester 1: Transcripts of Lectures Presented to an Honors Book of Mormon Class at Brigham Young University, 1988–1990*. Provo, UT: Foundation for Ancient Research and Mormon Studies, 1993.

———. *Tinkling Cymbals and Sounding Brass*. Salt Lake City: Deseret, 1991.

Nyman, Monte S., and Robert L. Millet, eds. *The Joseph Smith Translation: A Restoration of Plain and Precious Things*. Provo, UT: Religious Studies Center, Brigham Young University, 1985.

O'Connor, D. J. *The Correspondence Theory of Truth*. London: Hutchinson, 1975.

O'Dea, Thomas F. *The Mormons*. Chicago: University of Chicago Press, 1970.

Ostler, Blake. *Exploring Mormon Thought: The Attributes of God*. Salt Lake City: Greg Kofford, 2001.

———. *Exploring Mormon Thought: The Problem with Theism and the Love of God*. Salt Lake City: Greg Kofford, 2006.

Ostling, Richard and Joan. *Mormon America*. San Francisco: Harper, 2000.

Penrose, Charles W. *What the "Mormons" Believe*. Salt Lake City: Deseret News Press, 1900.

Peterson, Daniel C., and Stephen D. Ricks. *Offenders for a Word: How Anti-Mormons Play Word Games to Attack the Latter-day Saints*. Provo, UT: Foundation for Ancient Research and Mormon Studies, 1992.

Peterson, Michael, William Hasker, Bruce Reichenbach, and David Basinger. *Philosophy of Religion*. New York: Oxford University Press, 2001.

Pinnock, Clark. *Most Moved Mover*. Grand Rapids: Baker, 2001.

Pinnock, Clark, Richard Rice, John Sanders, William Hasker, and David Basinger. *The Openness of God*. Downers Grove, IL: InterVarsity, 1994.

Piper, John, Justin Taylor, and Paul Kjoss Helseth, eds. *Beyond the Bounds*. Wheaton, IL: Crossway, 2003.

Pratt, Orson. *The Essential Orson Pratt*. Salt Lake City: Signature, 1991.

———. *The Kingdom of God*. Liverpool: R. James, 1848.

Pratt, Parley P. *Key to the Science of Theology*. Salt Lake City: Deseret, 1965.

———. *Mormonism Unveiled*. New York: Joseph W. Harrison, 1842.

Quinn, Michael D. *Early Mormonism and the Magic World View*. Salt Lake City: Signature, 1998.

Quinn, Philip L., and Charles Taliaferro, eds. *A Companion to Philosophy of Religion*. Malden, MA: Blackwell, 1999.

Reynolds, George, and Janne M. Sjodahl. *Commentary on the Book of Mormon*. 7 vols. Edited by Philip C. Reynolds. Salt Lake City: Deseret, 1955.

Rhodes, Ron. *The 10 Most Important Things You Can Say to a Mormon*. Eugene, OR: Harvest House, 2001.

Rhodes, Ron, and Marian Bodine. *Reasoning from the Scriptures with the Mormons*. Eugene, OR: Harvest House, 1995.

Richards, LeGrand. *A Marvelous Work and Wonder*. Salt Lake City: Deseret, 1976.

Roberts, B. H. *A Comprehensive History of the Church of Jesus Christ of Latter-day Saints*. 6 vols. Orem, UT: Sonos, 1991.

———. *The Falling Away*. Salt Lake City: Deseret, 1931.

———. *The Mormon Doctrine of Deity: The Roberts and Catholic Priest Van Der Donckt Discussion*. Salt Lake City: Signature, 1998.

———. *Seventies Course in Theology*. 5 vols. Salt Lake City: Deseret News, 1907–1912.

Robertson, Judy. *Out of Mormonism*. Minneapolis: Bethany House, 2001.

Robinson, Stephen E. *Are Mormons Christians?* Salt Lake City: Bookcraft, 1991, 1998.

Robison, Parker Pratt, ed. *Orson Pratt's Works*. Salt Lake City: Deseret, 1945.

Rowe, David L. *I Love Mormons*. Grand Rapids: Baker, 2005.

Roy, Steven C. *How Much Does God Foreknow?* Downers Grove, IL: InterVarsity, 2006.

Schreiner, Thomas R. *New Testament Theology*. Grand Rapids: Baker, 2008.

———. *Paul: Apostle of God's Glory*. Downers Grove, IL: InterVarsity, 2001.

Schreiner, Thomas R., and Bruce A. Ware. *Still Sovereign*. Grand Rapids: Baker, 2000.

Scruton, Roger. *Modern Philosophy: An Introduction and Survey*. New York: Penguin, 1996.

Shipps, Jan. *Mormonism: The Story of a New Religious Tradition*. Urbana: University of Illinois Press, 1985.

Sire, James W. *Naming the Elephant*. Downers Grove, IL: InterVarsity, 2004.

———. *The Universe Next Door*. 4th ed. Downers Grove, IL: InterVarsity, 2004.

Skousen, Royal. *Book of Mormon Critical Text: A Tool for Scholarly Reference*. Provo, UT: Foundation for Ancient Research and Mormon Studies, 1984–1987.

Smith, Hyrum M., and Janne M. Sjodahl. *Doctrine and Covenants Commentary*. Edited by Joseph Fielding Smith, Harold B. Lee, and Marion G. Romney. Salt Lake City: Deseret, 1978.

Smith, Joseph Jr. *Discourses of the Prophet Joseph Smith*. Edited by Alma P. Burton. Salt Lake City: Deseret, 1977.

————. *History of the Church of Jesus Christ of Latter-day Saints.* 7 vols. Salt
    Lake City: Church of Jesus Christ of Latter-day Saints, 1948, 1951, 1978.
————. *Lectures on Faith.* Salt Lake City: Deseret, 1985.
Smith, Joseph F. *Gospel Doctrine.* Salt Lake City: Deseret, 1919, 1969.
Smith, Joseph Fielding. *Answers to Gospel Questions,* 5 vols. Salt Lake City:
    Deseret, 1957–1966.
————. *Church History and Modern Revelation.* Salt Lake City: Church of Jesus
    Christ of Latter-day Saints, 1953.
————. *Doctrines of Salvation: Sermons and Writings,* 3 vols. Compiled by
    Bruce McConkie. Salt Lake City: Bookcraft, 1954–1956.
————. *Essentials in Church History.* Salt Lake City: Deseret, 1972.
————. *The Restoration of All Things.* Salt Lake City: Deseret, 1945.
————, comp. *Teachings of the Prophet Joseph Smith.* Salt Lake City: Book-
    craft, 1976.
————. *The Way to Perfection.* Salt Lake City: Genealogical Society of Utah,
    1949.
Snow, Lorenzo. *The Teachings of Lorenzo Snow.* Edited by Clyde J. Williams.
    Salt Lake City: Bookcraft, 1984.
Spiegel, James S. *The Benefits of Providence.* Wheaton, IL: Crossway, 2005.
Stark, Rodney. *The Rise of Mormonism.* New York: Columbia University Press,
    2005.
Steup, Matthias, and Ernest Sosa, eds. *Contemporary Debates in Epistemology.*
    Malden, MA: Blackwell, 2005.
Stewart, David G. *The Law of the Harvest: Practical Principles of Effective
    Missionary Work.* N.p.: Cumorah, 2007. http://cumorah.com/index.php?
    target=law_harvest.
Stumpf, Samuel Enoch, and James Fieser. *Philosophy: History and Problems.*
    New York: McGraw Hill, 2003.
Taliaferro, Charles. *Contemporary Philosophy of Religion.* Malden, MA: Black-
    well, 1998.
Talmage, James. *Articles of Faith.* Salt Lake City: Signature, 2003.
————. *Jesus the Christ.* Salt Lake City: Deseret, 1990.
————. *The Philosophical Basis of Mormonism.* Salt Lake City: Press of Zion's,
    1931.
————. *The Vitality of Mormonism.* Boston: Gorham, 1919.
Tanner, Jerald, and Sandra Tanner. *3,913 Changes in the Book of Mormon.* Salt
    Lake City: Utah Lighthouse Ministry, 1996.
Thagard, Paul. *Coherence in Thought and Action.* Cambridge: MIT Press, 2000.
Ure, James W. *Leaving the Fold.* Salt Lake City: Signature, 1999.
Vogel, Dan, ed. *Early Mormon Documents.* 5 vols. Salt Lake City: Signature,
    1996–2003.
————. *The Word of God.* Salt Lake City: Signature, 1990.

Vogel, Dan, and Brent Lee Metcalfe, eds. *American Apocrypha*. Salt Lake City: Signature, 2002.

Walker, Ralph C. S. *The Coherence Theory of Truth: Realism, Anti-realism, Idealism*. New York: Routledge, 1989.

Ware, Bruce A. *God's Greater Glory*. Wheaton, IL: Crossway, 2004.

———. *God's Lesser Glory*. Wheaton, IL: Crossway, 2000.

Watson, Elden J., ed. *The Orson Pratt Journals*. Salt Lake City: E. J. Watson, 1975.

White, James R. *Is the Mormon My Brother?* Minneapolis: Bethany House, 1997.

———. *Letters to a Mormon Elder*. Minneapolis: Bethany House, 1993.

White, O. Kendall, Jr. *Mormon Neo-Orthodoxy: A Crisis Theology*. Salt Lake City: Signature, 1987.

Whitmer, David. *An Address to All Believers in Christ*. Richmond, MO: David Whitmer, 1887.

Whittaker, David J., ed. *The Essential Orson Pratt*. Salt Lake City: Signature, 1991.

Widtsoe, John A. *Evidences and Reconciliations*. Salt Lake City: Bookcraft, 1960.

———. *A Rational Theology as Taught by the Church of Jesus Christ of Latter-day Saints*. Salt Lake City: Deseret, 1965.

———, comp. *Discourses of Brigham Young*. Salt Lake City: Deseret, 1941, 1954.

Widtsoe, John A., and Joseph Fielding Smith. *Gospel Doctrine*. Salt Lake City: Deseret, 1919.

Williams, Clyde J., ed. *The Teachings of Harold B. Lee*. Salt Lake City: Bookcraft, 1996.

Williams, Drew. *The Complete Idiot's Guide to Understanding Mormonism*. Indianapolis: Alpha, 2003.

Woodruff, Wilford. *Leaves from My Journal*. Salt Lake City: Juvenile Instructor's Office of the Church of Jesus Christ of Latter-day Saints, 1881.

———. *Wilford Woodruff's Journals*. 9 vols. Midvale, UT: Signature Books, 1985.

Articles

Alexander, Thomas G. "The Odyssey of a Latter-day Prophet: Wilford Woodruff and the Manifesto of 1890." *Journal of Mormon History* 17 (1991): 169–206.

———. "The Reconstruction of Mormon Doctrine." *Sunstone* 22 (1999): 15–29.

Almeder, Robert. "Peirce's Thirteen Theories of Truth." *Transactions of the Charles S. Peirce Society* 21 (1985): 77–94.

Altholz, Josef L. "Truth and Equivocation: Liguori's Moral Theology and Newman's Apologia." *Church History* 44 (1975): 73–84.

Anderson, Richard L. "The Strength of the Mormon Position." *Dialogue* 1
(1996): 113–18.

Anderson, Robert D. "The Dilemma of the Mormon Rationalist." *Dialogue* 30
(1997): 71–94.

Armour-Garb, Bradley, and J. C. Beall. "Further Remarks on Truth and Contra-
diction." *Philosophical Quarterly* 52 (2002): 217–25.

Armstrong, John M. "Divine Reason: Historical Development in Mormon
Thought." *Dialogue* 30 (1997): 5–23.

Arrington, Leonard J. "The Intellectual Tradition of the Latter-day Saints." *Dialogue* 14 (1969): 13–26.

Ballard, M. Russell. "His Word Ye Shall Receive." *Ensign* (May 2001): 65–66.

———. "Members Are the Key." *Ensign* (September 2000): 8–15.

———. "The Miracle of the Holy Bible." Church of Jesus Christ of Latter-day
Saints. May 2007. https://www.lds.org/ensign/2007/05/the-miracle-of-the-
holy-bible?lang=eng.

Beckwith, Francis J. "Mormon Theism, the Traditional Christian Concept of
God, and Greek Philosophy: A Critical Analysis." *Journal of the Evangelical
Theological Society* 44 (2001): 671–95.

———. "With a Grain of Salt: Assessing a Mormon–Evangelical Dialogue."
Christianity Today 41 (1997): 57–59.

Bennion, Lowell. "A Mormon View of Life." *Dialogue* 24 (1991): 59–68.

Benson, Ezra Taft. "The Book of Mormon—Keystone of Our Religion." *Ensign*
(November 1986): 4–7.

———. "Fourteen Fundamentals in Following the Prophet." *Liahona*, June 1981.
https://www.lds.org/liahona/1981/06/fourteen-fundamentals-in-following-
the-prophet?lang=eng.

Benson, Ezra Taft, Gordon B. Hinckley, and Thomas S. Monson. "First
Presidency Statement on the Sabbath." *Ensign*, January 1993. https://www.
lds.org/ensign/1993/01/news-of-the-church/first-presidency-statement-on-
the-sabbath?lang=eng.

Bergera, Gary J. "Does God Progress in Knowledge?" *Dialogue* 15 (1982):
179–81.

———. "The Orson Pratt–Brigham Young Controversies: Conflict within the
Quorums." *Dialogue* 13 (1980): 7–49.

Best, Karl F. "Changes in the Revelation, 1833 to 1835: Mormon Book of Doctrine and Covenants." *Dialogue* 25 (1992): 87–112.

BonJour, Laurence. "Coherence Theory of Truth." In *The Cambridge Dictionary
of Philosophy*. 2nd ed. Edited by Robert Audi, 153–55. New York: Cambridge University Press, 1999.

Brown, Robert M., Richard M. Anderson, and David W. Bennett. "A New Step in Understanding: A Reply to a Book by S. M. McMurrin." *Dialogue* 1 (1966): 107–21.

Buerger, David J. "The Adam–God Doctrine." *Dialogue* 15 (1982): 14–58.

Burton, Alma P. "Follow the Brethren." *Ensign* (October 1972): 5–11.

Bush, Lester E., Jr. "Mormonism's Negro Doctrine: An Historical Overview." *Dialogue* 8 (1973): 11–68.

Bushman, Richard L. "The First Vision Story Revisited." *Dialogue* 4 (1969): 82–93.

Callister, Tad R. "The Book of Mormon—A Book from God." Church of Jesus Christ of Latter-day Saints. https://www.lds.org/general-conference/2011/10/the-book-of-mormon-a-book-from-god?lang=eng.

Canham, Matt. "Mormon Portion of Utah Population Steadily Shrinking." *Salt Lake Tribune*, June 22, 2006. http://www.sltrib.com/ci_2886596.

Cannon, Donald Q. "The King Follett Discourse: Joseph Smith's Greatest Sermon in Historical Perspective." *BYU Studies* 18 (1978): 170–92.

Carter, Joe. "The FAQs: Are Mormons Christian?" *Gospel Coalition*, April 2012. https://www.thegospelcoalition.org/article/the-faqs-are-mormons-christian.

Cavadini, John C. "The Quest for Truth in Augustine's *De Trinitate*." *Theological Studies* 58 (1997): 429–40.

Chappell, Timothy. "Plato on Knowledge in the Theaetetus." In *Stanford Encyclopedia of Philosophy*. Accessed August 5, 2008. http://plato.stanford.edu/entries/plato-theaetetus.

Church of Jesus Christ of Latter-day Saints. "Are Mormons Christian?" Church of Jesus Christ of Latter-day Saints. Updated September 1, 2016. https://www.lds.org/topics/christians?lang=eng&old=true.

———. "Crown of Gospel Is upon Our Heads." *Church News*. June 20, 1998. http://www.ldschurchnewsarchive.com/articles/31188/Crown-of-gospel-is-upon-our-heads.html.

———. "Is There Anything Wrong with Drinking Sodas with Caffeine in Them? Is Caffeine Bad? The Word of Wisdom Doesn't Mention It." Church of Jesus Christ of Latter-day Saints. Accessed April 23, 2017. Available from https://www.lds.org/new-era/2008/04/to-the-point/is-there-anything-wrong-with-drinking-sodas-with-caffeine-in-them-is-caffeine-bad-the-word-of-wisdom-doesnt-mention-it?lang=eng.

———. "Missionary Program." Mormon Newsroom. Accessed January 29, 2017. http://www.mormonnewsroom.org/topic/missionary-program.

———. "Mormonism in the News: Getting It Right." Mormon Newsroom, August 29, 2012. http://www.mormonnewsroom.org/article/mormonism-news--getting-it-right-august-29.

————. "Mother in Heaven." Church of Jesus Christ of Latter-day Saints. Accessed April 23, 2017. https://www.lds.org/topics/mother-in-heaven?lang=eng&old=true.

————. "Temple Garments." Mormon Newsroom. Accessed January 31, 2018. http://www.mormonnewsroom.org/article/temple-garments.

————. "Translation and Historicity of the Book of Abraham." Church of Jesus Christ of Latter-day Saints, 2016. Accessed April 5, 2017. https://www.lds.org/topics/translation-and-historicity-of-the-book-of-abraham?lang=eng&old=true.

————. "2016 Statistical Report." Mormon Newsroom. April 1, 2017. http://www.mormonnewsroom.org/article/2016-statistical-report-2017-april-conference.

Ciholas, Paul. "Knowledge and Faith." *Perspectives in Religious Studies* 3 (1976): 188–202.

Clayton, Philip. "Disciplining Relativism and Truth." *Zygon* 24 (1989): 315–34.

Cocks, Michael D. S. "What Is Truth?" *Journal of Religion and Psychical Research* 14 (1991): 154–57.

Collins, William P. "Thoughts on the Mormon Scriptures: An Outsider's View of the Inspiration of Joseph Smith." *Dialogue* 15 (1982): 49–59.

Corduan, Winfried. "Schleiermacher's Test for Truth: Dialogue in the Church." *Journal of the Evangelical Theological Society* 26 (1983): 321–28.

Crane, Richard. "Postliberals, Truth, *Ad Hoc* Apologetics, and (Something Like) General Revelation." *Perspectives in Religious Studies* 30 (2003): 29–53.

Cross, Charles B. "Coherence and Truth Conducive Justification." *Analysis* 59 (1999): 186–93.

Cummings, Richard J. "Quintessential Mormonism: Literal-Mindedness as a Way of Life." *Dialogue* 15 (1982): 93–102.

Dahms, John V. "The Nature of Truth." *Journal of the Evangelical Theological Society* 28 (1985): 455–65.

Depillis, Mario S. "Viewing Mormonism as Mainline." *Dialogue* 24 (1991): 59–67.

Dobay, Clara. "Intellect and Faith: The Controversy over Revisionist Mormon History." *Dialogue* 27 (1994): 91–108.

Duffy, John-Charles. "Defending the Kingdom, Rethinking the Faith: How Apologetics Is Reshaping Mormon Orthodoxy." *Sunstone* 132 (2004): 22–55.

Dunn, Loren C. "Receiving a Prophet." *Ensign* (May 1983): 29.

Edwords, Fred. "Is It Absolutely True that There Are No Absolutes?" *The Humanist* 66 (2006): 38.

Ehat, Andrew F. "'It Seems Like Heaven Began on Earth': Joseph Smith and the Constitution of the Kingdom of God." *BYU Studies* 20 (1980): 253–79.

Embry, Jessie L. "Ultimate Taboos: Incest and Mormon Polygamy." *Journal of Mormon History* 18 (1992): 93–113.

England, Eugene. "On Fidelity, Polygamy, and Celestial Marriage." *Dialogue* 20 (1987): 138–54.

———. "Perfection and Progression: Two Complimentary Ways to Talk about God." *Dialogue* 29 (1989): 31–47.

———. "Why the Church Is as True as the Gospel." *Sunstone* 21 (1999): 61–69.

Ensign editors, ed. "Elder Bruce R. McConkie: 'Preacher of Righteousness.'" *Ensign* (June 1985): 15–22.

Faulconer, James. "The Concept of Apostasy in the New Testament." In *Early Christians in Disarray: Contemporary LDS Perspectives on the Christian Apostasy*, edited by Noel Reynolds, 133–62. Provo, UT: Foundation for Ancient Research and Mormon Studies, 2005.

———. "Divine Embodiment and Transcendence: Propaedeutic Thoughts and Questions." *Element: A Journal of Mormon Philosophy and Theology* 1 (2005): 1–14.

———. "Foreknowledge of God." In *Encyclopedia of Mormonism*, edited by Daniel Ludlow, 521. New York: Macmillan, 1992.

———. "Room to Talk: Reason's Need for Faith." In *Revelation, Reason, and Faith: Essays in Honor of Truman Madsen*, edited by Donald W. Parry, Daniel C. Peterson, and Stephen D. Ricks, 85–120. Provo, UT: Foundation for Ancient Research and Mormon Studies, 2002.

———. "Scripture as Incarnation." In *Historicity and the Latter-day Saint Scriptures*, edited by Paul Y. Hoskisson, 17–61. Provo, UT: Religious Studies Center, Brigham Young University, 2001.

———. "Scripture, History, and Myth." *Sunstone* 14 (1979): 49–50.

First Presidency and the Council of the Twelve Apostles of the Church of Jesus Christ of Latter-day Saints. "Gospel Classics: A Doctrinal Exposition by the First Presidency and the Quorum of the Twelve Apostles from *Improvement Era*, Aug. 1916, 934–42; Capitalization, Punctuation, Paragraphing, and Spelling Standardized." Church of Jesus Christ of Latter-day Saints. June 2002. https://www.lds.org/ensign/2002/04/the-father-and-the-son?lang=eng.

Fjärstedt, Björn. "Religions as Reflections of Reality and Truth." *International Review of Mission* 74 (1985): 484–90.

Gardner, John H. "A Godlike Potential." *Dialogue* 6 (1971): 145–48.

Gibbard, Allan. "Truth and Correct Belief." *Philosophical Issues* 15 (2005): 338–50.

Givens, Terryl L. "The Book of Mormon and Religious Epistemology." *Dialogue* 34 (2001): 31–54.

Glasser, Arthur F. "Truth as Revealed in Scripture." *Religion and Intellectual Life* 3 (1986): 65–71.

Godfrey, Kenneth W. "The Coming of the Manifesto." *Dialogue* 5 (1970): 11–25.

Grant, Heber J. "Doctrine and Covenants 8:6–12." In *Latter-day Prophets and the Doctrine and Covenants*, compiled by Roy W. Doxey, 1:217. Salt Lake City: Deseret, 1978.

Grant, Heber J., Anthony W. Ivins, and Charles W. Nibley. "First Presidency Message of October 1942." BYUI.edu. Accessed April 23, 2017. http://emp. byui.edu/marrottr/FirstPresOct1942.htm.

Groothuis, Douglas. "Why Truth Matters Most: An Apologetic for Truth-Seeking in Postmodern Times." *Journal of the Evangelical Theological Society* 47 (2004): 441–54.

Grover, Mark L. "Religious Accommodation in the Land of Racial Democracy: Mormon Priesthood and Black Brazilians." *Dialogue* (1984): 23–34.

Hale, Van. "Defining the Mormon Doctrine of Deity." *Sunstone* 10 (1985): 23–27.

———. "The Doctrinal Impact of the King Follett Discourse." *BYU Studies* 18 (1978): 209–25.

Harris, James R. "Eternal Progression and the Foreknowledge of God." *BYU Studies* 8 (1967): 37–46.

Hempel, Carl G. "On the Logical Positivist's Theory of Truth." *Analysis* 2 (1935): 49–59.

Hinckley, Gordon B. "The Continuing Pursuit of Truth." *Ensign* (April 1986): 2–6.

———. "Converts and Young Men." *Ensign* (May 1997): 47–49.

———. "Find the Lambs, Feed the Sheep." *Ensign* (May 1999): 104–10.

Homer, Michael W. "The Judiciary and the Common Law in Utah Territory." *Dialogue* 21 (1988): 97–108.

Horwich, Paul. "Theories of Truth." In *A Companion to Metaphysics*, edited by Jaegwon Kim and Ernest Sosa, 492–95. Malden, MA: Blackwell, 1995.

Hunsinger, George. "Truth as Self-Involving." *Journal of the American Academy of Religion* 61 (1993): 41–56.

Ivins, Anthony W. "Doctrine and Covenants 20:11." In *Latter-day Prophets and the Doctrine and Covenants*, compiled by Roy W. Doxey, 1:220. Salt Lake City: Deseret, 1978.

Jessee, Dean C. "The Early Accounts of Joseph Smith's First Vision." *BYU Studies* 9 (1969): 275–96.

Jorgensen, Danny L. "The Mormon Gender-Inclusive Image of God." *Journal of Mormon History* 23 (1997): 95–126.

Kimball, Spencer W. "Revelation: The Word of the Lord to His Prophets." *Ensign* (May 1977): 76–78, https://www.lds.org/ensign/1977/05/ revelation-the-word-of-the-lord-to-his-prophets?lang=eng.

———. "The Sabbath—a Delight." *Ensign*, January 1978. https://www.lds.org/ ensign/1978/01/the-sabbath-a-delight?lang=eng.

Kimball, Stanley B. "Come Ye Disconsolate: Is There a Mercy Seat in Mormon Theology?" *Dialogue* 28 (1995): 69–75.

Kirkland, Boyd. "Elohim and Jehovah in Mormonism and the Bible." *Dialogue* 19 (1986): 77–93.

———. "Jehovah as the Father: The Development of the Mormon Jehovah Doctrine." *Sunstone* 9 (1984): 36–44.

Kunkle, Brett. "Are Mormons Christians?" *Stand to Reason*, August 2011. https://www.str.org/articles/are-mormons-christians#.WQFxJlLMxmA.

Larson, Stan. "Intellectuals in Mormon History: An Update." *Dialogue* 26 (1993): 187–89.

———. "The King Follett Discourse: A Newly Amalgamated Text." *BYU Studies* 18 (1978): 193–208.

Lewis, David. "Forget about the 'Correspondence Theory of Truth.'" *Analysis* 61 (2001): 275–80.

Linker, Damon. "Nietzsche's Truth." *First Things* 125 (2002): 50–60.

Linville, Mark. "Truth Café." *Touchstone* 19 (2006): 19–21.

Maffly-Kipp, Laurie. "A Mormon President?" *Christian Century*, August 21, 2007. http://www.christiancentury.org/article.lasso?id=3594. No longer accessible.

Makransky, John. "Buddhist Perspectives on Truth in Other Religions: Past and Present." *Theological Studies* 64 (2003): 334–61.

Maxwell, Neal. "A More Determined Discipleship." *Ensign* (February 1979): 69–73.

McMahon, Tim. "Historical Inflation Rate." Inflationdata.com, January 12, 2018. http://inflationdata.com/inflation/Inflation_Rate/HistoricalInflation.aspx.

McMurrin, Sterling M. "Comments on the Theological and Philosophical Foundations of Christianity." *Dialogue* 25 (1992): 37–47.

Mehr, Kahlile. "Women's Response to Plural Marriage." *Dialogue* (1985): 84–97.

Miles, Carrie A. "Polygamy and the Economics of Salvation." *Sunstone* 21 (1998): 34–45.

Miller, Alexander. "Russell, Multiple Relations, and the Correspondence Theory of Truth." *Monist* 89 (2006): 85–101.

Millet, Robert L. "Joseph Smith and Modern Mormonism: Orthodoxy, Neo-Orthodoxy, Tension, and Tradition." *BYU Studies* 29 (1989): 48–68.

Monson, Charles H. "On the Conditions Which Precede Revelation." *Dialogue* 2 (1967): 159–61.

Monson, Thomas S. "Follow the Prophets." *Ensign*, January 2015. https://www.lds.org/ensign/2015/01/follow-the-prophets?lang=eng.

———. "They Will Come." *Ensign*, May 1997.

Mulder, William. "Telling it Slant." *Dialogue* 26 (1993): 155–69.

Nibley, Charles W. "Doctrine and Covenants 50:17–24." In *Latter-day Prophets and the Doctrine and Covenants*, compiled by Roy W. Doxey, 2:164. Salt Lake City: Deseret, 1978.

Nine, Cara, and Keith Lehrer. "The Functional Role of Acceptance in Lehrer's Theory of Knowledge." *Philosophical Forum* 32 (2001): 95–103.

Nolan, Mark. "Materialism and the Mormon Faith." *Dialogue* 22 (1989): 62–75.

Oaks, Dallin H. "Criticism." *Ensign*, February 1987.

Ogden, Schubert M. "Faith and Truth." *Christian Century* 82 (1965): 1057–60.

Olsson, Erik J. "Why Coherence Is Not Truth-Conducive." *Analysis* 61 (2001).

Ostler, Blake T. "The Idea of Pre-Existence in the Development of Mormon Thought." *Dialogue* 15 (1982): 59–78.

———. "The Mormon Concept of God." *Dialogue* 17 (1984): 65–93.

———. "Mormonism and Determinism." *Dialogue* 32 (1999): 43–72.

———. "Worshipworthiness and the Mormon Concept of God." *Religious Studies* 33 (1997): 315–26.

Otterson, Michael. "Are Mormons Christians?" On Faith, accessed January 31, 2018, https://www.onfaith.co/onfaith/2007/12/10/are-mormons-christians/7620.

Pannenberg, Wolfhart. "The Nature of a Theological Statement." *Zygon: Journal of Religion and Science* 7 (1972): 6–19.

Parrish, Stephen E., and Francis J. Beckwith. "Mormon Theism and the Argument from Design: A Philosophical Analysis." *Criswell Theological Review* 6 (1993): 269–80.

Patterson, Douglas. "Correspondence and Metaphysics: Andrew Newman's *The Correspondence Theory of Truth*." *Inquiry* 47 (2004): 490–504.

Paul, Robert. "Joseph Smith and the Plurality of Worlds Idea." *Dialogue* 19 (1986): 13–36.

Paulsen, David L. "Are Christians Mormon? Reassessing Joseph Smith's Theology in His Bicentennial." *BYU Studies* 45 (2006): 35–128.

———. "Divine Determinateness and the Free Will Defense." *Analysis* 41 (1981): 150.

———. "Divine Embodiment: The Earliest Christian Understanding of God." In *Early Christians in Disarray: Contemporary LDS Perspectives on the Christian Apostasy*, edited by Noel Reynolds, 239-94. Provo, UT: Foundation for Ancient Research and Mormon Studies, 2005.

———. "The Doctrine of Divine Embodiment: Restoration, Judeo-Christian, and Philosophical Perspectives." *BYU Studies* 35 (1996): 6–94.

———. "Early Mormon Modalism and Other Myths." *FARMS Review* 13 (2001): 69–109.

———. "Joseph Smith and the Problem of Evil." *BYU Magazine* (October 2005): 37–38.

————. "Joseph Smith Challenges the Theological World." *BYU Studies* 44 (2005): 175–212.

————. "The Logically Possible, the Ontologically Possible, and Ontological Proofs of God's Existence." *International Journal for the Philosophy of Religion* 16 (1984): 41–49.

————. "Must God Be Incorporeal?" *Faith and Philosophy* 6 (1989): 76–87.

————. "A New Evangelical Vision of God: Openness and Mormon Thought." *FARMS Review* 15 (2003): 417–43.

————. "Omniscience, Omnipotence, and Omnipresence." In *Encyclopedia of Mormonism*, edited by Daniel Ludlow, 1030. New York: Macmillan, 1992.

————. "The Search for the Cultural Origins of Mormon Doctrines." In *Excavating Mormon Pasts: The New Historiography of the Last Half Century*, edited by Newell G. Bringhurst and Lavina Fielding Anderson, 27–52. Salt Lake City: Greg Kofford, 2004.

Peterson, Mark E. "Another Prophet Now Has Come!" *Ensign* (January 1973): 116–18.

Picht, Greg. "The God of the Philosophers." *Journal of the American Academy of Religion* 48 (1980): 61–79.

Porter, Perry. "A Chronology of Federal Legislation on Polygamy," xmission. com, January 4, 1998. http://www.xmission.com/~plporter/lds/chron.htm.

Pratt, Orson. "Celestial Marriage." In vol. 1 of *Journal of Discourses*, compiled by G. D. Watt, 53–66. London: Latter-day Saints' Book Depot, 1854.

————. "Celestial Marriage." *The Seer* (May 1853): 76.

————. "The Pre-Existence of Man." *The Seer* (February 1853): 24.

————. "The Pre-Existence of Man." *The Seer* (April 1853): 53.

————. "The Pre-Existence of Man." *The Seer* (August 1853): 120.

————. "The Pre-Existence of Man." *The Seer* (September 1853): 133.

Pratt, Parley. "A Letter to the Queen of England, Touching the Signs of the Times, and the Political Destiny of the World." *Times and Seasons* (15 November 1841): 591–93.

Quinn, D. Michael. "The Council of Fifty and Its Members, 1844 to 1945." *BYU Studies* 20 (1980): 163–92.

————. "The Mormon Succession Crisis of 1844." *BYU Studies* 2 (1976): 187–233.

Rampton, Vincent C. "The Fire of God: Thoughts on the Nature of the Divine Witness." *Dialogue* 29 (1996): 137–49.

Raschke, Carl A. "Religious Pluralism and Truth: From Theology to a Hermeneutical Dialogy." *Journal of the American Academy of Religion* 50 (1982): 35–48.

Rasmussen, Ellis T. "The Unchanging Gospel of Two Testaments." *Liahona*, September 1980. https://www.lds.org/liahona/1980/09/the-unchanging-gospel-of-two-testaments?lang=eng.

Rhodes, Michael D. "Why Do Latter-day Saints Believe that Jesus Was Jehovah of the Old Testament?" *Ensign* 18 (1988): 26–27.

Roberts, Allen D. "The Dilemma of the Mormon Rationalist." *Dialogue* 30 (1997): 71–94.

Robson, Kent E. "Omnis on the Horizon." *Sunstone* 8 (1983): 20–23.

———. "Time and Omniscience in Mormon Theology." *Sunstone* 5 (1980): 25–40.

Rodriguez-Pereyra, Gonzalo. "Searle's Correspondence Theory of Truth and the Slingshot." *Philosophical Quarterly* 48 (1998): 513–22.

Romney, Marion G. "The Book of Mormon." *Ensign* (May 1980): 65–67.

———. "The Holy Ghost." *Ensign* (May 1974): 90–92.

Ruprecht, Louis A. "Nietzsche, The Death of God, and Truth, or Why I Still Like Reading Nietzsche." *Journal of the American Academy of Religion* 65 (1997): 573–85.

Sears, Lannie Rex. "Determinist Mansions in the Mormon House?" *Dialogue* 31 (1998): 114–43.

———. "Philosophical Christian Apology Meets 'Rational' Mormon Theology." *Dialogue* 33 (2000): 66–96.

Siegel, Harvey. "Relativism." In *A Companion to Epistemology*, edited by Jonathan Dancy and Ernest Sosa, 428–30. Malden, MA: Blackwell, 1993.

Smith, George D. "Nauvoo Roots of Mormon Polygamy, 1841–46: A Preliminary Demographic Report." *Dialogue* 27 (1994): 1–72, https://www.dialoguejournal.com/wp-content/uploads/sbi/articles/Dialogue_V34N0102_135.pdf:123–58.

Smith, Joseph, Jr. "The Globe." *Times and Seasons* (15 April 1844): 508–11.

———. "Joseph Smith History, 1832." In *Early Mormon Documents*, edited by Dan Vogel, 1:26–31. Salt Lake City: Signature, 1996.

———. "Joseph Smith History, 1839." In *Early Mormon Documents*, edited by Dan Vogel, 1:54–144. Salt Lake City: Signature, 1996.

Smith, Joseph F. "Holy Ghost, Holy Spirit, Comforter." *Improvement Era* 12, no. 5 (March 1909). https://archive.org/details/improvementera1205unse.

Smith, Joseph Fielding. "Doctrine and Covenants 50:10–24." In *Latter-day Prophets and the Doctrine and Covenants*, compiled by Roy W. Doxey, 2:164. Salt Lake City: Deseret, 1978.

Sprinkle, Joe M. "Law." In *Baker Dictionary of Biblical Theology*, 467–70. Grand Rapids: Baker, 1996.

Stack, Peggy Fletcher. "Keeping Members a Challenge for LDS Church." *Salt Lake Tribune*, June 22, 2006. http://www.sltrib.com/cr_2890645?IADID.

Stark, Rodney. "The Rise of a New World Faith." *Review of Religious Research* 26 (1984): 18–27.

———. "So Far, So Good: A Brief Assessment of Mormon Membership Projections." *Review of Religious Research* 38 (1996): 175–78.

Starr, Lance. "'The Seer:' Reliable Source?" Fair Mormon. Accessed January 29, 2018. https://www.fairmormon.org/archive/publications/is_the_seer_a_reliable_source.

Stott, Michelle. "Of Truth and Passion: Mormonism and Existential Thought." *Dialogue* 22 (1989): 76–87.

Tanner, N. Eldon. "Ye Shall Know the Truth." *Ensign* (May 1978): 14–16.

Taylor, John. "The Government of God." *Times and Seasons* (15 July 1842): 855–58.

Teichmann, Roger. "Truth, Assertion and Warrant." *Philosophical Quarterly* 45 (1995): 78–84.

Tickemyer, Garland E. "Joseph Smith and Process Theology." *Dialogue* 17 (1984): 75–85.

Underwood, Grant. "Book of Mormon Usage in Early LDS Theology." *Dialogue* 17 (1984): 35–74.

Van Wagoner, Richard S. "Mormon Polyandry in Nauvoo." *Dialogue* 18 (1985): 67–83.

Vision, Gerald. "Lest We Forget 'the Correspondence Theory of Truth.'" *Analysis* 63 (2003): 136–42.

Walker, William R. "Follow the Prophet." *Ensign*, April 2014. https://www.lds.org/ensign/2014/04/follow-the-prophet?lang=eng.

Walters, Wesley P. "New Light on Mormon Origins from the Palmyra Revival." *Dialogue* 4 (1969): 59–81.

Watson, Michael L. "Statistical Report, 2006." *Ensign* (May 2007): 7.

White, O. Kendall. "A Reply to the Critics of the Mormon Neo-Orthodoxy Hypothesis." *Dialogue* 6 (1971): 97–100.

———. "The Transformation of Mormon Theology." *Dialogue* 5 (1970): 9–24.

Williamson, John. "Facts and Truth." *Philosophical Quarterly* 26 (1976): 203–16.

Wilson, William A. "The Study of Mormon Folklore: An Uncertain Mirror for Truth." *Dialogue* 22 (1989): 95–110.

Woodruff, Wilford. "Blessings Enjoyed by the Saints." In vol. 9 of *Journal of Discourses*, compiled by G. D. Watt and J. V. Long, 55–58. London: Latter-day Saints' Book Depot, 1862.

———. "The Church and Kingdom of God, and the Churches and Kingdoms of Men." In vol. 2 *Journal of Discourses*, compiled by G. D. Watt, 191–202. London: Latter-day Saints' Book Depot, 1855.

———. "The Gospel of Christ Unpopular in Every Age of the World—We Have to Live by Faith—God Has Decreed That His Kingdom Will Be Established—the Priesthood Conferred upon Joseph Smith by Holy Angels—All Blessings to Be Obtained from the God the Saints Worship." In vol. 17 *Journal of Discourses*, compiled by David W. Evans, 188–95. London: Latter-day Saints' Book Depot, 1875.

————. "The Gospel of Jesus Christ—Essential to Abide Its Laws." In vol. 12 of *Journal of Discourses*, compiled by G. D. Watt, E. L. Sloan, and D. W. Evans, 274–81. London: Latter-day Saints' Book Depot, 1869.

————. "The Holy Ghost—Laboring in Faith—the Kingdom of God—Patriarchal Marriage." In vol. 13 of *Journal of Discourses*, compiled by D. W. Evans and John Grimshaw, 156–69. London: Latter-day Saints' Book Depot, 1871.

————. "Intelligence Comes from God—Seek First the Kingdom of God—Great Changes to Take Place on the Earth—Israel of the Last Days—Why the Jews Cannot Be Converted." In vol. 4 of *Journal of Discourses*, compiled by G. D. Watt, 226–33. London: Latter-day Saints' Book Depot, 1857.

————. "Necessity of the Living Oracles Among the Saints—Exhortation to Obedience to Counsel." In vol. 9 of *Journal of Discourses*, compiled by G. D. Watt and J. V. Long, 323–26. London: Latter-day Saints' Book Depot, 1862.

————. "Preaching the Gospel to, and Helping the Lamanites—Obedience to Counsel." In vol. 9 of *Journal of Discourses*, compiled by G. D. Watt and J. V. Long, 221–29. London: Latter-day Saints' Book Depot, 1862.

————. "Testimony of the Spirit of Truth—Effects That Followed the Gospel Anciently and That Follow It Now." In vol. 8 of *Journal of Discourses*, compiled by G. D. Watt and J. V. Long, 261–67. London: Latter-day Saints' Book Depot, 1861.

Wrathall, Mark A. "Heidegger and Truth as Correspondence." *International Journal of Philosophical Studies* 7 (1999): 69–88.

Young, Brigham. "Comprehensiveness of True Religion, Etc." In vol. 7 of *Journal of Discourses*, compiled by G. D. Watt, 333–41. London: Latter-day Saints' Book Depot, 1854.

————. "Diversity Among Men as to Their Capacity for Receiving Truth." In vol. 8 of *Journal of Discourses*, compiled by G. D. Watt and J. D. Long, 158–62. London: Latter-day Saints' Book Depot, 1861.

————. "Effects and Privileges of the Gospel—The Latter-day Saints and the Christian World." In vol. 1 of *Journal of Discourses*, compiled by G. D. Watt, 233–45. London: Latter-day Saints' Book Depot, 1854.

————. "Government of God." In vol. 7 of *Journal of Discourses*, compiled by G. D. Watt, J. V. Long, et. al., 147–49. London: Latter-day Saints' Book Depot, 1860.

————. "How Divisions Were Introduced into the Christian World." In vol. 12 of *Journal of Discourses*, compiled by G. D. Watt, E. L. Sloan, and D. W. Evans, 64–71. London: Latter-day Saints' Book Depot, 1869.

————. "Intelligence, Etc." In vol. 7 of *Journal of Discourses*, compiled by G. D. Watt, J. V. Long, et. al., 282–91. London: Latter-day Saints' Book Depot, 1860.

———. "Joseph, A True Prophet-Apostates-Dream, Etc." In vol. 1 of *Journal of Discourses*, compiled by G. D. Watt, 80–84. London: Latter-day Saints' Book Depot, 1854.

———. "The Kingdom of God." In vol. 2 of *Journal of Discourses*, compiled by G. D. Watt, 308–17. London: Latter-day Saints' Book Depot, 1855.

———. "Knowledge, Correctly Applied, the True Source of Wealth and Power—Unity of Jesus and His Father—Miracles—Slavery—True Charity, Etc." In vol. 10 of *Journal of Discourses*, compiled by G. D. Watt and J. V. Long, 186–95. London: Latter-day Saints' Book Depot, 1865.

———. "A Knowledge of God Obtained Only through Obedience to the Principles of Truth." In vol. 9 of *Journal of Discourses*, compiled by G. D. Watt and J. D. Long, 329–34. London: Latter-day Saints' Book Depot, 1862.

———. "March of Mormonism." In vol. 1 of *Journal of Discourses*, compiled by G. D. Watt, 87–94. London: Latter-day Saints' Book Depot, 1854.

———. "The Necessity of the Saints Having the Spirit of Revelation—Faith and Works—the Power of God and of the Devil." In vol. 3 of *Journal of Discourses*, compiled by G. D. Watt, 152–60. London: Latter-day Saints' Book Depot, 1856.

———. "Opposition in All Things." In vol. 11 of *Journal of Discourses*, compiled by G. D. Watt, E. L. Sloan, and D. W. Evans, 233–41. London: Latter-day Saints' Book Depot, 1867.

———. "Salvation." In vol. 1 of *Journal of Discourses*, compiled by G. D. Watt, vii–6. London: Latter-day Saints' Book Depot, 1854.

———. "Self Government—Mysteries—Recreation and Amusements, Not in Themselves Sinful—Tithing—Adam, Our Father and Our God." In vol. 1 of *Journal of Discourses*, compiled by G. D. Watt, 45–53. London: Latter-day Saints' Book Depot, 1854.

———. "The Training of Children." In vol. 14 of *Journal of Discourses*, compiled by D. W. Evans, J. Q. Cannon, and Julia Young, 191–200. London: Latter-day Saints' Book Depot, 1872.

Young, S. Dilworth. "Elder Bruce R. McConkie of the Council of the Twelve." *Ensign* (January 1973): 5–11.

Unpublished Materials

Barlow, Phillip L. "The Bible in Mormonism." PhD diss., Harvard University, 1988.

Faulconer, James. "Why a Mormon Won't Drink Coffee but Might Have a Coke: The Atheological Character of the Church of Jesus Christ of Latter-day Saints." Lecture, Brigham Young University, Provo, UT, March 19, 2003.

Hinckley, Gordon B. "Be Not Afraid, Only Believe." Lecture, CES Fireside for Young Adults, Salt Lake City, UT, September 9, 2001.

Loomis, Roger. "Mormon Church Growth." Paper presented at the annual meet-
    ing of the Association for the Sociology of Religion, Chicago, IL, December
    19, 2002.

Lowder, Jay Scott. "Unresolved Tensions in the Mormon Doctrines of God, Man,
    and Salvation during Three Critical Periods of Development." PhD diss., The
    Southern Baptist Theological Seminary, 2007.

McConkie, Bruce R. "The Bible, a Sealed Book." Lecture, Brigham Young Uni-
    versity, Provo, UT, 1984.

Millet, Robert L. "The Development of the Concept of Zion in Mormon Theolo-
    gy." PhD diss., Florida State University, 1983.

Osborn, A. C. "The Mormon Doctrine of God and Heaven." Lecture, Baptist
    Ministers' Conference of South Carolina, Darlington, SC, November 29,
    1898.

Paulsen, David L. "Comparative Coherency of Mormon (Finitistic) and Classical
    (Absolutistic) Theism." PhD diss., University of Michigan, 1975.

Peterson, Mark E. "Race Problems—as They Affect the Church." Address, Con-
    vention of Teachers of Religion on the College Level, Provo, UT, August 27,
    1954.

Reid, Tim S. "Mormons and Evolution: A History of B. H. Roberts and His At-
    tempt to Reconcile Science and Religion." PhD diss., Oregon State Universi-
    ty, 1997.

Sears, Lannie Rex. "An Essay in Philosophical Mormon Theology." PhD diss.,
    Harvard University, 1996.

Tickemyer, Garland E. "A Study of Some Representative Concepts of a Finite
    God in Contemporary American Philosophy with Application to the God
    Concepts of the Utah Mormons." MA thesis, University of Southern Califor-
    nia, 1954.

Wider, Kurt. "Unity and Diversity in Mormon Thought." MA thesis, University
    of Calgary, 1994.

Wotherspoon, Daniel Wright. "Awakening Joseph Smith: Mormon Resources for
    a Postmodern Worldview." PhD diss., Claremont Graduate School, 1996.

Name Index

A

Abanes, Richard   *128, 199, 237*
Alexander, Thomas G.   *119, 228, 249, 255*
Allen, James B.   *118, 120–121, 237, 243, 258*
Allison, Gregg R.   *45, 237*
Allred, Gordon   *28–29, 31, 237*
Anderson, Neil L.   *194, 250–251, 257*
Arrington, Leonard J.   *112, 118, 237, 250*

B

Ballard, M. Russell   *7, 8, 17, 73–74, 105–106, 237, 250*
Beckwith, Francis   *19, 237, 238, 250, 256*
Bennion, Lowell L.   *28, 32, 238, 250*
Benson, Ezra Taft   *170, 187, 238, 250*
Bergera, Gary James   *34, 36–37, 42, 238, 250*
Bitton, Davis   *112, 118, 237*
Bringhurst, Newell G.   *1, 198, 238, 257*

C

Callister, Tad R.   *202–207, 225, 238, 251*
Canham, Matt   *5, 251*
Cannon, George Q.   *121, 130, 131, 239, 251, 261*
Carter, Joe   *224, 251*
Clark, James R.   *59, 109, 240, 246*
Clayton, William   *15*
Condie, Spencer J.   *107–108, 240*

D

Dana, Bruce E.   *29, 32–33, 241*
Dunn, Loren C.   *17, 252*
Durham, G. Homer   *107, 152, 241, 242*

E

Ehat, Andrew F.   *15, 253*

F

Faulconer, James   *20–21, 241, 253, 261*

G

Giles, Kevin   *45, 242*
Givens, Terryl L.   *83–85, 242, 253*
Godfrey, Kenneth W.   *15, 117–119, 254*
Gottlieb, Robert   *17, 125–128, 242*
Grant, Heber J.   *82, 83, 127, 151–152, 169, 170, 184, 242, 254, 259*

H

Hamer, John C.   *1, 198, 238*
Hansen, Klaus J.   *12, 14, 242*
Hardy, Grant   *82–83*
Henry, Carl F. H.   *71–72, 242*
Hinckley, Gordon B.   *7, 23, 170, 199, 217–218, 222–225, 227, 230, 231, 243, 250, 254, 261*
Homer, Michael W.   *107, 116–117, 152, 241–242, 254*
Hunter, Milton R.   *96, 180, 243*

I

Ivins, Anthony W.   *169, 170, 254*

K

Kimball, Spencer W.   *107–108, 121, 125–129, 169–170, 186, 193, 199, 241, 243, 254, 255*
Kunkle, Brett   *227–228, 255*

L

Lancaster, James E.   87–88
Lee, Harold B.   20, 111, 130, 247, 249
Leonard, Glen M.   112, 118, 120–121,
    237, 250
Long, J. V.   30, 123, 259–261
Loomis, Roger   4–5, 262

M

Maxwell, Neal A.   38, 38–42, 105, 244,
    255
McConkie, Bruce R.   28, 32–33, 37,
    56–58, 61, 64–65, 68, 74–78, 80, 92–98,
    102, 104–106, 111, 122, 125, 130,
    135–143, 146–147, 150–152, 154–157,
    159–161, 163–167, 171–176, 178–181,
    185, 189–190, 193–194, 204–208,
    210–212, 219, 229–231, 244–245, 248,
    253, 261, 262
McDermott, Gerald R.   21, 105–106, 237,
    245
McGuckin, John Anthony   45
McLachlan, James M.   244
McMurrin, Sterling   39–40, 245, 251, 255
McRay, J. R.   2–3
Millet, Robert L.   16, 19–22, 29, 37–38,
    51, 51–54, 75, 78–79, 81, 103–106, 109,
    142–143, 147, 159, 168, 169, 178, 184,
    188–190, 198, 207–208, 210, 218–219,
    228, 232–233, 244–247, 255, 262
Mohler, R. Albert   226
Monson, Thomas S.   7, 170, 186–187,
    250, 255
Mosser, Carl   18–19, 238
Musser, Joseph W.   29, 246

N

Newell, Coke   21, 246
Newquist, Jerreld L.   131, 239
Nibley, Charles W.   169, 170, 244, 246,
    254, 256

O

Oaks, Dallin H.   17, 256
Olson, Camille Fronk   159, 245
Ostler, Blake T.   29–30, 39–40, 246, 256
Ostling, Richard N. and Joan K.   11–12,
    129, 246

Otterson, Michael   221, 225, 256
Owen, Paul   18–19, 111, 238

P

Paulsen, David L.   38, 256, 262
Petersen, Mark E.   179–180
Peterson, Daniel C.   18–19, 123–125,
    185–186, 246, 253, 257, 262
Poll, Richard D.   117
Porter, Perry   3, 118, 257
Pratt, Parley   13–14, 30–31, 33–37, 62,
    69, 93, 112–116, 241, 244, 246–247,
    249, 250, 257

Q

Quinn, D. Michael   15–16, 247, 257

R

Richards, Franklin D.   15
Roberts, B. H.   28–29, 39, 237, 244, 247,
    258, 262
Robinson, Stephen F.   54, 219–220, 227,
    238, 247
Robson, Kent   38–39, 42–43, 258
Romney, Marion G.   33, 60, 121, 247

S

Sire, James W.   25–28, 43, 70, 247
Skinner, Andrew C.   167, 168, 190,
    207–208, 210, 212, 245
Smith, George Albert   176
Smith, George D.   110–111
Smith, Joseph Fielding   15, 58, 66, 68,
    122–123, 145, 151, 163, 168, 247, 249
Smith Jr., Joseph   10, 12–15, 19–20,
    28–31, 34, 38, 54, 62, 67, 78, 80–88,
    90, 92–96, 98–103, 105, 107, 110–112,
    115–116, 120, 121, 143, 145, 147, 158,
    176, 183, 186, 195, 197–199, 203, 205,
    214, 218, 220, 224–225, 227–228, 230,
    238–239, 243, 245–246, 248, 251–252,
    254, 255–256, 258–259, 262
Smith, Peter   2
Snow, LeRoi C.   31
Snow, Lorenzo   30–31, 248
Stack, Peggy Fletcher   4–5, 193, 258
Stapley, Delbert L.   186
Stark, Rodney   3–4, 6–8, 248, 258

Subject Index

A

age of accountability   *158*
alcoholic beverages   *176*
Ancient Americans   *89*
archaeology   *82*
area presidency   *209*
Articles of Faith   *28–29, 96*

B

baptism   *156–159*
baptism for the dead   *77, 159*
baptismal regeneration   *47*
Beneficial Financial Group   *8*
Bible   *73–81*
bigamy   *110*
bishop   *207–208*
Bonneville International Corporation   *9*
Book of Abraham   *98–101*
Book of Commandments   *93*
Book of Mormon   *81–92*
Book of Moses   *96–97*

C

caffeine   *176*
Cain   *123–124*
canon of scripture   *105–106*
celestial bodies   *135, 147*
celestial glory   *135, 147*
celestial kingdom   *113, 125, 134–137, 139, 147, 157*
celestial law   *135, 147*
celestial marriage   *77, 137*
charity   *178–181*
coffee   *176*
conditional salvation   *146*
confession   *153*
continuing revelation   *101–129*
Council of Fifty   *15–16*

Cullom–Struble Bill   *120*

D

damnation   *174*
deification   *31, 82, 135, 138*
Deseret Book Company   *9*
Deseret Management Corporation   *8*
Deseret News   *9*
Doctrine and Covenants   *92–95*

E

Edmunds Act   *118, 198*
Edmunds–Tucker Act   *118, 198*
Egyptian papyrus   *95, 98–100*
Egyptologists   *99*
Elohim   *47–48*
endure to the end (ETTE)   *146*
eternal families   *82, 189*
eternal life   *137, 147, 151*
eternal progression   *48, 136*
evangelism   *2–3, 27*
exaltation   *32, 113, 135–137, 145, 147, 189*
Excel Entertainment   *9*

F

faith   *148–150*
family   *187–189, 207*
family history work   *190–193*
fasting   *171–172*
fatalism   *41*
finitism   *39*
First Presidency   *211*
First Vision   *196*
"Following the Prophet"   *187*
foreknowledge   *41*
foreordination   *38, 40–41*
forgiveness   *154*

Scripture Index

LDS Scripture Index